Research Perspectives on Social Media Influencers and their Followers

Research Perspectives on Social Media Influencers and their Followers

Edited by
Brandi Watkins

LEXINGTON BOOKS

Lanham • Boulder • New York • London

Published by Lexington Books
An imprint of The Rowman & Littlefield Publishing Group, Inc.
4501 Forbes Boulevard, Suite 200, Lanham, Maryland 20706
www.rowman.com

6 Tinworth Street, London SE11 5AL, United Kingdom

British Library Cataloguing in Publication Information Available

Library of Congress Cataloging-in-Publication Data

Names: Watkins, Brandi, editor.
Title: Research perspectives on social media influencers and their
    followers / edited by Brandi Watkins.
Description: Lanham : Lexington Books, [2021] | Includes bibliographical
    references and index. | Summary: "This book analyzes social media
    influencers and their relationship with their online followers. Each
    chapter represents a unique theoretical and methodological approach to
    examining the importance of this relationship from a variety of
    perspectives and contexts"—Provided by publisher.
Identifiers: LCCN 2020050654 (print) | LCCN 2020050655 (ebook) |
    ISBN 9781793613646 (cloth) | ISBN 9781793613660 (pbk)
    ISBN 9781793613653 (epub)
Subjects: LCSH: Online social networks. | Social media—Influence. | Social influence.
Classification: LCC HM742 .R468 2021 (print) | LCC HM742 (ebook) |
    DDC 302.30285—dc23
LC record available at https://lccn.loc.gov/2020050654
LC ebook record available at https://lccn.loc.gov/2020050655

This book is for you, Dad. Thank you for all you do.

Contents

Acknowledgments

I would like to thank the staff at Lexington Books, especially Nicolette Amstutz and Jessica Tepper, for their help with making this project become a reality. Thank you to all the authors who contributed thoughtful and interesting chapters. Editing chapters and seeing firsthand the creativity and variety of approaches to examining the phenomenon of social media influencers was an absolute joy. Last, but certainly not least, I would like to thank my family and friends for their constant support and encouragement.

List of Figures and Tables

FIGURES

TABLES

List of Figures and Tables

Introduction

Brandi Watkins

In the fall of 2019, Buzzfeed published an article titled, "Who Is Caroline Calloway and Why Is Everyone Talking About Her. Let Us Explain." Following the headline was a screenshot of an Instagram account. The image featured a blonde woman with a floral headdress against a pink background. The caption accompanying the photo read, "I don't make a lot of sense as a person if you don't believe that all my life I've loved above all else telling stories about myself. Swipe for proof!" (McNeal, 2019). At the time of the screenshot, the post had 2,428 likes. The article is an explainer on the rise and fall of Instagram influencer Caroline Calloway.

According to the article, Calloway first started posting on Instagram in 2012 with the goal of "writing an autobiographical story that carried across multiple Instagram posts and introduced different people in my life as 'characters'" (McNeal, 2019, para. 7; also cited in Ross, 2018). An article in *Man Repeller* lauded Calloway as being the first Instagram influencer who was "famous for something that didn't exist until a few years ago: a personal brand" (Ross, 2018, para. 1). Calloway's followers on Instagram grew to 800,000 by 2017 (McNeal, 2019).

In 2016, she entered into a book deal with Flatiron Publishing to write her memoir. However, in 2017, she posted for her followers on Instagram that she had decided to pull out of the book deal because, as McNeal (2019) puts it, "she had pulled out because she felt the proposal she had sold was a 'lie' that didn't represent who she actually was" (para. 13). Shortly after the book debacle, Calloway became entangled in another controversy—what journalist Kayleigh Donaldson dubbed a scam (McNeal, 2019). Calloway announced that she would be hosting creativity workshops in the spring of 2019 which her followers could attend for $165 (McNeal, 2019; Park, 2019). The forty-five-person, four-hour workshops to be held in various locations was reported by W to include lectures covering topics including "physical and mental health, discovering your voice, harnessing your creativity, and getting over heartbreak" (Park, 2019, para. 5). In addition to the lectures, participants could expect a homemade lunch, care package, and handwritten personalized letter from Calloway (McNeal, 2019; Park, 2019). W reported that the events sold out immediately (Park, 2019).

The event did not go as advertised. After facing the mounting logistics of a multi-city workshop tour, Calloway announced to her followers that she was canceling most of her tour dates (McNeal, 2019). A workshop was held on January 12 in Brooklyn. Park (2019) attended the event and wrote about her experience, citing that many of the advertised accoutrements were not going to be included in the workshop (see Park, 2019 for full article). As McNeal (2019) notes, "Many of the things fans were promised, such as personal letters to each attendee, a flower crown, and a care package, either did not come to fruition or, as one reporter in attendance wrote, fell woefully short of expectations" (para. 24). Similar to the previous book debacle, Calloway's reputation took another hit as news of the disappointing workshop and Donaldson's tweet about the event being a scam went viral (Park, 2019). This would not, however, be the last controversy surrounding Calloway. In September 2019, Natalie Beach announced in *The Cut* that she was actually the author of Calloway's long Instagram captions, not Calloway (Beach, 2019). The article, written in first person by Beach, chronicled her friendship and financial entanglements with Calloway that resulted in her ghostwriting the influencer's Instagram captions and parts of her unpublished book (see Beach, 2019).

After involvement with so many controversies in such a short amount of time, it would be logical to think that Calloway's Instagram presence would suffer too. That is not to be the case. McNeal (2019) reported that she gained about 3,000 new followers after Beach's article was published. Some of that number is reflected in people with a genuine curiosity or self-described "obsession" with Calloway's story, but still there are some followers who seem to genuinely care for Calloway. McNeal (2019) wrote in response to Beach's article in *The Cut*:

> The reaction to the essay has been polarizing. Despite people calling her a scammer, a grifter, or worse, Calloway has almost 1 million fans and rabid followers who watch her every move. Some of those followers genuinely like her, and are sending her messages of love and support. "You are so loved and supported (heart emoji). this [*sic*] is hard, but you are strong. we [*sic*] can do hard things," Wrote on one Instagram. (paras. 39–40)

Calloway's story not only points to the lengths that a person will go to in order to maintain their status as influencer but also illustrates the lengths followers will go to in order to maintain their relationship with the influencer. The chapters presented in this manuscript present a variety of research perspectives, questions, and methodologies all exploring the dynamic, and often puzzling, relationship between followers and social media influencers (SMIs).

ABOUT SOCIAL MEDIA INFLUENCERS

A conversation about the influencer–follower relationship should begin with the influencer and create a better understanding of the phenomenon that is the social media influencer. Abindin and Ots (2015) define *social media influencers* as:

> One form of microcelebrities who document their everyday lives from the trivial and mundane, to exciting snippets of the exclusive opportunities in their line of work. Influencers are the shapers of public opinion who persuade their audience through the conscientious calibration of personae on social media, as supported by "physical" space interactions with their followers in the flesh to sustain their accessibility, believability, emulatability, and intimacy—in other words, their "relatability." (p. 3)

This definition captures the characteristics that make following a SMI appealing to many—they present a lifestyle on social media that people find to be relatable in a way that gives followers hope that they too can live such an idyllic life. Audrezet et al. (2018) suggest that successful SMIs are adept at blending "real life" with branded content in a way that is not intrusive for followers, thus making SMIs instrumental tastemakers who communicate information about trends to their followers. Content created by SMIs are used to develop long-lasting relationships with followers (Hwang & Zhang, 2018).

Successful social media is about relationships (Luttrell, 2015). Luttrell (2015) writes that "social media should be viewed as how a company or brand effectively utilizes each of the aforementioned technologies to connect, interact, and cultivate trusting relationships with *people*" (p. 23, emphasis included in the quote). Successful brands on social media know that they must create content that is entertaining or useful to followers, that they must respond promptly to follower inquiries, and generally engage with followers as if they were friends. This same principle holds true for successful SMIs—they recognize the value of the relationship they have with their followers.

Through social media content, SMIs create intimacy and thus enhance their relationship with followers. Abindin and Ots (2015) identified four strategies used by SMIs to create intimacy: (1) endearment and personal language, (2) authenticity through unaltered behind-the-scenes material, (3) establishing common ground with followers by sharing mundane practices (despite the influencer promoting a more luxurious lifestyle), and (4) real-life meet-ups with followers. One example of this comes from the realm of beauty influencers on YouTube, where SMIs frequently ask for video ideas from followers, which as Rasmussen (2018) explains, "may show that they do care about user interests in an attempt to connect with the audience" (p. 290). Rasmussen (2018) goes on to suggest that "simply responding to comments on YouTube or any other social media create the allusion to audiences that celebrities care about them" (pp. 290–291). As a result, followers describe SMI content as relatable, non-commercial, and from ordinary people just like themselves (Audrezet et al., 2018) and that SMI content is "one of the last forms of real, authentic communication" (Scott, 2015, p. 295; as cited in Audrezet et al., 2018).

Business-savvy SMIs have leveraged their large following and status into a lucrative brand for themselves. Abindin (2017) notes that SMIs are "a contemporary incarnation of Internet celebrity for whom microcelebrity is not merely a hobby or a supplementary income but an established career with its own ecology and economy" (p. 1). It is the reach and status of SMIs as tastemakers and opinion leaders that make them ideal for marketing and brand communication efforts (Archer & Harrington, 2016).

In light of the success of SMIs, brands have incorporated influencer marketing into their brand communication strategies. Influencer marketing is "promoting brands through the use of specific key individuals who exert influence over potential buyers" (Audrezet et al., 2018, para. 3) and includes collaborations between brands and SMI to integrate product promotion into their social media content. Influencer marketing has been found to be the second most effective marketing strategy (Audrezet et al., 2018). Influencer Marketing Hub (2020) reported that 91 percent of their survey respondents indicated influencer marketing was effective. In 2019, more than 380 influencer marketing agencies were created (Influencer Marketing Hub, 2020) and in 2022, brands are projected to spend upwards of $15 billion on Influencer Marketing (Influencer Marketing Hub, 2021). Thus, there is real economic impact and value from better understanding the influencer–follower relationship.

BOOK OVERVIEW

At the time of the writing of this introduction, we are in the midst of a global pandemic due to the novel coronavirus. In the wake of widespread business closures, quarantines, and social distancing, many have turned to the Internet as a space for social connection. Families and friends are meeting using technologies such as FaceTime, Zoom, and Skype. Emerging social media platforms, like TikTok, are growing as people are finding ways to connect with others in a new environment. Thus, in this "new normal," that the world finds itself in, enhances the need and importance of research that looks at how the Internet and social media can be used effectively as a relationship building tool as well as the gratifications that can be achieved by each party in an online relationship. This book, specifically, looks at the online (and often parasocial) relationship between SMI and their followers.

The goal of this book is to provide readers with an overview of the current research into the relationship between SMI and their followers, which is still in its early stages. As the influencer marketing industry continues to grow and evolve, so too should our understanding of the relationship that makes influencer marketing relevant—the influencer–follower relationship. The chapters selected for inclusion in this volume represent a number of theoretical, methodological, and disciplinary approaches to examining the influencer–follower relationship. Contributors examine how SMIs build relationships with followers through creating content, the science behind the effectiveness of social media influencer marketing, how to leverage expertise to become an SMI, legal and ethical considerations for SMIs, and how SMIs manage crises. To date, there are limited resources for practitioners and scholars to access information about the influencer–follower relationship. As such, the chapters presented in this book represent a first effort at organizing and providing direction for future research on the influencer–follower relationship.

REFERENCES

Abindin, C. (2017). #familygoals: Family, influencers, calibrated amateurism, and justifying young digital labor. *Social Media + Society, 3*(2), 1–15. https://doi.org/10.1177/2056305117707191

Abindin, C., & Ots, M. (2015, August). The influencer's dilemma: The shaping of new brand professions between credibility and commerce. In AEJMC 2015: Annual conference. San Francisco, CA: Association for Education in Journalism and Mass Communication.

Archer, C., & Harrigan, P. (2016). Show me the money: How bloggers as stakeholders are challenging theories of relationship building in public relations. *Media International Australia, 160*(1), 67–77. https://doi.org/10.1177/1329878X16651139

Audrezet, A., de Kerviler, G., & Guidry Moulard, J. (2018). Authenticity under threat: When social media influencers needs to go beyond self-presentation. *Journal of Business Research.* http://doi.org/10.1016/j.busres.2018.07.008

Beach, N. (2019, September 10). The story of Caroline Calloway & her ghostwriter Natalie. https://www.thecut.com/2019/09/the-story-of-caroline-calloway-and-her-ghostwriter-natalie.html

Hwang, K., & Zhang, Q. (2018). Influence of parasocial relationship between digital celebrities and their followers on followers' purchase and electronic word-of-mouth intentions, and persuasion knowledge. *Computers in Human Behavior, 87*, 155–173. https://doi.org/10.1016/j.chb.2018.05.029

Influencer Marketing Hub. (2020). The state of influencer marketing 2020: Benchmark report. https://influencermarketinghub.com/influencer-marketing-benchmark-repo rt-2020/

Influencer Marketing Hub. (2021). Influencer marketing: Social media influencer marketing stats and research for 2021. https://www.businessinsider.com/ influencer-marketing-report

Luttrell, R. (2015). *Social media: How to engage, share, and connect*. Lanham, MD: Rowman & Littlefield Publishers.

McNeal, S. (2019, September 13). Who is Caroline Calloway and why is everyone talking about her? Let us explain. https://www.buzzfeednews.com/article/stephani emcneal/caroline-calloway-the-cut

Park, A. (2019, January 14). Caroline Calloway's "creativity workshop" taught me nothing about creativity, but a lot about scamming. https://www.wmagazine.com/ story/caroline-calloway-creativity-workshop/

Rasmussen, L. (2018). Parasocial interaction in the digital age: An examination of relationship building and the effectiveness of YouTube celebrities. *The Journal of Social Media in Society, 7*(1), 280–294.

Ross, H. (2018, June 20). Caroline Calloway talks social media, book deals and fans. https://www.manrepeller.com/2018/06/caroline-calloway-interview.html

Chapter 1

The Science of Social Media Influencer Marketing

Kelli S. Burns

Influence and persuasion theories have long been applied to the fields of marketing, advertising, public relations, and communication to understand how awareness, attitudes, and behavior can be raised, changed, or maintained. In this new era of social media influencer marketing, many of the same theories remain applicable and can enhance our understanding of the influence process. Marketers are still learning how to effectively use influencer marketing as an integral part of many marketing campaigns and are focused on improving their return on investment from this tactic (Armano, 2019). The literature review presented in this chapter will summarize and categorize academic research by the theoretical foundations used to understand influencers and provide frameworks for future research.

The literature review detailed in this chapter examined research studies from 2014 to 2019 published in journals representing the disciplines of advertising, public relations, marketing, and social media to uncover insights for effective influencer marketing and theoretical approaches used to build knowledge of the influencer process. The first step in the literature review was to select journals from the following disciplines: advertising, public relations, social media, and marketing; this process identified fifteen journals. Journals with the longest histories and highest impact factors in those disciplines were first selected, but newer journals were also included to reflect the rise of digital and social media communication. Through EBSCOhost, the keyword "influencer" was searched in each journal during the six-year period of 2014–2019, a timeframe chosen because it corresponded with the year that the search term "influencer" started its meteoric rise on Google Trends. Also, in 2014, more than one-quarter of all online adults were using Instagram, a popular platform for influencers, as well as half of the young adults aged between eighteen and twenty-nine (Duggan et al., 2014). All results were

Table 1.1   Journals Ranked by Number of Influencer Articles Published 2014–2019

Journal Name	Year Founded	H Index	Articles on Influencers
International Journal of Advertising	1982	37	5
Computers in Human Behavior	1985	137	4
Journal of Interactive Advertising	2000	n/a	4
Journal of Advertising	1972	89	2
Journal of Marketing	1936	218	1
Journal of Social Media in Society	2012	n/a	1
Public Relations Review	1978	67	1
Total			18

then reviewed to determine those that were directly related to the topic of social media influencers. Case studies and other non-empirical studies were excluded from this review.

Seven of the fifteen journals included articles relevant for this study. The advertising journals were *Journal of Advertising, International Journal of Advertising,* and *Journal of Interactive Advertising. Journal of Marketing* represented marketing, and *Public Relations Review* represented public relations. Finally, *Computers in Human Behavior* and *Journal of Social Media in Society* were included for their focus on digital and social media communication and for having published relevant articles. The eight journals dropped from this study as a result of having no articles about influencers included *Journal of Advertising Research, Journal of Marketing Research, Journal of Interactive Marketing, Journal of Consumer Marketing, Journal of Consumer Research, Journal of Public Relations Research, Journal of Computer-Mediated Communication,* and *Social Media + Society.*

Table 1.1 shows the total number of relevant articles about influencers in each of the reviewed journals as well as the year the journal was founded and the H Index. Overall, these advertising, public relations, marketing, and social media journals produced eighteen articles focused on influencer marketing, despite the growth of and increasing budgets for this tactic among marketers, and eleven of these articles were published in advertising journals. The search was conducted in late 2019, but one publication was already available dated 2020.

FRAMEWORK FOR ORGANIZING THEORIES

McGuire's (1989) communication-persuasion matrix is applicable to understanding and analyzing persuasion in influencer contexts. McGuire identified five classes of input variables, described as "the independent variables and persuasive messages that can be manipulated" (1989, pp. 44–45), that should direct the construction of persuasive communication campaigns. According to McGuire, "when one is mastering or keeping up with the literature, the matrix provides a conceptual framework for assimilating new findings about relations making up the attitude-change process so that this new material is available for creative retrieval" (1999, pp. 154–155). For this reason, the theories and frameworks that emerged from the review of the literature are presented and organized in accordance with four of McGuire's (1989) five classes of input variables: source, message, receiver/audience, and intent/destination. None of the articles used a theoretical framework related to the channel. It is also important to note that many of the studies applied several theories or frameworks to the study of influencers.

RESULTS

Source Input Variable Studies

Endorser marketing studies often focus on source variables that impact the relationship between endorsers and advertising effectiveness, which fall under McGuire's source input variables. McGuire's (1989) source input factors that impact the effectiveness of a message include credibility, attractiveness, and power. This review will cover three theories and models that align with McGuire's source input factors: Source Credibility Theory, Uses and Gratifications Theory, and the Two-Step Flow Model.

Source Credibility

Social media influencers serve as brand endorsers, and thus source effects literature can highlight critical qualities of the source that may be relevant to understanding the effectiveness of influencers. Source effects literature commonly measures the trustworthiness, expertise, and attractiveness of the source to determine source credibility (Ohanian, 1990). Likeability has also been explored in other studies of source effects (Bergkvist & Zhou, 2016). Of the eighteen journal articles reviewed for this chapter, eight referenced the role of source effects.

Several of these studies manipulated the source, such as the study by Schouten et al. (2019), who compared the impact of celebrity and influencer endorsement on advertising effectiveness, including attitude toward the ad, attitude toward the product, and purchase intentions. According to the researchers, this study is grounded in endorsement marketing research that has mostly focused on celebrities. The moderating variable was product-endorser fit. The mediators were identification, defined as perceived similarity and wishful identification, and credibility, defined as trustworthiness and expertise. The results showed that consumers identify more with, feel more similar to, and are more trusting of influencers than celebrities. Similarity, wishful identification, and trust mediated the relationship between the type of endorser and advertising effectiveness. Product-endorser fit was not found to produce interaction effects with endorser type, nor did expertise mediate the relationship between endorser type and advertising effectiveness. A key finding for marketers was that influencers can be more effective than celebrities if they can engender wishful identification, similarity, and trust. The researchers acknowledged that the line between traditional celebrities and social media influencers is blurring, as some celebrities have become very active on social media as influencers and that some social media influencers have become celebrities in their own right by launching clothing lines, modeling for fashion brands, and landing television deals.

Rasmussen (2018) also manipulated the source characteristics in a study that compared the effectiveness of highly popular YouTube vloggers (i.e., two million or more subscribers) to moderately popular vloggers (i.e., 100,000–250,000 subscribers). Their study found no significant difference in terms of popularity of the influencer on credibility (both were viewed as credible), but that the highly popular influencer treatment was more likely to influence purchase intent than the moderately popular influencer treatment. Because both types of influencers were viewed as credible, Rasmussen questioned whether it was the platform (YouTube) or the production value that created the illusion of credibility or whether the endorsers conveyed credibility on their own. Furthermore, they suggested that YouTubers with fewer subscribers also be included in additional research.

Lou and Yuan (2019) had respondents consider their own source, which provided variability in the independent variable. The researchers examined information value and entertainment value of the message and expertise, trustworthiness, attractiveness, and similarity of the influencer. Moderating the relationship between these variables and the outcomes of brand awareness and purchase intention was trust in the post. This study found significant relationships between the information value (not entertainment value) of the posts and the trustworthiness, attractiveness, and similarity (not expertise) of the source with trust in the posts, which led to brand awareness and purchase intention. Expertise and attractiveness also had direct and positive significant correlations with brand awareness (bypassing trust in the posts), while the trustworthiness of the influencer had a direct and negative correlation. None of the source credibility dimensions had a direct and positive significant impact on purchase intention. The findings suggested that users value the information provided by influencers and that it builds trust, leading to desirable advertising outcomes such as awareness and purchase intention. The researchers noted that the dimension of trust in the posts deserves more attention because it demonstrated the strongest impact on purchase intentions.

In other studies, source effects are a result of the manipulation of another variable, such as advertising literacy intervention and advertising disclosure. De Jans et al. (2018) examined the relationship between influencer effects, such as trustworthiness, and advertising effects, such as purchase intention, in their study of advertising literacy intervention. They found that affective advertising literacy, which is defined as being critical toward advertising content, negatively impacted the trustworthiness of the influencer, but that an advertising literacy intervention through an informational vlog could have a positive impact on influencer effects.

Hughes et al. (2019) manipulated the social media platform (either a blog or Facebook) and the stage in the consumer decision journey (either awareness or trial) and then analyzed the role of blogger expertise as a moderator for engagement. Blogger expertise was found to moderate engagement for awareness campaigns (vs. trial) for sponsored posts on a blog, but expertise made no difference in engagement when the post was on Facebook. The researchers noted the importance of including campaign intent in studies of the relationships among source, content, and engagement. On high-involvement, low-distraction social media platforms (e.g., blogs), expert endorsement is valuable for an awareness campaign, while a novice endorsement is effective for a trial campaign. In contrast, on low-involvement, high-distraction social media platforms (e.g., Facebook), source expertise did not have an impact on engagement.

Similarly, De Veirman and Hudders (2019) also manipulated other variables to measure the impact on source credibility, namely disclosure and sidedness of the message (either one-sided or two-sided). The researchers found that disclosure had a negative impact on credibility through ad recognition, then ad skepticism. Furthermore, a moderated mediation effect occurred with sidedness of the message whereby source credibility and then brand attitude were only negatively affected when the message was one-sided as opposed to two-sided.

Another study that manipulated advertising disclosure and measured source credibility was Carr and Hayes (2014). The researchers found a positive relationship between perceptions of blogger credibility and the blogger's perceived word-of-mouth influence. They also found that explicit disclosures of third-party influence, as well as no mention of third-party influence, resulted in the highest perceptions of credibility, followed by an explicit mention that there is no third party involved (i.e., impartiality). Implicit disclosures of third-party influence led to the lowest perceptions of credibility.

De Veirman et al. (2017) examined the variable of follower count and the role it plays in impacting perceptions of opinion leadership and also likeability. The follower–followee ratio was also explored to understand its impact on likeability. The researchers found that a high number of followers led to higher perceptions of popularity and then more likeability, but not necessarily the perception that the influencer is an opinion leader. The researchers found a negative relationship between followers and likeability when the influencer follows few accounts but noted this relationship might only be true for female influencers.

In summary, the source effects used in these studies included trustworthiness (De Jans et al., 2018; De Veirman & Hudders, 2019; Lou & Yuan, 2019; Rasmussen, 2018; Schouten et al., 2019), expertise (De Veirman & Hudders, 2019; Hughes et al., 2019; Schouten et al., 2019), similarity (Lou & Yuan, 2019), identification (Schouten et al., 2019), likeability (De Veirman et al., 2017), attractiveness (De Veirman & Hudders, 2019; Lou & Yuan, 2019), and also credibility in general (Carr & Hayes, 2014).

Uses and Gratifications Theory

Uses and Gratifications Theory generally attempts to understand the needs of audience members who have expectations of the mass media or other sources that lead to various patterns of media exposure or engagement to gratify those needs (Katz et al., 1974). While Uses and Gratifications Theory can be applied to understanding the audience of influencers, the following two studies examined uses and gratifications from the perspective of the source, or influencer, thus falling under McGuire's source input variable.

Erz et al. (2018) found influencers to include more hashtags and use the platform for self-presentation, as they tend to score higher on narcissism, extraversion, and self-monitoring than other users. In the other study, Lahuerta-Otero and Cordero-Gutierrez (2016) found that, among almost 4,000 tweets related to Toyota and Nissan, influencers used more hashtags and mentions but fewer words and embedded links than non-influencers. Influencers also followed many more people and expressed positive and negative opinions and feelings while using Twitter.

Both of these studies explore content shared by influencers (i.e., hashtags, mentions, words, and links), but only Erz et al. (2018) examined motivations such as self-presentation and the predictors of self-presentation (i.e., narcissism, extraversion, and self-monitoring). When applied to influencers, this theory can tap many more dimensions to build an understanding of both uses and gratifications. Other social gratifications besides self-presentation can be explored. Additionally, the studies reviewed did not address uses and gratifications of users who follow influencers, which is another area of inquiry.

Two-Step Flow Model

The Two-Step Flow Model predicts that media indirectly influence the public through information gatekeepers, or opinion leaders, who pass media messages along to their networks (Katz & Lazarsfeld, 1955). Only one study used the Two-Step Flow Model as a theoretical framework (Carr & Hayes, 2014). Because two-step flow starts with the opinion leader, it is classified under McGuire's source variable in this literature review.

Carr and Hayes (2014) applied two-step flow to understand the effect perceived third-party influence would have on the credibility of the influencer and then on product attitudes and purchase intentions of the readers of product reviews on blogs. The researchers described the relationship between information from organizations and then mavens (influencers) in the Two-Step Flow Model as a volatile one, which can create issues for the flow of information if relationships are not disclosed (Carr & Hayes, 2014). When this happens, the status of the influencer is jeopardized, which can impact the ability of these opinion leaders to influence others.

Message Input Variable Studies

McGuire's (1989) message input variables include delivery and message style, types and structure of the argument, and types of appeals. A common influencer research topic among the journal articles reviewed in this analysis was the effect of disclosure of paid promotion, which can be classified under McGuire's message input variable. These studies all apply the Persuasion-Knowledge Model (Friestad & Wright, 1994) and manipulate the disclosure message.

Persuasion-Knowledge Model

The Persuasion-Knowledge Model (PKM) (Friestad & Wright, 1994) focuses on the persuasion knowledge of consumers that allows them to recognize persuasion attempts and then select and implement coping strategies to deal with those persuasion attempts. According to the PKM, messages that are considered persuasion will be processed differently than those not considered persuasion. PKM is widely applied in studies of advertising disclosure in influencer posts or videos.

Of the eighteen influencer articles in this analysis, eight used PKM. In all these studies, persuasion knowledge is measured and used as a mediator of other outcomes. Many of these studies started with the manipulation of advertising disclosure, a practice that is required of marketers by the Federal Trade Commission (FTC). In these studies, disclosure was manipulated in a variety of ways, with most of them comparing a sponsored message or versions of a sponsored message with a non-sponsored message.

Kim and Song (2018) examined the main effect of content sponsorship type (either organic or sponsored) and the interaction between sponsorship and content type (either experience-centric or promotional) on consumer responses to brand-related user-generated content, including inferences of manipulative intent, brand attitude, and intention to click on a URL. Experience-centric content included personal opinions or experiences by the influencer, whereas promotional content focused on factual and objective information, such as the promotion of a sale or discount.

De Veirman and Hudders (2019) examined disclosure in the context of sidedness of the message. Sponsorship disclosure was manipulated to be either material compensation, financial compensation, not sponsored, or not disclosed. The message was manipulated to be either one-sided or two-sided, whereby a one-sided message only focused on the positive aspects of the product and failed to mention any negatives, while a two-sided message mentioned both the benefits and downsides to the product.

Evans et al. (2018) manipulated sponsorship text disclosure (either present or absent) and sponsor pre-roll (either sponsor pre-roll, non-sponsor pre-roll, or no pre-roll) on persuasion knowledge, perceptions of sponsorship transparency, and other outcomes, such as perceptions of these types of videos, attitudes toward the brand, attitudes toward the sponsor, and attitudes toward regulation. Stubb and Colliander (2019) focused on disclosure that an influencer's post is organic and not sponsored (often indicated by the disclosure that "this is not a sponsored post") and compared these "impartial" posts to those that disclosed sponsorship or had no mention of sponsorship at all in terms of the impact on perceptions of advertising and then source and message credibility.

De Jans et al. (2018) examined the impact of advertising disclosure (i.e., disclosure vs. no disclosure) on recognition of advertising and advertising literacy among adolescents. They found that disclosure increased advertising recognition and affective advertising literacy and that affective advertising literacy negatively impacted influencer trustworthiness and parasocial interactions, and then purchase intention. They found that using an informational vlog as an intervention can result in advertising disclosure having a positive impact on advertising effects. Evans et al. (2017) measured the impact of disclosure in the form of "Paid Ad," "Sponsored," "SP" (sponsored post), and no disclosure on attitudes, purchase intention, and intention to spread electronic word-of-mouth messages, and advertising recognition, which was measured as a mediator between disclosure and the other effects. Boerman (2020) examined whether the standard Instagram disclosure led to advertising recognition and in turn, how advertising recognition impacted online behavioral intentions, parasocial interactions, and brand recall for both micro-influencers (less than 10,000 followers) and meso-influencers (10,000 to 1 million followers).

After manipulating the advertising disclosure, these studies then measured the persuasion knowledge of participants. Studies looked at persuasion knowledge leading to manipulative intent (Kim & Song, 2018), advertising recognition (Boerman, 2020; De Jans et al., 2018; Evans et al., 2017, 2018; Stubb & Colliander, 2019), and advertising recognition leading to skepticism (De Veirman & Hudders, 2019). One disclosure study (Dhanesh & Duthler, 2019) asked respondents to consider influencers and whether they were aware that influencers were paid, therefore not manipulating this variable in the same way the previous experimental studies did. Some of the other message variables manipulated in these disclosure studies included sidedness of the message (De Veirman & Hudders, 2019) and promotional vs. experience-centric content (Kim & Song, 2018).

Despite the widespread use of PKM in influencer studies, the findings have limited applications to improving influencer performance, given that the FTC regulates advertising disclosure. One conclusion is that these studies demonstrate that the FTC's guidelines are having an impact on advertising recognition, which is the purpose of the guidelines. Because disclosure is not optional, researchers should focus on building knowledge about influencers using variables that can be manipulated in the real world.

Receiver Input Variable Studies

McGuire's (1989) receiver input variables are related to the audience and can include demographics, personality, and lifestyle. This review will cover four theories or models related to receivers: the Elaboration Likelihood Model, Relationship Management Theory, the Six-Segment Strategy Wheel, and Parasocial Interaction Theory.

Elaboration Likelihood Model

The Elaboration Likelihood Model (ELM) (Petty & Cacioppo, 1986) proposes two routes to persuasion based on the communication receiver's ability and motivation to process a message: the central route and the peripheral route. Receivers who are able and willing to process messages will follow the central route to persuasion. As they elaborate more on the message arguments, they will experience more enduring attitude change. Receivers who are neither able nor willing to process messages will follow the peripheral route to persuasion and will rely on peripheral cues or heuristics to process information, which may result in attitude change, but it is less likely to be long-lasting. In applying this theory to influencers, researchers are asking what elements can impact the route to persuasion and also what cues are relevant in the peripheral route. With its focus on message receivers, ELM can be categorized under McGuire's receiver variables, but the following study, the only one to use ELM, also manipulated the medium.

Hughes et al. (2019) applied ELM in a study that examined the social media platform (either a blog or Facebook) and the stage in the consumer decision process (either awareness or a trial). When a sponsored post was shared on a blog, the expertise of the blogger was found to drive advertising intent more effectively for awareness campaigns rather than trial campaigns. On Facebook, source expertise was not effective in driving engagement, but it depended more on high hedonic content, which was found to be more effective for trial campaigns as opposed to awareness campaigns. ELM can explain these findings in that blog readers are generally in a high-involvement, low-distraction, central route environment where an expert endorsement can be useful, whereas Facebook users are in a low-involvement, high-distraction, peripheral route environment where expertise is less relevant and hedonic content can be persuasive.

Relationship Management

Influencers are utilized in marketing campaigns because they can form online relationships with consumers. For this reason, Hon and Grunig's (1999) relationship management theory can be applied to measure the outcomes of these relationships, namely the dimensions of trust, satisfaction, commitment, and control mutuality. Only one study in this review measured the variables from relationship management theory.

Dhanesh and Duthler (2019) measured persuasion knowledge as well as the outcomes from relationship management theory and found a positive and significant relationship between awareness of paid endorsement and two of the four relationship variables—trust and satisfaction. Therefore, they concluded the FTC requirement that influencers are open and transparent about their endorsement deals is beneficial to the relationship between the influencer and the consumer, particularly on these two key dimensions. The researchers also found that two other relationship outcomes—control mutuality and commitment—were the strongest predictors of behavioral intentions.

Six-Segment Strategy Wheel

Another theoretical framework for influencer research is the Six-Segment Strategy Wheel (SSSW) (Taylor, 1999). The wheel encompasses both the transmission view of communication and the ritual view of communication in six message segments (three for each view of communication). Representing the transmission view are three message strategies classified as rational, acute, and routine. Rational strategies suggest that consumers can process information from ads and make a rational purchase decision; acute strategies apply when consumers need to make a decision quickly because of time constraints; and routine strategies rely on habit to motivate consumers to make a decision (Taylor, 1999). The three ritual message strategies are classified as ego, social, and sensory. Ego strategies allow consumers to fulfill emotional needs to define themselves by the products they purchase; social strategies allow purchase decisions to be shown off to others or communicate membership in a social community; and sensory strategies play on the association between the product and the emotional response by consumers, such as pleasure or happiness (Taylor, 1999). One study in this literature review focused on comments made by receivers of messages; therefore, the SSSW is categorized under McGuire's receiver variables.

Daniel et al. (2018) examined whether the SSSW was relevant to discussions in the vaping community found in the comments of videos published in the Vape Capitol YouTube Channel. The researchers found categories of the SSSW to be present in 42 percent of comments, with the ritual side representing 86.3 percent of those comments and the transmission side representing 13.7 percent. The authors proposed a model whereby social message strategies, such as having a relevant and likable influencer, lead to feelings of parasocial interaction, which can deliver a range of benefits for the advertiser.

Parasocial Interaction Theory

Developed by Horton and Wohl (1956), parasocial interaction (PSI) describes a pseudo-relationship that develops between a celebrity and the audience. Prior to digital and social media, parasocial interaction was often a one-sided and mediated relationship, such as when an audience member felt a connection to a celebrity on television. With the advent of digital and social media, audiences now have more ways to connect with celebrities, such as mentioning them on Twitter, posting a comment on their blogs or YouTube videos, or sending an email. It is possible that the relationship becomes two-way if the celebrity responds in some way.

In an experimental study, Rasmussen (2018) found that parasocial interaction can occur between YouTube influencers and viewers, who felt that they knew the influencer, the influencer seemed like a friend, and they enjoyed the influencer's personality. In comparing effectiveness of a highly popular YouTube vloggers to moderately popular vloggers, they found popularity to be significantly related to all three parasocial interaction variables. They concluded that parasocial interaction occurs not only between audiences and traditional celebrities, but also with vloggers on platforms such as YouTube in the digital world.

Boerman (2020) used parasocial interaction as an outcome of disclosure and ad recognition. Their study of micro- and meso-influencers found neither disclosure nor advertising recognition to have an impact on parasocial interaction, but explained that the sample had low PSI with the influencer. Future research could use an influencer who experiences a higher PSI among followers.

Daniel et al. (2018) also explored parasocial interaction in their study of comments in a YouTube vaping community. Parasocial interactions were present in 68 percent of comments. They concluded that parasocial interaction can lead to feelings of a parasocial relationship after repeated interactions, and then finally brand loyalty, sales, and word of mouth.

Intent Input Variable Studies

Intent input variables, also called destination variables, focus on the actions a persuasive campaign attempts to achieve. McGuire (2001) recognized that when messages are able to change beliefs, attitudes, or behavior, the other two variables are generally impacted. Furthermore, McGuire (2001) noted that the persuasive impact may be strongest immediately after a communication but may also increase over time. Finally, persuasive campaigns may use or be impacted by techniques to induce resistance to persuasion. For the intent variable, this review will cover Reactance Theory, which focuses on a negative reaction to a persuasive attempt, and electronic word of mouth, which may be generated as a result of a communication and is related to other outcomes, such as beliefs, attitudes, and behaviors. Because intent variables concern factors that lead people to resist persuasion, the PKM could have been discussed in this section but was instead included in the message input section because the message was manipulated in many of those studies.

Reactance Theory

The reaction to a persuasive attempt, such as an advertisement, could be critical emotions toward the ad, including skepticism (Boerman et al., 2012). These reactions are explained by reactance theory, which argues that consumers desire autonomy and independence and will develop "reactance" to advertising if their ability to make decisions is compromised by manipulation attempts (Brehm & Brehm, 1981).

In the only study to use reactance theory as a framework, De Veirman and Hudders (2019) explored whether consumers experience reactance when exposed to Instagram posts containing disclosure through a process of advertising recognition, then skepticism, which was predicted to negatively impact influencer credibility and then brand attitudes. The researchers found support for the role of reactance and additionally used it to explain the unexpected result of a difference between the treatments of disclosure of material compensation and disclosure of financial compensation (De Veirman & Hudders, 2019). The researchers reasoned that consumers are more aware of the influencers' motives when they are being paid but less clear when free products are being provided, causing them to question whether the marketer required a recommendation in return for the free products or only hoped for this recommendation. The uncertainly around the relationship may lead to more skepticism about the authenticity of the review.

Electronic Word of Mouth

Word of mouth (WOM) has been described by Katz and Lazarsfeld (1955) as an exchange of marketing information between consumers that impacts their attitudes and behaviors toward the discussed products and services. The messages that flow in this process are not influenced or perceived to be influenced by a commercial third party but rely on consumer knowledge and experience. Research has demonstrated that WOM is one of the key influencers of consumer behavior, making it a particularly fruitful research stream (Daugherty & Hoffman, 2014). Electronic word of mouth (eWOM) is an extension of traditional word of mouth involving communications that occur informally over the Internet. eWOM has also been defined as "any positive or negative statement made about a product or company, which is made available to a multitude of people and institutions via the Internet" (Hennig-Thurau et al., 2004). Huete-Alcocer (2017) compared WOM to eWOM across four dimensions: credibility, privacy, diffusion speed, and accessibility. They described credibility as being positively impacted in WOM since the receiver knows the sender, but negatively impacted in eWOM because the sender might be anonymous to the receiver. WOM conversations are more likely to be private where eWOM may be shared on public sites and available to others. Messages spread slowly in WOM because the process generally happens through synchronous communication while online messages spread more quickly. Finally, WOM is less accessible to many people, whereas eWOM is easily accessible.

Influencer literature on eWOM is often related to the factors that impact the transmission of eWOM, namely disclosure. The research also examines the direction of the impact. Seven studies included eWOM as a theoretical framework. Some of these studies specifically measure eWOM by the audience of the influencer (Boerman, 2020; Dhanesh & Duthler, 2019; Evans et al., 2019). Others do not directly measure eWOM, but may consider eWOM from the perspective of followers and whether they will be inspired to generate eWOM after exposure to an influencer's post (Kim & Song, 2018), while others consider eWOM from the perspective of the influencer in his or her effectiveness to inspire eWOM among followers (Carr & Hayes, 2014; De Veirman et al., 2017). Finally, Araujo et al. (2017) examined retweets of a brand's tweets to determine how to generate eWOM by followers.

One of the three studies that measured the intention of followers to spread eWOM was conducted by Evans et al. (2017), who examined the impact of advertising disclosure on advertising recognition and then on outcomes such as attitudes, purchase intention, and intention to spread eWOM messages. Attitude toward the brand was found to be significantly higher when the post had no disclosure, but there were no significant differences for the other variables, including eWOM. An interaction between disclosure recall and advertising recognition produced a negative indirect effect on the intention to spread eWOM.

Another study that specifically included eWOM measures of the audience was conducted by Dhanesh and Duthler (2019), who used Evans et al.'s (2017) scale to measure eWOM along with purchase intention as outcomes of awareness of paid endorsement by influencers. The study found that awareness of paid endorsement as a practice led to ad recognition for a specific ad, which was a driver of purchase and eWOM intentions. Paid endorser awareness was also positively correlated with the influencer–follower relationship, but did not impact purchase and eWOM intentions. Finally, the influencer–follower relationship correlated with behavioral intentions, with commitment having the most impact on eWOM intention.

Boerman (2020) also used eWOM measures as an outcome of disclosure and ad recognition, although they were referred to as online behavioral intentions. Their study of micro- and meso-influencers found disclosure to have an indirect impact through advertising recognition on higher behavioral intentions, which was the opposite of hypothesized direction, and on higher brand recall.

Kim and Song (2018) applied eWOM principles from the perspective of the audience in their study of brand-sponsored and organic (unpaid) brand-related user-generated content (UGC) on Twitter. They attempted to identify conditions under which consumer skepticism is decreased and persuasion efforts are enhanced by manipulating not only whether the post was paid or organic but also whether the content of the post focused specifically on the product promotion or the experience of using the product. The researchers found that for organic brand-related UGC, experience-centric content generated more favorable brand attitudes and greater intention to click on a URL than promotional content on Twitter. However, for brand-sponsored UGC, promotional content was more effective than experience-centric content for yielding greater intention to click on a URL. The researchers concluded that their research advances

WOM literature by exploring how inferences of manipulative intent impact the effectiveness of brand-related UGC and the ability to generate eWOM. According to the researchers, the content of the communication has not been explored as much as other variables that impact eWOM. Their study added to the literature by differentiating when organic brand-related, unpaid content can be most effective (when it is experience-centric) and when sponsored content can be most effective (when it is promotional). The implications of this study for marketers are that consumers are more accepting of promotional content in sponsored posts but can be frustrated with content that seems organic and experience-centric, but turns out to be sponsored.

De Veirman et al. (2017) used experimental research to examine the characteristics of Instagram influencers that lead to effectiveness within the framework of eWOM literature. Their study included the variable of follower count and the role it plays in impacting perceptions of opinion leadership and likeability. Although the variable is not directly measured, this study frames eWOM from the perspective of how an influencer can generate it through opinion leadership.

Another study that examined eWOM from the perspective of the influencer was Carr and Hayes (2014), who framed the concept in terms of a reader's perception of a blogger's word-of-mouth influence. Perceived word-of-mouth influence was measured using Bansal and Voyer's (2000) scale that included items related to the blogger providing new information, influencing views about the product's features, or helping the receiver make a decision but not the word of mouth that occurs after the reader was exposed to the information. The researchers found a positive relationship between perceptions of blogger credibility and the blogger's perceived word-of-mouth influence, but there was no direct relationship between perceived third-party influence and the blogger's eWOM influence.

Taking a different approach were Araujo et al. (2017), who studied how eWOM, in the form of retweets of a brand's tweets, can be the most effective. The researchers explored whether the following variables led to more retweets of a brand's tweet: the number of "influentials" (aka influencers) who retweet, whether the tweet mentions influentials, the number of information brokers who retweet, and the number of users with strong ties who retweet. All variables were related to more retweets, except for users with strong ties.

CONCLUSION

The literature review presented in this chapter used McGuire's (1989) five classes of input variables to organize theoretical frameworks applied in eighteen research studies about influencers published across seven journals from advertising, public relations, marketing, and social media. This overview demonstrates that there is still much more to explore across each of McGuire's input variables.

Much of the source research revolves around source credibility, and also similarity, likeability, and attractiveness. Influencer follower count was also considered in some of these studies, as well as a comparison of influencers to celebrities. Other source variables to explore in future research include relevance, engagement, and authenticity of the influencer. Future studies could also compare influencers with many endorsement deals to influencers with fewer deals. Marketers generally look at metrics such as followers and engagement when choosing influencers, but survey research could also be applied to measure perceptions of influencer trustworthiness, attractiveness, and similarity as well as trust in the posts.

Additionally, research could consider the source as not only the influencer but also the sponsoring organization. None of the studies presented in this review explored the relationship between the organization and the influencer, how influencers can contribute to meeting organizational goals, or how organizations can incorporate what is learned from the feedback provided by the audience of influencers.

The primary message variable manipulated in these studies was advertising disclosure and its impact on persuasion knowledge. Because disclosure is required for influencer posts, research should move into new areas to better understand the message variable. One study in this review compared promotional posts to experience-centric posts. Type of content, such as informational or entertaining, could also be explored through additional research. De Veirman and Hudders (2019) noted that research on how the sponsored post should look is limited and that more research on how to best position products in influencer posts is needed in terms of both the post's image and its caption.

As previously mentioned, no studies in this review used a theoretical framework that could be classified as being related to channel variables, although one study in the review compared one social media platform to another. More research could highlight the differences between platforms, how influencers can be effective given the platform, or how marketers can choose the best platform given their objectives. Users also receive messages from different social media channels, including some from the same brand in various formats, such as promoted posts, paid influencer posts, and pre-roll advertising. Research could explore the impact of viewing brand advertising in multiple formats across different channels.

From the perspective of the audience, this literature revealed no studies that compared demographic or cultural groups, and more research in this area is warranted to understand the effectiveness for different groups. Similarly, research could explore differences in the audience on the basis of social media usage, lifestyles, and buyer behavior. Additionally, audience involvement is a key variable that was barely explored in these studies. In the digital space, the audience can quickly become the influencer, and therefore, more research could focus on how to motivate consumers to become influencers. The audiences also provide helpful feedback to both the influencer and the organization, and more research could be used to understand how this feedback is being monitored and utilized. Additionally, Uses and Gratifications Theory, which was applied only to influencers in the studies included in this review, could also be useful here in exploring audience motivations.

Reactance Theory and eWOM were discussed under the input of intent, and researchers have more opportunities to apply other theories that could be classified as intent. McGuire (2001) discussed factors that impact the persistence of the persuasive impact, which may decline or increase over time. For example, further research could study the role of the discounting-cue sleeper effect. Similarly, Cialdini's (2008) six principles of persuasion (liking, social proof, consistency, scarcity, reciprocity, and authority) may play a role in persuasive intent and can be applied to understand how influencers can be more effective.

The literature in this review is overwhelmingly experimental, and one issue with experimental research that was acknowledged by some of the researchers was that their stimuli were not realistic. For example, Schouten et al. (2019) placed a product image next to the endorser's face in their stimuli despite the fact that social media influencers usually present products in a more organic and natural way. Previous research on product placement revealed that integrating the product into the story in a visually compelling way enhanced endorser effectiveness (Russell, 1998). Others used stimuli that had been previously produced, such as the beauty vlogger videos viewed by Rasmussen's (2018) participants. De Jans et al. (2018) used informational vlogs about advertising featuring influencers created for them by a Belgian influencer marketing agency.

Other studies in this chapter employed survey methodology, such as Lou and Yuan (2019), who asked respondents to consider the influencers they follow on social media, and Dhanesh and Duthler (2019), whose respondents identified one social media influencer to consider when responding to the survey items. In addition to experimental research used in one study, Hughes et al. (2019) analyzed field data from a large set of influencer marketing campaigns in a second study. Content and/or network analysis was employed by Erz et al. (2018), Araujo et al. (2017), and Lahuerta-Otero and Cordero-Gutierrez (2016) in studies of Twitter.

In addition to examining McGuire's (1989) inputs, many of these studies measure a range of outcome variables, including brand recall, attitude toward the ad and brand, intention to engage with the post, and purchase intention. Most of the research covered in this chapter focused on intent and not actual behavior, and further research could analyze the relationships between source, message, and channel variables and relevant outcome variables in more realistic settings.

The literature review presented in this chapter presents a range of theories with applications to social media influencers as an overview for understanding the influencer process. It should be noted that relevant studies may have been missed when searching with the keyword "influencer," including studies that use terminology such as "sponsored posts." Also important to mention is that despite the presentation of theoretical frameworks related to the influencer process in a delineated manner in this chapter, the process actually moves in many different directions. Users could become influencers, influencer messages can be viewed from many different sources and on different platforms, and users can provide important feedback to influencers and the sponsoring organization. Further research should consider influencer communication as both a fluid and an integrated process to tap into innovative ways to answer relevant questions.

REFERENCES

Araujo, T., Neijens, P., & Vliegenthart, R. (2017). Getting the word out on Twitter: The role of influentials, information brokers and strong ties in building word-of-mouth for brands. *International Journal of Advertising, 36*(3), 496–513. https://do i.org/10.1080/02650487.2016.1173765

Armano, D. (2019, December). Three ways influencer marketing will further mature in 2020. *Adweek.* https://www.adweek.com/brand-marketing/3-ways-influencers -marketing-will-come-further-mature-in-2020/

Bansal, H. S., & Voyer, P. A. (2000). Word-of-mouth processes within a services purchase decision context. *Journal of Service Research, 3*(2), 166–177. https://doi .org/10.1177/109467050032005

Bergkvist, L., & Zhou, K. Q. (2016). Celebrity endorsements: A literature review and research agenda. *International Journal of Advertising, 35*(4), 642–663. https://doi .org/10.1080/02650487.2015.1137537

Boerman, S. C. (2020). The effects of the standarized Instagram disclosure for micro- and meso- influencers. *Computers in Human Behavior, 103*, 199–207. https://doi .org/10.1016/j.chb.2019.09.015

Boerman, S. C., Willemsen, L. M., & Van der Aa, E. (2012). "This post is sponsored": Effects of sponsorship disclosure on persuasion knowledge and electronic word of mouth in the context of Facebook. *Journal of Interactive Marketing, 38*, 89–92. https://doi.org/10.1016/j.intmar.2016.12.002

Brehm, S. S., & Brehm, J. W. (1981). *Psychological reactance: A theory of freedom and control.* San Diego, CA: Academic Press.

Carr, C. T., & Hayes, R. A. (2014). The effect of disclosure of third-party influence on an opinion leader's credibility and electronic word of mouth in two-step flow. *Journal of Interactive Advertising, 14*(1), 38–50. https://doi.org/10.1080/152520 19.2014.909296

Cialdini, R. (2008). *Influence: Science and practice* (5th ed.). Boston, MA: Allyn and Bacon.

Daniel, E. S., Jr., Crawford Jackson, E. C., & Westerman, D. K. (2018). The influence of social media influencers: Understanding online vaping communities and parasocial interaction through the lens of Taylor's six-segment strategy wheel. *Journal of Interactive Advertising, 18*(2), 96–109. https://doi.org/10.1080/152520 19.2018.1488637

Daugherty, T., & Hoffman, E. (2014). eWOM and the importance of capturing consumer attention within social media. *Journal of Marketing Communications, 20,* 82–102. https://doi.org/10.1080/13527266.2013.797764

De Jans, S., Cauberghe, V., & Hudders, L. (2018). How an advertising disclosure alerts young adolescents to sponsored vlogs: The moderating role of a peer-based advertising literacy intervention through an informational vlog. *Journal of Advertising, 47*(4), 309–325. https://doi.org/10.1080/00913367.2018.1539363

De Veirman, M., Cauberghe, V., & Hudders, L. (2017). Marketing through Instagram influencers: The impact of number of followers and product divergence on brand attitude. *International Journal of Advertising, 36*(5), 798–828. https://doi.org/10.1 080/02650487.2017.1348035

De Veirman, M., & Hudders, L. (2019). Disclosing sponsored Instagram posts: The role of material connection with the brand and message-sidedness when disclosing covert advertising. *International Journal of Advertising, 39*(1), 1–37. https://doi .org/10.1080/02650487.2019.1575108

Dhanesh, G. S., & Duthler, G. (2019). Relationship management through social media influencers: Effects of followers' awareness of paid endorsement. *Public Relations Review, 45*(3). https://doi.org/10.1016/j.pubrev.2019.03.002

Duggan, M., Ellison, N. B., Lampe, C., Lenhart, A., & Madden, M. (2015). Social media update 2014. *Pew Research Center.* https://www.pewresearch.org/internet /2015/01/09/social-media-update-2014/

Erz, A., Marder, B., & Osadchaya, E. (2018). Hashtags: Motivational drivers, their use, and differences between influencers and followers. *Computers in Human Behavior, 89,* 48–60. https://doi.org/10.1016/j.chb.2018.07.030

Evans, N. J., Hoy, M. G., & Childers, C. C. (2018). Parenting "YouTube Natives": The impact of pre-roll advertising and text disclosures on parental responses to sponsored child influencer videos. *Journal of Advertising, 47*(4), 326–346. https:// doi.org/10.1080/00913367.2018.1544952

Evans, N. J., Phua, J., Lim, J., & Jun, H. (2017). Disclosing Instagram influencer advertising: The effects of disclosure language on advertising recognition, attitudes, and behavioral intent. *Journal of Interactive Advertising, 17*(2), 138–147. https://doi.org/10.1080/15252019.2017.1366885

Friestad, M., & Wright, P. (1994). The persuasion knowledge model: How people cope with persuasion attempts. *Journal of Consumer Research, 21*(1), 1–31. https://doi.org/10.1086/209380

Hennig-Thurau, T., Gwinner, K. P., Walsh, G., & Gremler, D. D. (2004). Electronic word-of-mouth via consumer-opinion platforms: What motivates consumers to articulate themselves on the Internet. *Journal of Interactive Marketing, 18*(1), 38–52. https://doi.org/10.1002/dir.10073

Hon, L. C., & Grunig, J. E. (1999). *Guidelines for measuring relationships in public relations*. Gainesville, FL: Institute for Public Relations Research. http://www.inst ituteforpr.org/research_single/guidelines_measuring_relationships/

Horton, D., & Wohl, R. R. (1956). Mass communication and para-social interaction. *Psychiatry, 19*(3), 215–229. https://doi.org/10.1080/00332747.1956.11023049

Huete-Alcocer, N. (2017). A literature review of word of mouth and electronic word of mouth: Implications for consumer behavior. *Frontiers in Psychology, 8*(1256). https://doi.org/10.3389/fpsyg.2017.01256

Hughes, C., Swaminathan, V., & Brooks, G. (2019). Driving brand engagement through online social influencers: An empirical investigation of sponsored blogging campaigns. *Journal of Marketing, 83*(5), 78–96. https://doi.org/10.1177/0022242919854374

Katz, E., Blumler, J. G., & Gurevitch, M. (1974). Utilization of mass communication by the individual. In J. G. Blumler, & E. Katz (Eds.), *The uses of mass communications: Current perspectives on gratifications research* (pp. 19–32). Beverly Hills, CA: Sage.

Katz, E., & Lazarsfeld, P. F. (1955). *Personal influence: The part played by people in the flow of mass communications*. Glencoe, IL: Free Press.

Kim, M., & Song, D. (2018). When brand-related UGC induces effectiveness on social media: The role of content sponsorship and content type. *International Journal of Advertising, 37*(1), 105–124. https://doi.org/10.1080/02650487.2017.1349031

Lahuerta-Otero, E., & Cordero-Gutierrez, R. (2016). Looking for the perfect tweet: The use of data mining techniques to find influencers on Twitter. *Computers in Human Behavior, 64*, 575–583. https://doi.org/10.1016/j.chb.2016.07.035

Lou, C., & Yuan, S. (2019). Influencer marketing: How message value and credibility affect consumer trust of branded content on social media. *Journal of Interactive Advertising, 19*(1), 58–73. https://doi.org/10.1080/15252019.2018.1533501

McGuire, W. J. (1989). Theoretical foundations of campaigns. In R. E. Rice, & C. K. Atkin (Eds.), *Public communication campaigns* (pp. 43–65). Newbury Park, CA: Sage.

McGuire, W. J. (1999). *Constructing social psychology: Creative and critical aspects*. Cambridge, UK: Cambridge University Press.

McGuire, W. J. (2001). Input and output variables currently promising for constructing persuasive communications. In R. E. Rice, & C. K. Atkin (Eds.), *Public communication campaigns* (pp. 22–48). Thousand Oaks, CA: Sage.

Ohanian, R. (1990). Construction and validation of a scale to measure celebrity endorsers' perceived expertise, trustworthiness, and attractiveness. *Journal of Advertising, 19*(3), 39–52. https://doi.org/10.1080/00913367.1990.10673191

Petty, R. E., & Cacioppo, J. T. (1986). *Communication and persuasion: Central and peripheral routes to attitude change.* New York, NY: Springer.

Rasmussen, L. (2018). Parasocial interaction in the digital age: An examination of relationship building and the effectiveness of YouTube celebrities. *The Journal of Social Media in Society, 7*(1), 280–294. https://thejsms.org/tsmri/index.php/TSMR I/article/view/364

Russell, C. A. (1998). Toward a framework of product placement: Theoretical propositions. *Advances in Consumer Research, 25*(1), 357–362. https://www.acrwebsite .org/volumes/8178/volumes/v25/na-25

Schouten, A. P., Janssen, L., & Verspaget, M. (2019). Celebrity vs. influencer endorsements in advertising: The role of identification, credibility, and product-endorser fit. *International Journal of Advertising, 39*(2), 258–281. https://doi.org /10.1080/02650487.2019.1634898

Stubb, C., & Colliander, J. (2019). "This is not sponsored content": The effects of impartiality disclosure and e-commerce landing pages on consumer responses to social media influencer posts. *Computers in Human Behavior, 98*, 210–222. https:/ /doi.org/10.1016/j.chb.2019.04.024

Taylor, R. (1999). A six-segment message strategy wheel. *Journal of Advertising Research, 39*(6), 7–17.

Chapter 2

#FitnessGoals and Brands on Instagram

Influencers and Digital Dialogic Communication

Alison N. Novak

As social media platforms increased in popularity over the past ten years, practitioners and academics have grappled with its impact on digital advertising, brand communication, and digital dialogic communication. As these fields grew to become dominant features of promotional practices, some products and services were quick to adapt and adopt new techniques of communication. One category that particularly embraced social media influencers (SMIs) as a part of the promotion mix is the fitness industry. Audrezet et al. (2018) found that the fitness industry spent approximately 8 percent of marketing budgets on Instagram influencers in 2018 and projected that the number will continue to rise in 2019. Further, fitness SMIs attract brands beyond the traditional scope of the industry to include companies such as Audible (Amazon), Hilton, and CoverGirl. For example, fitness SMI Sjana Elise Earp frequently promotes products from Bioessence, a skincare company, which she says pays her $25,000 per post (House, 2016). Despite this multi-billion-dollar industry that continues to expand to include new brands, few academic studies examine the result of paying SMIs to promote brands, particularly as it relates to improved brand communication.

Digital dialogic communication is one route to improve brand identity, salience, and communication. The theory, originating in the late 1990s to examine how organizations could use chat rooms to communicate directly with the public, suggests that brands should use digital spaces to achieve two-way communication with mutual adjustment (Vooveld, 2019). However, today, academics question if true digital dialogic communication takes place in online spaces such as Instagram or if organizations use the illusion of communication without the labor required to achieve mutual adjustment. This study seeks to expand on current theories of digital dialogic communication to examine its presence within fitness SMI accounts. To do this, the chapter provides findings from a discourse analysis of thirty randomly sampled "#ad" posts from the ten most followed fitness SMIs on Instagram, or 300 total posts.

INFLUENCERS AND BRAND COMMUNICATION

Uzunoğlu and Misi Kip (2014) define *brand influencers* as individuals who communicate information about an organization or product using persuasive messaging through digital media to a mass audience. These individuals are hired by organizations to use and share branded information with their followers to increase public awareness, liking, or consumption of a related product (Iqani et al., 2019). Influencers are hired for several tasks, including introducing a new product or service to an audience already familiar with a brand, reinforcing the popularity of an existing product or service, or addressing developing crises or issues facing a product or service (Godey et al., 2016). In these cases, the influencer speaks on behalf of a product or service, usually in the first-person voice, to explain its value (Godey et al., 2016). In addition, influencers might demonstrate a product or service through a picture or video, or they may promote the product through a giveaway or discount specific to their account and followers (Godey et al., 2016).

Bryant and Mawer (2016) suggest that SMIs are an extension of traditional promotional techniques such as spokespersons and celebrity endorsements. These techniques date back to the early 1930s, with the hiring of radio broadcasters to sell or verbalize support for specific products or services (Bryant & Mawer, 2016). In the ninety years since these first promotional messages, advertisers and public relations practitioners have developed best practices for selecting and using influencers, including (1) selecting an individual with matching interests and aesthetics of the brand, (2) selecting an individual with a large following specifically interested in an industry (i.e., fashion, sports, food, etc.), (3) asking the influencer to only post one promoted message per week, (4) demonstrating the product or services use in pictorial and text form, and (5) demonstrating a genuine interest in follower satisfaction and experience (Joker, 2018). However, as Joker (2018) reflects, these best practices are more abstract recommendations than practically implementable strategies. More work is needed to develop specific steps or tasks associated with the best practices and to evaluate the success of branded communication using SMIs.

Nechita (2018) posits that although influencers are now a regular part of the digital promotional mix (along with promoted posts, targeted messages, and use of big data warehouses), there is still a lot of uncertainty in the industry about the effectiveness of this approach. In part, consumers are seemingly more aware and critical of the role of SMIs, a likely result of growing literacy in digital media and skepticism of account credibility (Nechita, 2018). As consumers grow more familiar with accounts that regularly feature "ads" or promoted messages, and as more incidents of SMIs promoting products without genuine ties to the brand are publicized, members of the public grow critical of promoted messages (Nechita, 2018).

Hughes and Brooks (2019) reflect that in the early 2000s, users were less familiar with the concept of SMIs, and influencers, on the other hand, were less likely to self-identify or note when a post was sponsored (because of limited regulations and policies). However, by 2018, 90 percent of users indicated that they followed at least one account on social media that includes paid posts or uses "#ad" (Hughes & Brooks, 2019). This growing awareness matches the increase in both profits and uses in the SMI industry (Bratu, 2019). Bratu (2019) argues that the SMI industry has proliferated since 2009, which includes the development of influencer agents, influencer advocacy and lobbying groups, influencer conferences and workshops, and specific divisions and interest groups in professional organizations such as the Public Relations Society of America. This formalization of the industry drove the increase in SMI revenue as well as the number of self-identified SMIs on social media sites like Instagram (Bratu, 2019).

However, despite the growth of the SMI industry, scholars question the impact and effectiveness of this strategy within the digital promotions mix. Freberg et al. (2011) note that in the effort to celebrate and utilize a new form of promotion, the public relations profession failed to carefully evaluate the success of influencers and critically consider the ethics involved in selecting and using this strategy. Voorveld (2019) reflects that the industry lacks specific influencer models of communication, and as a result, there are limited recommendations for advertiser actions after a promoted post-debut on an SMI's account. Beyond concerns of campaign measurement, most advertisers have started responding to follower comments or directing SMIs to go beyond just one post and instead engage followers through the comments section (Vooveld, 2019). These actions, while new to the industry, perhaps reflect changes in advertising in general, such as the use of digital dialogic communication rather than one-way asymmetrical messaging (Vooveld, 2019). In short, scholars have only just begun to identify the ways that advertiser expectations of SMI actions and services continue to evolve.

THE FITNESS INDUSTRY, INSTAGRAM, AND INFLUENCERS

While research on digital dialogic communication on social media platforms is still in its early stages, most scholarship agrees that social media platforms are now a large part of the marketing and branding mix (Humphreys, 2018). Most organizations have some presence on social media, ranging from organizational accounts, promoted messages/posts, and the use of SMIs to promote products and services (Martinus & Anggraini, 2018). According to Edney et al. (2018), the fitness and health industries have specifically embraced social media as a mechanism for disseminating organizational messages and reaching target audiences. Some products, such as the Garmin smartwatches, is marketed exclusively using social media, demonstrating the reliance and perceived effectiveness of these platforms by marketers (Edney et al., 2018).

Gagnon and Sabus (2015) found that working with SMIs was a prominent theme in fitness industry conferences, with many professional associations paying for SMIs to come to annual meetings and conferences to teach best practices to brand managers and industry representatives. Higgins (2016) notes that the use of SMIs is synonymous with fitness industry promotions and most companies assume that they will need to partner with SMIs at some point in their promotion cycles.

While there is no standard definition of "influencer" for the fitness industry, Bokunewicz and Shulman (2017) consider that influencers are individuals possessing social capital with a dedicated group of followers and the ability to influence this group. Kádeková and Holienčinová (2018) add that influencers have social capital, meaning they have perceived power because of their ability to influence large masses of followers and direct attention, attitudes, and behavior. The number of required or expected followers can vary from platform to platform and from industry to industry, but most paid influencers have over one million followers (Bokunewicz & Shulman, 2017). Abidin (2016) notes that influencers do much more than just simply get paid to post information about products; they are required (like all promotional channels) to conduct research and demonstrate the effectiveness of the product. The most effective influencers do more than garner likes—they inspire conversation within the comments section, they engage the audience in a discussion about products, and they introduce content or messaging in a credible way to a difficult-to-reach audience (Abidin, 2016).

SMI effectiveness is measured on the "influencer index," a tool that compares influencers and quantitatively defines their social capital and ability to affect change in a target demographic (Arora et al., 2019). The influence index combines measures of followers, engagement, screen-time, and click-through to determine an SMI's effectiveness (Arora et al., 2019). Most organizations use the index to select SMIs and negotiate pricing (Booth & Matic, 2011)—a practice that continues to develop and reflect the growing standards and formalization of SMI practices (Doupnik, 2017).

Despite industry research on SMI effectiveness and recognition, limited academic studies have examined how SMIs actively communicate with followers or how SMI accounts become active spaces of digital dialogic communication between the public and the organizations. Scholars have called for more research looking at how the comments section of an influencer's post can be used by organizations to engage potential consumers or solicit feedback (Ungerman & Myslivcova, 2014; Dutot et al., 2016; Chokroverty et al., 2018; Voorveld, 2019). This study aims to answer that call.

DIGITAL DIALOGIC COMMUNICATION

In an effort to improve brand identity, salience, and communication, theorists developed digital dialogic communication. Since its inception in the 1990s, the theory was used to study how organizations can use the mechanisms of online technology to solicit feedback and mutually adjust opinions and actions. In digital dialogic communication, the goal is for organizations to listen to the public and use feedback to effect change within the organization (Kent & Taylor, 2002). Additionally, the public must listen to the organization and incorporate information into their knowledge, emotions, or actions. In this way, both the public and the organization adjust themselves through the information exchanged in a digital space.

There are five original components of digital dialogic communication that must occur in order to benefit from this form of communication:

mutuality, or the recognition of organization–public relationships; propinquity, or the temporality and spontaneity of interactions with publics; empathy, or the supportiveness and confirmation of public goals and interests; risk, or the willingness to interact with individuals and publics on their own terms; and finally, commitment, or the extent to which an organization gives itself over to dialogue, interpretation, and understanding in its interactions with publics. (Kent & Taylor, 2002, p. 22)

At its core is the concept of "dialogue" that is a valuable exchange between an organization and the public. Sommerfeld and Yang (2018) note that although digital dialogic communication may use different platforms than it did during the 1990s, the end goal of "dialogue" remains the same—mutual adjustment. However, contemporary questions arise regarding the changing nature of social media platforms and the decentralization of organization representatives (Sommerfeldt & Yang, 2018). With the use of SMIs and the engagement of groups outside the organization, challenges to the dialogic promise of digital media arise and allow for future areas of scholarship (Ciszek & Logan, 2018).

A consistent method to digital dialogic communication is two-way communication, or where an organization and the audience can exchange ideas and information with each other. Organizational chat rooms are ideal spaces for two-way communication because both the public and the organization can post messages, respond to each other, and engage in conversation with multiple parties at any time. However, as the Internet developed, more spaces for two-way communication emerged, such as social media platforms. Like chat rooms, social media platforms allow the public to post comments and feedback about an organization, and the organization has space to respond. Tewes and Nee (2016) note that the public is most likely to engage in two-way communication on social media platforms because these spaces have added third-party credibility and are less controlled by the organization. For example, the public believes that negative feedback on social media is more likely to be listened to because they assume the feedback will not be deleted. As a result, organizations are forced to listen or engage in two-way communication in order to address negativity.

The goal of digital dialogic communication is mutual adjustment or affecting change in both the audience and the organization based on the dialogue established in digital spaces (Uysal, 2018). When organizations listen authentically to the feedback from the public, they are more likely to adjust their own behaviors in order to meet the needs and concerns of potential consumers (Dhanesh, 2017). In this way, mutual adjustment is the goal state for an organization and the public who maximize the benefits of digital engagement (Dhanesh, 2017). Bruning et al. (2006) note that public relations and organizational communication is now in an era of mutual adjustment, where all "best practices" in each industry direct organizations to attain or reach for changing behaviors based on public feedback. In the past, mutual adjustment was primarily studied through experimental research design on controlled communication platforms, such as an organization's own chat room or website messaging system (Tewes & Nee, 2007). However, there is growing evidence that mutual adjustment also occurs through uncontrolled communication channels such as social media and the comments section of news websites (Knustad, 2018; Novak & Sebastian, 2018).

In any case, there is limited research on digital dialogic communication in social media platforms, particularly as it (may or may not) produce mutual adjustment. Further, no studies look at how digital dialogic communication occurs through brand ambassadors or SMIs who are paid to speak on behalf of an organization. If, as the research demonstrates, users trust social media platforms more because of their perceived credibility and the lack of organizational control, more research is necessary to understand this relationship when engaging a paid representative of the organization on these platforms.

While marketing research clearly identifies that social media promotion is effective at improving brand recognition and purchasing, no studies have used the digital dialogic framework to examine this industry and how organizations and the public use two-way communication on social media platforms (Dunlop et al., 2016). Nöcker et al. (2014) call for research on this topic, suggesting that although most research focuses on the effectiveness of social media promotions, few studies examine the communication mechanisms behind it. As such, this project seeks to study mutual adjustment within Instagram as mediated through SMI accounts in order to expand these assertions that the process of digital dialogic communication can produce mutual adjustment even when mediated by third-party communicators, specifically fitness SMIs on Instagram.

METHODOLOGICAL APPROACH

This project adopts a discourse analysis methodology to study if and how digital dialogic communication takes place between organizations and the public within the comments section of paid posts on Instagram influencer accounts. The goal is to apply the five components of digital dialogic communication to the comments sections, as well as understand the role of the SMI within digital dialogic communication and relationship building between fitness brands and consumers. In short, a series of discourses will illustrate the communication that takes place within these comments sections, as well as how the five components are (or are not) present to identify and critique this communication.

Sample

The fitness market was selected as a focus of this project because of the presence and early adoption of SMIs in the industry. For data collection purposes, the study analyzed thirty randomly sampled "#ad" posts from the ten most followed fitness SMIs on Instagram, or 300 total posts. All paid posts were collected from December 1, 2014, to June 1, 2019, with a total of 1,495 promoted posts (see table 2.1 for statistical information on posts). From this collection, 300 posts were randomly selected for analysis. The date December

Table 2.1   Influencers and Posts

Name and link	Number of followers	Number of total posts	Number of #ad posts
Michelle Lewin	13.4 million followers;	1,468	112
Jen Setler	12.5 million followers	1,467	80
Kayla Itsines	11.5 million followers	9,072	366
Simeon Panda	5.1 million followers	6,321	201
Lauren Kagan	3.9 million followers	2,487	55
Massy Arias	2.5 million followers	3,679	159
Emily Skye	2.6 million followers	3,060	219
Joe Wicks	2.6 million followers	9,779	91
Rachel Brathen	2.1 million followers	7,454	77
Alexa Jean	1.7 million followers	1,353	135

1, 2014, was selected as the starting date for data collection because this was the period when Instagram started requiring paid posts to include "#ad" to identify themselves. Although this practice was readily adopted earlier, it was formally announced only in 2014, thus providing a starting date for data collection.

It is important to note that the ten accounts were selected based on their popularity in 2019; thus, not all accounts were as popular throughout the four-and-a-half-year data collection period. While other accounts were likely popular and garnered similar attention during this time period, this project adopts the methodological recommendations of Chien-Wen and Chin-Jin (2017) as well as Dhanesh and Duthler (2019) to limit the scope to the ten accounts of those popular at the time of data collection (for improved reliability and completeness of data archives purposes).

Data Analysis

Once 300 randomly sampled posts were selected for this project, a team of two researchers read through the posts and comments section, identifying instances where commenters engaged with the SMI, where the SMI responded directly to user comments, and places where the organization posted responses (such as the SMI's comment section). After reading the posts, the researchers applied Gee and Handford's (2012) seven meaning-making tasks and identified a set of discourses (see table 2.2 for posts and descriptions). Following Gee's (2016), Johnson et al.'s (2017), and Zappavigna et al.'s (2016) framework and methodology, the researchers met to identify a final set of discourses that comprehensively identified and described how digital dialogic communication in the posts of SMIs. For reliability purposes, examples and quotes are provided within each discourse.

Table 2.2 Gee's Meaning-Making Tasks

Task	Description	Example
Significance	Post reflects importance of product, brand, or service	"If you know me, you know not a day goes by that I don't have some chocolate."
Practices	Post describes the product, brand, or service for other users; or engages/provides action for other users in conversation	"I'm so glad you all like the new collection!"
Identities	Post uses nouns and adjectives to describe the brand, product, or movement	"My favorite is the big statement moon ring."
Relationships	Post connects brand, product, or service to other events, or foci	"I had the ultimate driving experience."
Politics	Post reflects on the social, historical, civic, or political nature of the brand, product, or service	"But nobody is going to catch me angry. I should be mad about a lot of things that have happened to me, but I put my energy toward results."
Connections	Post discusses relevance of the brand, product, or service by comparing or relating to other issues	"These aren't like everyone else's leggings, these are the best ones out there."
Sign systems and knowledge	Identifies common language practices, jargon, or cultural knowledge	"@vqfit bio BLACK FRIDAY is coming! Up to 75% off. 25% sitewide sale going live at 7pm GMT on Sunday 24th do not miss it!"

RESULTS

Discourse 1: Influencers as Surrogates and Partners

As paid communicators, SMIs acted as brand surrogates by speaking on behalf of an organization. For most posts within this study, SMIs reflected on how a brand or product impacted their lives. For example, Jen Selter (@ JenSetler) posted this advertisement on a chocolate giveaway:

> #ad #GIVEAWAY!! If you know me, you know not a day goes by that I don't have some chocolate. . . . I'm so happy that @kinderbuenous is FINALLY COMING TO THE US!! To celebrate, it's giveaway time! If you're a chocolate lover, I'll be picking 3 winners to send some boxes to!! All you have to do is Tag 3 friends who love chocolate below Follow @kinderbuenous. (Selter, 2019)

Like most promoted posts, Setler (1) gives a quick summary of her relationship to the product, (2) introduces the brand, and (3) instructs followers about future actions to take part in the promotion. This formula appeared frequently throughout the posts, allowing for both personal reflection by the SMI and positive promotive communication about the brand or product. In most cases, the accompanying image featured the SMI using the product. In Selter's case, she posted a GIF of her popping out of a large pile of kinder bars.

Importantly, the language used within posts is personal and reflects a close relationship between the brand and the SMI. For example, all 300 posts included "I," "me," and "mine" illustrating a rhetorical closeness between the products being featured and the speaker. In eight cases, the SMIs used "we" or "our" in order to demonstrate that they considered themselves part of the brand. In these cases, SMIs spoke as less like a third-party endorser and more as a member of the brand's team or organization. For example, Rachel Brathen (@yoga_girl) promoted a collection of jewelry from Satya Jewelry by posting:

Link in bio or go to yogagirl.com/shop to see all our gems. My favorite is the big statement moon ring. . . . And the moon bar necklace. . . . And the HOOPS ah the hoops! Ok it's too hard to pick just one I think you will love the collection as much as I do! (Brathen, 2019a)

In this case, Brathen is more than speaking on behalf of the organization, since she uses "our" to denote closeness with the company and a mutual interest in the success of the collection.

This type of brand surrogacy is further identified in the comments section. When users post questions that would usually be intended for organizational representatives, SMIs like Brathen post responses. For example, one user asks: "Love love love this collection. It's so beautiful. Do they ship to the Netherlands?" and Brathen responds to the follower, "yes worldwide!" (Brathen, 2019b) In cases like this, the SMI fields questions normally intended for customer service representatives. Inherent in these exchanges is trust between the follower and the SMI; the follower must believe that the SMI has genuine insight into the organization and can answer (sometimes) technical questions about organizational policies.

In other cases, SMIs also field compliments and complaints by followers. For example, one follower commented, "this collection is freaking gorgeous? It's got such 'Rachel vibezzz' I adore the vibration of them all and the patterns. The moon phase earring is calling me." Brathen responded to the follower, "thank you!!!!!!" accepting the compliment on behalf of the organization (Brathen, 2019b). In complimentary posts, the SMIs reinforce their identity as a brand surrogate by accepting praise intended for the collection's designers and manufacturers. In this way, the posts blur the boundaries between the organization and the influencers.

Discourse Two: Selecting Partnerships and Branding Authenticity

Because all posts featuring paid promotion use the "#ad" identifier, many interactions within the comments section featured questions about the nature of the promotion and selection process of promoted brands. In one such interaction, Simeon Panda (@SimeonPanda) promoted a collection from Vanquish athletic wear, a frequent partnership featured on his Instagram page. He posted the following:

> the New @vqfit tracksuit is clean Ultimate technical detailing Bonded Zipper Pockets Two Way Front Zips Thumb Holes Premium Fused Branding Hidden Inner Pockets Bespoke Premium Fabric Blend Enhanced Tapered Fit Check it out, visit vqfit.com/Simeon or tap the link in the @vqfit bio BLACK FRIDAY is coming! Up to 75% off. 25% sitewide sale going live at 7pm GMT on Sunday 24th do not miss it! #vqfit #visit #WeAreVanquish #elevate. (Panda, 2019)[1]

After Panda posted this, one user asked, "Panda how did you get sponsorship from VQ?" to which Panda responded, "take a look at my page" and provided a link to his website that explained how he selected partnerships based on his personal use, not the amount of money provided.

SMIs frequently defended or explained their partnership choices, often directing followers to their personal websites and policy statements. These statements range from personal manifestos about how the SMI selects products to legal statements regarding the liability of an SMI after promotion takes place. For example, Kayla Itsines (@Kayla_Itsines) includes an exhaustive 3,500+ words of set policies that cover everything from third-party sales to privacy to customer dissatisfaction. The policies, clearly written by a legal team, serve to both reduce Itsines's liability when customers have a negative interaction with promoted products or organizations and explain the limits of her responsibilities as a promoter to interested organizational partners. Similarly, Panda also provides an explanation of his responsibilities regarding third-party promotions:

> We are not responsible for examining or evaluating the content or accuracy and we do not warrant and will not have any liability or responsibility for any third-party materials or websites, or for any other materials, products, or services of third-parties. . . . Complaints, claims, concerns, or questions regarding third-party products should be directed to the third-party. (Panda, 2020)

Beyond the reflections provided on official websites, SMIs also reflect on the authenticity of partnerships within individual posts and in the comments section. This seems to appear most frequently when SMIs introduce a new partnership or respond to criticism about a partnership. For example, Massy Arias (@Massy.Arias) featured a partnership with Porsche on her Instagram account, asking her followers to help her select a color for a test drive. While most followers posted suggested colors, one individual criticized the brand partnership by saying, "this is so not like you," seemingly referencing her partnership with a luxury brand while simultaneously posting videos about low-cost fitness ideas (such as working out at a state park) (Massy, 2019). While Arias did not reply to the follower directly, she did modify her original post to include a short reflection on why Porsche was selected for a partnership: "I had the ultimate driving experience which is not so bad for a New Yorker who just started driving two years ago. Check my story I have a little giveaway" (Massy, 2019). Her story then featured a link to her website and her brand partnership selection process, as well as a giveaway for a test drive in a Porsche.

However, there are also partnerships that SMIs must work harder to defend or eventually even apologize for. In a 2018 partnership with the NFL, Arias was forced to defend a campaign she shared on Instagram that promoted NFL programs. Arias, a Dominican Republic–born fitness influencer, partnered with the NFL during a time of controversy regarding the organization's support (or lack thereof) of black athletes and related sociopolitical movements. After followers criticized her original post, she provided an interview with ESPN to defend her partnership, saying:

> But what am I going to do? I'm going to make sure that I am the best at what I do. This is where I put my anger—making sure that I am a professional. Making sure that there is no way you're not going to include me in what you do because I am this good. I work twice as hard, three times as hard if I need to. But nobody is going to catch me angry. I should be mad about a lot of things that have happened to me, but I put my energy toward results. (Petit, 2019)

For Arias, the partnership made sense because she aimed to improve the representation of minority athletes within the NFL, but for some followers, the partnership was problematic due to the NFL's actions. While Arias continued the partnership, she also continued to defend it outside Instagram, through news media channels.

There also appears to be a broadening of the "fitness industry" throughout fitness SMI accounts. All ten SMIs identified in this study simultaneously partner fitness with other forms of wellness, including fashion and beauty, mental health, home furnishings, and relationship building. When selecting partnerships, fitness SMIs often partnered with brands outside the traditional boundaries of fitness. Emily Skye (@emilyskyefit) partnered with the beauty brand James to promote 24-karat gold under-eye masks to alleviate dark circles. Her post featured an image of her wearing the mask while playing with her toddler-daughter wearing matching pajamas (Skye, 2019). Followers were receptive to the advertisement, often remarking how the masks helped their own skin (and asking questions about the matching pajamas brand as well). Similarly, Joe Wicks (@thebodycoach) promoted a campaign for BBC's Children in Need foundation that featured literacy as a component of wellness. Again, followers were receptive to his posts, seemingly supporting the connection between childhood literacy, wellness, and physical fitness: "Well done Joe, think about how many people you have inspired and helped!" (Wicks, 2019) For the most part, followers were complementary toward partnerships that focused on non-profits or fundraising, even when they fell outside the scope of fitness.

Discourse Three: Missing the Digital Dialogic Communication

Because fitness SMIs act as surrogates for the organizations and invoke first-person language when introducing products or brands, there is a possibility of engaging consumers in the following section to illustrate two-way communication and potentially digital dialogic communication. SMIs frequently answered questions about brands and products, responded to compliments and critiques about follower experiences, and provided feedback such as "hearts" (or likes). In this way, SMIs communicated on behalf of the brand to engage the audience in sometimes lengthy comment-based conversations about the brand or product.

These interactions indicate the presence of two-way communication, where the original post by the SMI initiates conversation, then followers respond by posting comments and the SMI then replies to the followers' post (and the pattern continues). Importantly, this two-way communication requires both the SMI and the followers to post specific responses and address each other. For example, Lauren Drain Kagan (@laurendrainfit) posted an advertisement for a maternity outfit, to which a follower replied, "Congrats!!!! Loving that jumper on you." Kagan then liked the comment and posed "thanks!" in response (Drain Kagan, 2019). In most cases, interactions between SMIs and followers were short but still indicated two-way communication.

However, it is unclear (and unlikely) that mutual adjustment takes place in these spaces. Although SMIs communicate on behalf of a brand and act as a surrogate in brand communication, it is unclear if feedback obtained in two-way communication is referred back to the organization itself. While it is likely that marketers maintain a close watch over the comments section of paid SMI posts, there were no instances where the sponsoring organization directly replied to comments or engaged followers in the comments section.

This is likely strategic, in that comments by the organization would likely challenge the third-party credibility established by trusted SMIs and infringe on the community-centric nature of the SMI's account. The comments sections revealed communication taking place between followers, not just with the SMI. For example, when followers respond with questions on posts by Itsines about sponsored workout plans, other users jump in and answer the questions:

User one: are the post pregnancy workouts ok if you're still breastfeeding? (I was told by my physio the other week that HIIT type workouts can affect your milk production, but I've never heard that before and don't know how true that is?!)

User two: [user one] The calories you intake matter most when breastfeeding, so definitely keep a watchful eye on that. If you drop them too low, your milk production will be affected because our bodies need the extra calories while breastfeeding.

User three: [user one] Hi there, sorry to jump in middle. Just wanted to share my experience with you. I am using BBG and breastfeeding. I have started BBG when my son was 5 months old and now he is 8 months and breastfeed 100%. We didn't have any problem. As long as you keep a healthy diet, your milk production won't be impacted. Good luck. (Itsines, 2019)

In this case, Itsines does not respond to questions about the sponsored fitness plan, but instead other followers and purchasers of the *BBG (Bikini Body Guide)* answered the questions. Again, this indicates two-way communication, but it is unclear if the questions were referred to the BBG brand managers so that they could adjust marketing or communication to accommodate this feedback. Thus, while the followers adjust their behavior and information base because of the information provided in the comments section, there is no evidence throughout the 300 posts that the organization adjusted its behavior.

Beyond a failure to see a mutual adjustment, three of the original five components of digital dialogic communication are missing. First, by working with SMIs, there is evidence of mutuality or the recognition of organization–public relationships that are necessary for success. By paying SMIs to share content with the public, organizations recognize the value of public-centered communication and the use of a platform that facilitates engagement. Similarly, propinquity is demonstrated by paying for content on a platform that encourages frequent updates and constant new material. By using Instagram, organizations understand that posts are featured for a limited time before new content replaces them. Interactions with the public are, therefore, temporary and occur only after instigated by an SMI post. Risk is also demonstrated by using an uncontrolled platform and account where an organization has little ability to control public feedback or comments. A paying organization takes a risk by allowing a highly visible SMI to control communication about a brand or product with limited ability to respond, edit, or shape comments by users.

Despite these three components, organizations failed to demonstrate the traditional practices of empathy or commitment when working with fitness SMIs on Instagram. The lack of demonstrated empathy by the organization may be strategic. By allowing the SMI to directly respond to user comments (rather than the organization), the credibility of the partnership and the post is maintained. Further, although the organization does not demonstrate empathy, the SMI does by responding to comments and liking user feedback. In this way, empathy is demonstrated through the surrogate qualities of the SMI rather than by the organization. Perhaps a more nuanced way of understanding empathy through the lens of SMIs should recognize the surrogacy potential of SMIs, not relying on behaviors specifically from organizational accounts.

Finally, there was limited evidence of commitment to the digital dialogic process established through SMI posts. While SMIs respond frequently to follower comments, there is no evidence that the SMI is committed to sharing feedback with the organization or that the organization uses user comments to update practices. This is crucial to the digital dialogic communication process and is likely the issue with achieving mutual adjustment. Without demonstrating a commitment to the feedback from followers, organizations do not adjust their own communication, practices, or structures, therefore limiting the impact of user suggestions and comments. This may perhaps be the limit of SMIs as surrogates; once the post is completed and the SMI contract is fulfilled, there is no longer a relationship between the SMI and the organization and no guarantee that comments on a post are relayed to the organization. The reflection provides more considerations for digital dialogic communication in SMI posts.

Discourse Four: Responses to Criticism

For most SMIs, the comments section was an opportunity to respond to user questions, reinforce a relationship with followers, and demonstrate appreciation for follower interest. All ten influencers responded and liked user feedback inconsistently but frequently throughout their posts. For example, there were instances where Alexa Jean Hunt (@AlexaJeanFitness) liked every comment, and then there were sponsored posts where she never responded or liked any comments (Hunt, 2019). There were no identified patterns of what type of comments instigated a reply or like within or between accounts. However, there were occasional instances where SMIs referred users directly to the organization instead of addressing questions or concerns themselves (as a surrogate). This usually occurs primarily after negative feedback. For example, after a user criticized a pair of yoga pants promoted by Michelle Lewin (@michelle_lewin), the SMI failed to acknowledge or respond to the critique (despite liking all other comments and responding to others). She then updated the original post with a referring link to the "one0one_101" sales team for questions (Lewin, 2019). This pattern similarly occurred on Simeon Panda's and Massy Arias's pages.

Surprisingly, this did not occur during technical questions about shipping or return policies. In these questions, SMIs continued their surrogate brand communication by answering questions typically reserved for customer service representatives. It is unclear whether they are provided with answers by the organization or if they are giving educated guesses, but their ability and willingness to answer technical questions seemingly reinforces their surrogacy status.

DISCUSSION

This study confirmed the richness of user comments and replies to SMI posts on Instagram as an asset to brand managers. SMIs act as brand surrogates, using their third-party credibility to engage followers, answer questions, cultivate community, and solicit feedback and information. In doing so, SMIs help shape and reflect branded information on behalf of an organization but stop short of achieving mutual adjustment and true digital dialogic communication. As noted, only three (mutuality, propinquity, and risk) of the traditional components of digital dialogic communication were identified within this dataset, and the outlying two (empathy and commitment) are either impossible or need revision to address the SMI and Instagram context. Traditionally, the notion of empathy requires the organization demonstrating a genuine interest in public goals or interest. However, the point of using an SMI is that the organization's official accounts stay out of communication allowing the credibility of the SMI to impact followers. While SMIs demonstrate empathy, the organizations do not. Therefore, this component needs to accept influencers as surrogates who can demonstrate empathy on behalf of an organization.

The component of commitment is more complicated and would require additional actions by the organization, such as eventual responses to follower comments, following up with specific commenters, or creating a sustainability plan that illustrates how user feedback will be incorporated into organizational practices. Currently, organizations fail to participate in the comments section, meaning they rely upon the SMI to share feedback or reply to compliments and criticism. To demonstrate commitment, organizations should post within the comments section, privately respond to user comments, or demonstrate how feedback obtained in these posts influences practices.

Similarly, the nuances and intersectionality of the "fitness" category make these types of SMI accounts an important area of future work. Although this project was limited to fitness accounts, the SMIs promoted products well outside that industry, including television stations, transportation, hotels/travel, and fashion. Future work should examine how SMIs position their own accounts and use the rhetoric of "well-being" to promote related industries and products. All ten SMIs offered fitness program subscriptions, and some promoted their own cookbooks, athletic equipment, and sports beverages, which further necessitates research that looks at products that are specifically created by the SMIs, not just the third-party brands they are paid to support. Comparative studies examining the best practices of paid promotion versus authentic promotion of self-developed products could reveal how to maximize the impact of each category.

As the use of SMIs continues to grow, organizations will need to find ways to incorporate the feedback developed in the comments sections of paid posts. When SMIs act as surrogates for an organization and engage in two-way communication, they use most of the components of digital dialogic communication; however, they fail to achieve real mutual adjustment because of a lack of commitment from the organization. With additional work, organizations can demonstrate this commitment, but more research is necessary to maximize its impact and determine if real mutual adjustment is possible through Instagram influencers.

NOTE

1. Posts, like this one, also contain emoticons, which are removed for analysis.

REFERENCES

Abidin, C. (2016). "Aren't these just young, rich women doing vain things online?": Influencer selfies as subversive frivolity. *Social Media + Society, 2*(2). https://doi .org/10.1177/2056305116641342

Arias, M. [@Massy.arias.] (2019, Nov. 7). I started the day never having driven a @Prorche, and now I understand why people love this Macan [Instagram photo]. https://www.instagram.com/p/B4lvt3UgPNH/

Arora, A., Bansal, S., Kandpal, C., Aswani, R., & Dwivedi, Y. (2019). Measuring social media influencer index-insights from Facebook, Twitter, and Instagram. *Journal of Retailing and Consumer Services, 49*, 86–101. https://doi.org/10.1016/j.jretconser.2019.03.012

Audrezet, A., de Kerviler, G., & Guidry Moulard, J. (2018). Authenticity under threat: When social media influencers need to go beyond self-presentation. *Journal of Business Research*. doi:10.1016/j.jbusres.2018.07.008

Bethany Johnson, Margaret M. Quinlan, & Nathan Pope. (2019). #ttc on Instagram: A multimodal discourse analysis of the treatment experience of patients pursuing in vitro fertilization. *Qualitative Research in Medicine & Healthcare, 3*(1). https://doi.org/10.4081/qrmh.2019.7875

Bokunewicz, J., & Shulman, J. (2017). Influencer identification in Twitter networks of destination marketing organizations. *Journal of Hospitality and Tourism Technology, 8*(2), 205–219. https://doi.org/10.1108/JHTT-09-2016-0057

Booth, N., & Matic, J. (2011). Mapping and leveraging influencers in social media to shape corporate brand perceptions. *Corporate Communications: An International Journal, 16*(3), 184–191. https://doi.org/10.1108/13563281111156853

Brathen, R. [@yoga_girl]. (2019a, Nov. 6). I am so, so, so proud to finally be able to share with you: The Yoga Girl Collection [Instagram photo]. https://www.instagram.com/p/B4hspPmBNhf/

Brathen, R. [@yoga_girl]. (2019b, Nov. 6). Love love love this collection [Instagram photo]. https://www.instagram.com/p/B4iFES2hH7D/

Bratu, S. (2019). Can social media influencers shape corporate brand reputation? Online followers' trust, value creation, and purchase intentions. *Review of Contemporary Philosophy, 18*. https://doi.org/10.22381/RCP18201910

Bruning, S., DeMiglio, P., & Embry, K. (2006). Mutual benefit as outcome indicator: Factors influencing perceptions of benefits in organization-public relations. *Public Relations Review, 32*(1), 33–40. https://doi.org/10.1016/j.pubrev.2005.10.005

Bryant, A., & Mawer, C. (2016). *The TV brand builders: How to win audiences and influence viewers*. London, UK: KoganPage.

Chien-Wen, S., & Chin-Jin, K. (2017). Analysis of social media influencers and trends on online and mobile learning. *International Review of Research in Open and Distributed Learning, 18*(1), 1–224. https://doi.org/10.19173/irrodl.v18i1.2640

Chokroverty, L., Sobowale, K., & Beckert, D. (2018). Disaster communication using social media: Trends and best practices. *Journal of the American Academy of Child and Adolescent Psychiatry, 57*(10), S40–S41. https://doi.org/10.1016/j.jaac.2018.07.173

Ciszek, E., & Logan, N. (2018). Challenging the dialogic promise: How Ben & Jerry's support for Black Lives Matter fosters dissensus on social media. *Journal of Public Relations Research, 30*(3), 115–127. https://doi.org/10.1080/1062726X.2018.1498342

Dhanesh, G. (2017). Putting engagement in its proper place: State of the field, definition and model of engagement in public relations. *Public Relations Review, 43*(5), 925–933. https://doi.org/10.1016/j.pubrev.2017.04.001

Dhanesh, G., & Duthler, G. (2019). Relationship management through social media influencers: Effects of followers' awareness of paid endorsement. *Public Relations Review, 45*(3), 40–52. https://doi.org/10.1016/j.pubrev.2019.03.002

Doupnik, E. (2017). Social media: Online retailers lead brick-and-mortar in influencer marketing. *WWD,* 14. http://search.proquest.com/docview/2196325904/

Drain Kagan, L. [@Laurendrainfit]. We finally have a home! Outfit: @prettylittlething We looked at so many houses this summer and finally fell in love! [Instagram photo]. https://www.instagram.com/p/B3ax5b-llTf/

Dunlop, S., Freeman, B., & Jones, S. (2016). Marketing to youth in the digital age: The promotion of unhealthy products and health promoting behaviours on social media. *Abstracts, 4*(3), 35–49. https://doi.org/10.17645/mac.v4i3.522

Dutot, V., Lacalle Galvez, E., & Versailles, D. (2016). CSR communications strategies through social media and influence on e-reputation. *Management Decision, 54*(2), 363–389. https://doi.org/10.1108/MD-01-2015-0015

Edney, S., Bogomolova, S., Ryan, J., Olds, T., Sanders, I., & Maher, C. (2018). Creating engaging health promotion campaigns on social media: Observations and lessons from Fitbit and Garmin. *Journal of Medical Internet Research, 20*(12), e10911. https://doi.org/10.2196/10911

Freberg, K., Graham, K., McGaughey, K., & Freberg, L. (2011). Who are the social media influencers? A study of public perceptions of personality. *Public Relations Review, 37*(1), 90–92. https://doi.org/10.1016/j.pubrev.2010.11.001

Gagnon, K., & Sabus, C. (2015). Professionalism in a digital age: Opportunities and considerations for using social media in health care. *Physical Therapy, 95*(3), 406–414. https://doi.org/10.2522/ptj.20130227

Gee, J. (2016). Discourse analysis matters: Bridging frameworks. *Journal of Multicultural Discourses, 11*(4), 343–359. https://doi.org/10.1080/17447143.2016.1226316

Gee, J., & Handford, M. (2012). *The Routledge handbook of discourse analysis.* Routledge.

Godey, B., Manthiou, A., Pederzoli, D., Rokka, J., Aiello, G., Donvito, R., & Singh, R. (2016). Social media marketing efforts of luxury brands: Influence on brand equity and consumer behavior. *Journal of Business Research, 69*(12), 5833–5841. https://doi.org/10.1016/j.jbusres.2016.04.181

Handy Martinus, & Liza Anggraini. (2018). The effect of sales promotion in social media on the students: Purchase intention of face cleaner water product. *Humaniora, 9*(1), 15–22. https://doi.org/10.21512/humaniora.v9i1.4101

Higgins, J. (2016). Smartphone applications for patients' health and fitness. *American Journal of Medicine, 129*(1). https://doi.org/10.1016/j.amjmed.2015.05.038

House, L. (2016, January 18). "Choose a theme, let tagging be your friend and don't forget the rule of thirds: Instagram star reveals her secrets to social media fame (and how she edits her own snaps)." *Daily Mail.* https://www.dailymail.co.uk/femail/article-3404115/Instagram-star-Sjana-Earp-reveals-secrets-social-media-fame.html

Hughes, C., & Brooks, G. (2019). Driving brand engagement through online social influencers: An empirical investigation of sponsored blogging campaigns. *Journal of Marketing, 83*(5), 78–96. https://doi.org/10.1177/0022242919854374

Humphreys, L. (2018). *The qualified self social media and the accounting of everyday life*. MIT Press.

Iqani, M., Alacovska, A., & Gill, R. (2019). Picturing luxury, producing value: The cultural labour of social media brand influencers in South Africa. *International Journal of Cultural Studies, 22*(2), 229–247. https://doi.org/10.1177/1367877918821237

Itsines, K. [@KaylaItsines]. The calories you intake matter most when breastfeeding, so definitely keep a watchful eye on that [Instagram photo]. https://www.instagram.com/kayla_itsines/?hl=en

Jean Hunt, A. [@AlexaJeanFitness]. Profile. https://www.instagram.com/alexajeanfitness/

Joker, K. (2018). Insights + advice from industry influencers. *Brand Packaging, 22*(2), 31–31. http://search.proquest.com/docview/2102831018/

Kádeková, Z., & Holienčinová, M. (2018). Influencer marketing as a modern phenomenon creating a new frontier of virtual opportunities. *Communication Today, 9*(2), 90–105. http://search.proquest.com/docview/2137429273/

Kent, M., & Taylor, M. (2002). Toward a dialogic theory of public relations. *Public Relations Review, 28*(1), 21–37. https://doi.org/10.1016/S0363-8111(02)00108-X

Knustad, M. (2018). How platform affects comments on news articles. A qualitative analysis of comments from a newspaper's comment section and Facebook page. The University of Bergen.

Lewin, M. [@Michelle_Lewin]. Un ejercicio muy efectivo para agregar firmeza y volumen a los glúteos. Aprieta fuerte en la parte superior del movimiento. Regresa hacia abajo, lentamente y controlado, sin tocar el piso con los glúteo [Instagram photo]. https://www.instagram.com/p/B4-wDUah8L0/

Men, L., Tsai, W., Chen, Z., & Ji, Y. (2018). Social presence and digital dialogic communication: Engagement lessons from top social CEOs. *Journal of Public Relations Research, 30*(3), 83–99. https://doi.org/10.1080/1062726X.2018.1498341

Nechita, A. (2018). Online brand awareness. A case-study on creating associations and attachment. *Journal of Media Research, 11*(31), 91–111.

Nöcker, G., Siegert, S., Tomse, M., Quast, T., & Höwner, J. (2014). How can health promotion institutions/services effectively use social media in health communication? *European Journal of Public Health, 24*(2). https://doi.org/10.1093/eurpub/cku165.109

Novak, A., & Sebastian, M. (2018). *Network neutrality and digital dialogic communication: How public, private, and governmental forces shape internet policy*. Routledge.

Panda, S. (2020). "Terms of service." *Simeon Panda.com*. https://simeonpanda.com/policies/terms-of-service

Panda, S. [@simeonpanda]. (2019, Nov. 20). tracksuit is clean, Ultimate technical detailing [Instagram photo]. https://www.instagram.com/p/B5GAFuPhRuu/

Petit, A. (2019, Feb 28). Health coach Massy Arias on the Afro-Latinx fitness conundrum. *ESPN*. https://www.espn.com/espnw/culture/story/_/id/26105707/health-coach-massy-arias-afro-latinx-fitness-conundrum

Pinto, M., & Yagnik, A. (n.d.). Fit for life: A content analysis of fitness tracker brands use of Facebook in social media marketing. *Journal of Brand Management, 24*(1), 49–67. https://doi.org/10.1057/s41262-016-0014-4

Selter, J. [@JenSelter]. (2019, Nov. 13). #ad #GIVEAWAY!! If you know me, you know not a day goes by that I don't have some chocolate . . . . [Instagram photo]. https://www.instagram.com/p/B40FLE-BZKZ/

Sommerfeldt, E., & Yang, A. (2018). Notes on a dialogue: Twenty years of digital dialogic communication research in public relations. *Journal of Public Relations Research, 30*(3), 59–64. https://doi.org/10.1080/1062726X.2018.1498248

Syke, E. [@emilyskyefit]. Monkeying around with my mini! How's her face in the second pic! Seriously matching PJs are LIFE! [Instagram photo]. https://www.instagram.com/p/B0oEOjfB14X/

Tewes, R., & Nee, R. (2016). Two-way symmetrical communication and Twitter in professional sports public relations. *ProQuest Dissertations Publishing*. http://search.proquest.com/docview/1809782668/

Ungerman, O., & Myslivcova, S. (2014). Model of communication usable for small and medium-sized companies for the consumer communication in social media. (Marketing and Trade/Marketing a obchod). *E+M Ekonomie a Management, 17*(1), 167–184. https://doi.org/10.15240/tul/001/2014-1-013

Uysal, N. (2018). On the relationship between dialogic communication and corporate social performance: Advancing dialogic theory and research. *Journal of Public Relations Research, 30*(3), 100–114. https://doi.org/10.1080/1062726X.2018.1498344

Uzunoğlu, E., & Misci Kip, S. (2014). Brand communication through digital influencers: Leveraging blogger engagement. *International Journal of Information Management, 34*(5), 592–602. https://doi.org/10.1016/j.ijinfomgt.2014.04.007

Voorveld, H. (2019). Brand communication in social media: A research agenda. *Journal of Advertising, 48*(1), 14–26. https://doi.org/10.1080/00913367.2019.1588808

Wicks, J. [@thebodycoach]. The UK tour is officially over. It's been such an incredible week travelling around with Pudsey. Thank you to everyone who took part in the big morning move today. We estimate that over 1 million kids have taken part so far. [Instagram photo]. https://www.instagram.com/p/B44mRGMHFab/

Zappavigna, M., Adami, E., & Jewitt, C. (2016). Social media photography: Construing subjectivity in Instagram images. *Visual Communication, 15*(3), 271–292. https://doi.org/10.1177/1470357216643220

Chapter 3

#MarketingFaith

The Megachurch Pastor as Social Media Influencer

Elizabeth B. Jones, Sydney O. Scheller, and Nathan A. Vick

Social media influencers (SMIs) have become crucial in many brands' marketing strategies. For most brands, the business objective driving the use of SMI marketing tactics is to increase profits by leveraging the preexisting trust (Lou & Yuan, 2019) and relationship between SMIs and consumers (Hwang & Zhang, 2018). However, when the definition of "brand" expands to include a wider swath of organization types, the SMI's role and goals may become multifarious and encompass both tangible and intangible objectives. This chapter examines one such non-traditional brand context: the Christian megachurch. Specifically, we examine the Twitter communication practices of megachurch pastors from an SMI perspective. Although all SMIs strategically construct their online identity through the technological affordances available to them (Marwick, 2016), megachurch pastors arguably face unique challenges as they attempt to create a social media presence that simultaneously sates followers and honors God.

To frame the current investigation, we focus on three central questions that capture the tensions confronting megachurch pastors as SMIs: (1) What is the megachurch, and can it be conceptualized as a brand? (2) Can megachurch pastors legitimately be defined as SMIs? and (3) How might documented SMI communication practices shape megachurch pastors' online self-presentation strategies? These questions will culminate in an original qualitative content analysis of the Twitter communication of the pastors of the largest churches in America.

CONCEPTUALIZING THE MEGACHURCH AS A BRAND

Defining the *Megachurch*

The megachurch is defined as "any Protestant Christian congregation with a sustained average weekly attendance of 2,000 persons or more in its worship services" (Hartford Institute, 2015, "Megachurch Definition" section). In addition to size, megachurches tend to share other traits, including massive recreational programs, large staffs and volunteer ranks, and flourishing communication departments, all intended to meet the spiritual, emotional, and educational needs of members and spiritual seekers (Eagle, 2015; Hartford Institute, 2015). The megachurch, in its current form, first proliferated in the United States during the 1970s and 1980s (Hartford Institute, 2015). Of particular relevance to the current investigation is the role of the megachurch's leader, the senior pastor,[1] a position typically defined as the elder in the church in charge of teaching, preaching, and leading. In the United States, almost all megachurch pastors are male, display an authoritative leadership style, and demonstrate personal charisma (Hartford Institute, 2015). Given this definition of the *megachurch*, can this institution accurately be defined as a *brand*? This question has been widely debated, and we next present a brief summary of relevant positions.

Defining a *Brand*

Brands originally served a legal function to denote the origin of a particular good and to prevent theft (e.g., a cattle brand designated the owner of livestock; Kapferer, 2012). This term has since evolved into a "name that influences buyers, becoming the purchase criterion" (Kapferer, 2012, p. 8). The brand name exerts its influence through the mental associations the customer holds that engender positive emotions such as trust and respect (Kapferer, 2012). These positive mental associations add intangible but real equity to an organization (Keller, 2009). Brand management, therefore, strategically separates one's brand from other competitors through the process of differentiation, in which a brand highlights its unique attributes and value (Kapferer, 2012). Narratives, stories that surround and inform brands, play a crucial role in this brand differentiation process and are "utilized whenever there is a surplus of interchangeable goods" (Twitchell, 2004, p. 4).

Given this definition of "brand," two primary schools of response emerge when weighing whether or not to include religious institutions within its purview. The first position opposes the branding of faith. The critiques in this camp center on a resistance to the "commodification" of faith and argue that this commodification leads to deleterious outcomes such as a cheapened faith practice and an unjust evangelical industrial complex (e.g., Miller, 2003; Johnson, 2017; Wigg-Stevenson, 2009).

The second and arguably more popular position accepts megachurch branding as largely unproblematic and, pragmatically, as necessary and even desirable. From this view, commodification is a sociologic reality that permeates all spheres of life, including the religious (Kaperferer, 2012; Twitchell, 2004). If brands emerge whenever there is a surplus of interchangeable goods, then religion must follow suit, for it is also fungible, in that all varieties offer some permutation of salvation and epiphany (Twitchell, 2004). Further, in a nation with no state-sponsored religion and a bombardment of commercial advertisements that promise earthly meaning, fulfillment, and transcendence, religious institutions must market themselves as a valuable commodity (Einstein, 2008). Rather than seek new converts, many religious institutions tend to compete for congregants internally amid—to use marketing parlance—an already existing "target market" of believers (Twitchell, 2004).

Although church leaders reject the premise that Christianity is a fungible good, they nonetheless also tend to embrace the branding of faith enthusiastically. Church how-to resources train pastors in marketing strategies and argue that church leaders must become conversant in the lingua franca of self-branding or else suffer missional aphasia. Pastors view branding through social media as one important way to communicate the Christian gospel message and to foster worship attendance, goodwill, and fundraising support (e.g., Cooke, 2012).

This impulse within many churches to adopt new communication channels for evangelistic goals has strong precedent. First, it reflects the *optimistic* stance that the Church has historically adopted toward new communication technologies, rather than the concurrent strands of technological pessimism or ambiguity (Campbell & Garner, 2016). This optimistic position holds that the benefits of technology for the salvation of souls and betterment of earthly injustices outweigh potential problems. Further, the contemporary megachurch's embrace of social media marketing strategies builds upon a long Protestant history of using entertainment and new communication for mass evangelism (Eagle, 2015). It is plausible that many current megachurch pastors identify with this optimistic technology stance and view faith branding as instrumentally useful. However, as Einstein (2008) notes, "Marketing religion is a balancing act—a delicate dance of how far one must go to remain relevant while at the same time remaining true to one's faith. This is no easy task" (p. 15). When megachurch pastors act as SMIs, they use various communication strategies in service of this negotiation.

THE MEGACHURCH PASTOR AS
SOCIAL MEDIA INFLUENCER

If the megachurch is to be branded, a logical next step is the selection of a brand endorser. For most megachurches, that endorser is, de facto, the senior pastor. As Christian ministry consultant Phil Cooke (2012) notes, "One thing I've discovered is that the pastor or ministry leader is the hub of the brand. Everything else revolves around his or her role" (p. 94). The contemporary focus on the senior pastor as a church representative is not entirely novel. Protestant church architecture, for instance, has long reflected the primacy of the speaker within worship (Eagle, 2015). Eagle (2015), for example, described a 1601 church structure as possessing a roof with the "characteristic lantern shape of many Protestant Temples, which *amplified the speaker's voice* [emphasis added]" (p. 592). We do not wish to stretch the comparison too thin; however, we argue that contemporary social media affords new and historically coherent possibilities for pastoral amplification through digital channels. Although the pastor plays a clear role in supporting the church brand, little research has explored if and how they function as an SMI. We next define the term "SMI" and compare our conceptualization of megachurch pastor as SMI with existing definitions, which focus on commercial contexts.

SMI *Definition*

Scholars define "SMI" in varying ways within the research literature. The burgeoning of social media that affords SMI marketing is relatively recent (Fox & McEwan, 2019), and thus multiple conceptualizations of SMIs are unsurprising. One oft-cited definition designates SMIs as "a new type of independent third-party endorser who shape audience attitudes through blogs, tweets, and the use of other social media" (Freberg et al., 2011, p. 90). Other academic definitions emphasize varying dimensions of the role, including the technical competencies needed to create sophisticated social media content that appeals to a niche audience (e.g., Audrezet et al., 2018), or the identification of social influence through the examination of online social network structures (e.g., Agonisto et al., 2019). Others have argued that SMIs are professionals who approach the cultivation of their online persona as a job and generate income (Albindin, 2017). Some scholars have proposed boundary conditions for SMIs, in order to differentiate SMIs from traditional celebrities and to highlight instead their "micro-celebrity" (e.g., Khamis et al. 2017; Marwick, 2016; Schoutten et al., 2019). Instructional marketing resources in the popular press tend to be more inclusive in their definition of an *SMI*, proposing a continuum of SMIs ranging from traditional celebrity to micro-celebrity. What all of these definitions hold in common is an emphasis on social influence and the creation or amplification of that influence through the strategic exploitation of social media.

Situating the Megachurch Pastor within Commercial *SMI* Definitions

Many megachurch pastors demonstrate qualities that would categorize them as SMIs as thus defined. For example, some megachurch pastors are preexisting celebrities by virtue of their "well-knownness" (Boorstin, 1962; Gamson, 2011), and are sometimes referred to as "holy mavericks" (Lee & Sinitiere, 2009) who command social media followings of millions. Further, many of the most engaged-with tweets on Twitter are not from traditional celebrities like Justin Bieber but from pastors like Joel Osteen (O'Leary, 2012). As well-known megachurch pastors enter the realm of social media and fame becomes more easily attained, the line between pastor and influencer becomes blurred.

Not all megachurch pastors, however, can be classified as celebrities, and there is likely considerable variation in a given pastor's level of engagement with the strategies for social media communication. Pastors, or their social media communication teams, potentially also demonstrate varying amounts of technical skill and content-creation acumen. Given these concerns, we argue that the question of how megachurch pastors function as SMIs requires additional research attention. To that end, we next briefly review research on how the technological affordances of social media shape influencer communication practices and the unique tensions megachurch pastors may encounter.

SOCIAL MEDIA INFLUENCER COMMUNICATION PRACTICES

Several bodies of work inform our study of the communication practices of SMIs, most notably from computer-mediated-communication, public relations, and digital religion studies. First, it is important to note that all SMI communication is shaped by the technological affordances of a given communication channel. These technological affordances are the attributes of a particular object that enable or constrain use in interaction (Gibson, 1979). We understand communication technologies in part by the various affordances they possess, which include their level of interactivity, accessibility, visibility, and personalization (Baym, 2015; Fox & McEwan, 2019). Social media affordances allow SMIs to create a desired identity of authenticity, to engage in relationship management through dialogue, relational labor, and parasocial interaction, and to co-construct pastoral authority.

In terms of identity, social media allows users to construct the persona they wish to present to the world through identity cues (Baym, 2015; Goffman, 1959), including markers of storied religious identity (Campbell & Garner, 2016). This identity construction is social, in that SMIs assemble their identity in light of an imagined social media audience, whose true size and composition can seldom fully be known by the online content creator (Marwick & boyd, 2010). As research has suggested, one valued identity characteristic of SMIs is authenticity (e.g., Audrezet et al., 2018). *Authenticity* is a term that is elusive but tends to encompass ideas of being true to a "real" self and behaving in a manner consistent with that ideal.

One of the ways SMIs create perceived authenticity is through relationship management. *Relationship management* involves two-way communication between the SMIs and their followers, though this communication is often asymmetrical. One such form of communication is the dialogue between content creator and audience, as afforded by the structural capabilities of interactive social platforms (e.g., Watkins & Lewis, 2014). These dialogic relationship studies often build on the work of Kent and Taylor (1998), who defined *dialogic communication* as "any negotiated exchange of ideas and opinions" (p. 325). In addition to dialogue between an SMI and their followers, SMIs engage in other forms of relational labor, which is conceptualized as the "ongoing, interactive, affective, material, and cognitive work of communicating with people over time" (Baym, 2018, p.19). This relational labor facilitates a sense of ongoing access to the day-to-day, "backstage" (Goffman, 1959) life of the SMI. Prolonged relational labor may facilitate parasocial interaction, defined as the relationships that audiences form with media figures (Horton & Whol, 1956). This parasocial interaction between an SMI and their audience may engender positive attitudes toward the SMI (e.g., Rasumussen, 2018). We argue that megachurch pastors who desire to be successful SMIs must attend to all of the aforementioned communication concerns. However, we also posit that megachurch pastors may face unique SMI challenges. To date, the most extensively studied area of potential tension is online pastoral authority.

Campbell (2007) notes that religious authority "differs from the general concept of authority, in that it draws on a particular form of legitimization, often linked to a divine source" (p. 1046). However, religious authority, even with the addition of divine legitimization, also relies on "systems, roles, and personified beliefs" (Campbell, 2007, p. 1046). Given the extensive reach and democratic opportunities that social media affords to SMIs (Baym, 2015), many religious institutions have feared that voices unsanctioned by the religious establishment will rise to prominence (Campbell & Garner, 2016). At the same time, religious institutions have viewed social media as a way to reassert traditional forms of authority. As Campbell and Garner (2016) note, "Religious institutions are increasingly learning to leverage social media to build their influence and harness the power of the web to display their expert knowledge online" (p. 74). The limited body of work related to the communication of pastoral online authority corroborates the stance that social media tends to reinforce, rather than undermine, traditional religious authority (e.g., Campbell, 2010; Cheong et al., 2011). However, traditional understandings and enactments of religious authority have arguably shifted with the widespread adoption of social media.

For example, Cheong (2016) argues that contemporary religious authority is "discursive, relational, and emergent" (p. 84). From this perspective, ministers do not abdicate their pastoral authority when they communicate online; rather, they engage in practices of strategic arbitration (Cheong et al., 2011). Strategic arbitration involves the communicative process of self-presentation as a sage and sociable curator of spiritual wisdom in a highly fragmented information landscape (Cheong et al., 2011). For example, in a study of how megachurch pastors used Twitter to engage in strategic arbitration, Cheong (2016) found that ministers cultivated an approachable yet authoritative online persona through their Twitter bios, personal promotion, connections to offline religious institutions and rites, "behind the scenes" glimpses into the pastoral profession, and spiritual teachings.

Taken together, these findings help determine the unique situations mega-church pastors may face as they attempt to maintain and reinforce clerical authority. An additional challenge pastors as SMIs may encounter is pressure to represent their churches and the Christian faith well. Pastoral exposure on social media can invite unwanted censure. For example, the Instagram account @PreachersNSneakers lampoons prominent faith leaders' social media photos by identifying the materialistic displays of consumption, such as designer sneakers and handbags, found therein (Rojas, 2019). This commentary captures the incongruity between laypeople's expectation of pastoral austerity and the observation of (possibly) tithe-funded excess. In sum, past research on the social media communication of megachurch pastors has tended to focus on ministers as an undifferentiated group or to present case studies of one or two pastors. The current study updates these findings and expands theorizing into the area of SMIs.

METHOD

This study examined the Twitter communication practices of megachurch pastors from the twenty largest megachurches in the United States through the method of qualitative content analysis, defined by Hseih and Shannon (2005) as "a research method for the subjective interpretation of the content of text data through the systematic classification process of coding and identifying themes or patterns" (p. 1278). Twitter is a microblogging platform that allows users to communicate with "tweets," short posts that are no more than 280 characters long (Twitter, 2019, "Getting started" section). We selected Twitter as our focal social media for several reasons. First, it is widely used in the United States, with 22 percent of adults using the platform (Pew Research, 2019). Forty-two percent of these Twitter users report that they use the platform at least once a day (Pew Research, 2019). Second, it is relatively simple to acquire Twitter data for research purposes. Twitter web scrapers are readily available, and unlike platforms such as Facebook, Twitter does not draw a distinction between posts and comments.

Sample

Megachurch Identification

This study focused on the Twitter presences of the megachurch senior pastors from twenty of the largest Protestant churches in the United States. Identifying the twenty largest megachurches is admittedly fraught, as church attendance is self-reported, and may not be made available. To construct our sampling frame, we first consulted a megachurch size ranking available through the Hartford Institute for Religion Research (2015, "Database of megachurches in the U.S. section"). We then updated and cross-referenced this list against each megachurch's website information and Outreach 100's (2019) self-report list of the largest U.S. congregations. Reported estimates of weekly worship attendance for the churches in the sample ranged from 17,294 (New Life Church in Arkansas) to 43,500 (Lakewood Church in Texas).

Tweet Identification

Once the megachurch sampling frame was completed, the senior pastors from each congregation were identified. Two churches did not have a senior pastor at the time of sampling and thus were removed from the study. Next, Twitter was searched to establish which of the identified pastors had an active Twitter presence, defined as posting a tweet (i.e., "tweeting") at least once during the sampling period. In this step, two pastors were eliminated; one who had not tweeted in over one year and one who did not appear to have an account. Thus, sixteen pastors were included in the final sample.

Once the list of senior pastors was determined, study data was scraped from each pastor's Twitter profile. The unit of analysis was each individual tweet sent by each pastor within a designated timeframe. We chose a three-month period lasting from July 1, 2019 to September 30, 2019, in order to provide both a manageable sample from prolific Twitter users and sufficient data from infrequent Twitter users. This period contained 636 tweets with an average number of 37.4 tweets per pastor, with one being the lowest number of tweets sent by a pastor and 68 being the highest number. The data was

Table 3.1   Senior Pastor Twitter Following and Church Affiliation

Senior Pastor	Twitter Followers	Church Affiliation	Estimated Weekly Worship Attendance
Joel Osteen	9.04M	Lakewood Church	43,500
Rick Warren	2.33M	Saddleback Church	22,055
Steven Furtick	652K	Elevation Church	25,998
Andy Stanley	595K	North Point Community Church	30, 629
Craig Groeschel	378K	Life.Church	30,000
Ed Young	302K	Fellowship Church	24,162
Robert Morris	113K	Gateway Church	28,000
Chris Hodges	99.5K	Church of the Highlands	44,872
Joseph W. Walker III	73.2K	Mount Zion Baptist Church	19,723
Kyle Idleman	44.7K	Southeast Christian Church	21,764
Jud Wilhite	43.4K	Central Church	21,055
Rick Bezet	23.6K	New Life Church	17,294
Jim Burgen	6.3K	Flatirons Community Church	16,703
Dr. Ed Young	5.0K	Second Baptist Church	20,656
Bob Merritt	3K	Eagle Brook Church	22,211
Ashley Wooldridge	2.9K	Christ's Church of the Valley	35,000

Note. Pastors are presented in order of highest number of Twitter followers to lowest number of Twitter followers. *M* designates "million"; *K* designates "thousand."

acquired with a Twitter Advanced Search web scraper. See table 3.1 for senior pastor, Twitter following, and church affiliation information.

Data Analysis

We adopted grounded theory techniques in order to analyze the data (e.g., Corbin & Strauss, 2008). Thus, to analyze the final sample of pastors' Twitter communication, the researchers immersed themselves in the tweets of each megachurch pastor. The individual tweet, therefore, constituted the primary unit of analysis. We subjected each tweet to a close reading to break apart the data for ideas and to ascertain the number of tweets within a given megachurch pastor's Twitter presence that coalesced on a particular topic. Initial codes emerging from the data were formed and refined into overarching conceptual categories (Corbin & Strauss, 2008). Themes were generated inductively by the team of three researchers, rather than adopted a priori. Last, we compared and contrasted these themes across pastors.

RESULTS

We examined the Twitter communication practices of megachurch pastors from an SMI perspective. We thus investigated if megachurch pastors adopted similar self-presentation and relational labor strategies to market themselves, their churches, and their Christian faith, as those used by secular SMIs. We were particularly attuned to the practices used to reconcile self-branding and the divine imperatives of the pastoral role. We observed commonalities in SMI practice across pastors in the sample, as well as patterns of meaningful variation. Findings related to the chapter's aims are thus presented here in turn. Three overarching themes of influencer practice emerged across the sample: *promotion, rapport building*, and *edification*. Throughout these results, tweets are quoted verbatim to illustrate findings. We then describe how the pastors created unique configurations of these practices in their Twitter communication.

Promotion

In the marketing literature, "promotion" involves the process of coordinating "channels of information and persuasion in order to sell goods and services or promote an idea" (Belch & Belch, 2012, p. 12). Commercial SMIs engage in promotion frequently through, for example, brand partnerships (e.g., Audrezet et al., 2018). Megachurch pastors also used Twitter to publicize goods and to encourage action. Similar to secular micro-celebrities who promote goods that will resonate with the idiosyncratic desires of their niche audience (Marwick, 2016), so too did megachurch pastors cast promotions as the fulfillment of the needs of the online flock. Three subcategories were identified within the larger *promotion* theme: *personal promotion, network promotion*, and *church promotion*.

First, tweets that fell into the category of *personal promotion* emphasized the pastor, as a self-branded entity, selling or publicizing his independent ventures, most commonly in the form of books, podcasts, and speaking tours. Andy Stanley and Robert Morris are examples of pastors who exemplified this category. These promotional tweets did not engage in "hard sell" tactics (i.e., "take it or leave it"); rather, they noted the unique and positive values that this commodity offered to the disciple or the way that the item would solve a felt problem. For example, Andy Stanley (2019) promoted a link to an online store that sold an audiobook version of his recent book *Irresistible*:

Andy Stanley (@AndyStanley) on August 13, 2019, at 7:43 a.m.: Don't have time to read Irresistible? How 'bout I read it to you? [Link to audiobook and image attached].

Also, one common motif within the promoted materials was that of "leadership," through which megachurch pastors indirectly modeled how leaders should promote themselves and their offerings. Further, some pastors engaged in name-dropping within their self-promotional tweets, which may have served to bolster the perceived credibility of a given endeavor. For example:

> Andy Stanley (@AndyStanley) on September 21, 2019, at 11:15 a.m.: Had an amazing day with Reggie Joiner, Joel Thomas, and the fine folks at Mission Community Church talking about Irresistible. On to Kansas City & Austin! Click here for more info: [Link and image attached].

Second, in addition to promoting their independent endeavors, many senior pastors also engaged in *church promotion*, defined here as tweeting about church events and worship services. Rick Warren, Robert Morris, Ed Young, and others exhibited this communication practice. Within this tweet category, pastors used Twitter's digital affordances to attract online followers to a physical locale. Similar to the *self-promotion* category, church promotion tweets also described the unique values of participating in a physical worship experience. For example, Robert Morris (2019) tweeted:

> Robert Morris (@PsRobertMorris) on September 21, 2019, at 12:05 p.m.: God is 100% grace all the time. I hope you'll join me at @gatewaypeople this weekend as I continue the "God Is . . ." series. For service times & locations, visit http://times.gatewaypeople.com.
>
> #GatewayPeople #GatewayLife #GodIs [Sermon video attached].

This tweet accomplished several communicative functions simultaneously, as it evoked positive emotion through an emphasis on a winsome attribute of God (his grace), invited a potentially lonely online populace to join a community (@gatewaypeople; #GatewayPeople), and informed about both the nature of the divine and worship service logistics.

The third and final subcategory associated with the *promotion* theme was *network promotion*, in which pastors publicized the products and services of friends, colleagues, and organizations. Many pastors, including Idleman, Morris, and Warren, promoted the books, podcasts, and events of other individuals and organizations. For instance:

> Chris Hodges (@Chris_Hodges) on September 3, 2019, at 5:18 p.m.: Excited about this new book from my friend @pastorbrady. Check it out here: [Image with link attached].

Through these forms of network promotion, pastors ostensibly introduced their online followers to organizations and individuals of value to them. Through this practice, pastors also solidified their own religious identity in connection to those with whom they associated (Baym, 2015). This established the in-group identity as a demarcated, yet accessible, class of faith leaders.

Rapport Building

The second overarching theme we identified was that of *rapport building*, whereby pastors engaged in relationship building with their online Twitter followers. As noted previously, secular SMIs tend to be adept at communicating with audiences in a manner that creates the perception of an interactive relationship (e.g., Rasmussen, 2018). Pastors also engaged in these rapport-building practices, though in a manner that infused an undercurrent of pastoral care for the online community. The subcategories that emerged within *rapport building* were *audience engagement*, *persona construction*, and *celebration*.

Audience engagement included tweets in which the pastor demonstrated two-way interaction with the Twitter community. Common forms of audience engagement included live videos, responses to individual Twitter followers, solicitation of prayer requests, and asking questions of followers. Bishop Joseph Walker, III, for example, frequently used Twitter's live broadcast feature (i.e., Periscope) to engage with his followers. The affordances of the live broadcast allowed Bishop Walker to present his audience with a seemingly authentic, "raw and unedited" view into his life (e.g., "Bishop JWW3 Sunday Night Reflections"). Further, the live broadcast format allowed for synchronous interaction, as live viewers could chat, ask questions, and indicate liking or agreement by tapping their mobile screens to share hearts. Other pastors also deviated from the one-to-many tweet structure typically adopted for promotional tweets in order to interact with individual users. For instance, Kyle Idleman (2019) engaged regularly with individual followers, often in a pastoral tone:

> Kyle Idleman (@Kyleidleman) on July 28, 2019, at 8:53 a.m.: So sorry you are feeling that way and experiencing this—saying a prayer for you now. It's no accident I saw your tweet! Hold on though, He's in the business of making beauty from ashes.

In terms of the solicitation of prayer requests, Ed Young (2019) notes the following:

> Ed Young (@EdYoung) on September 3, 2019, at 1:30 p.m.: We should never underestimate the power of prayer; it undeniably moves the heart of God. Our team here @fc wants to pray for YOU! Send us your prayer requests in the comment section below.

Other pastors provoked discussion and engagement by asking questions, which often focused on a spiritual theme like heaven or forgiveness.

In addition to audience engagement, the pastors also demonstrated *persona construction*, which included efforts to convey authenticity through tweets that emphasized identity aspects *other than* the pastoral role. Through these tweets, followers were able to view the pastor not only as a divinely appointed leader but also as an embodied and multifaceted person. Tweets about marriage, familial relationships, vacations, and hobbies such as fishing and sports occurred most frequently. Tweets in this subcategory, more than others, tended to use humor—often self-deprecating. They also sometimes referenced pop culture and Internet culture, such as memes and hashtags. For example, Ed Young tweeted a short video of comical photoshoot outtakes with the caption "#Mood." Others encouraged their followers to engage with online content in accordance with general Internet conventions, such as photos with "caption this" prompts and #tbt (throwback Thursday) tweets. Although tweets in this category did not tend to be explicitly religious in nature, they all could be described as wholesome and upbeat.

The *celebration* subcategory included tweets in which the pastor explicitly rejoiced over the actions of the members of either his physical church congregation or online following. Examples included the pastor celebrating baptisms in the church or highlighting the production staff. This category exemplified the pastor's ability to be "one of" the community himself, and to share the success of his followers with a large audience.

Edification

Edification was the final theme that was identified. This theme is arguably the SMI Twitter communication practice unique to the pastoral role. Through tweets that focused on *edification*, pastors emphasized their status as shepherds and teachers vertically connected to the divine. Thus, these pastors acted as conduits who translated complex theological principles into 280-character tweetable snippets. Of note, some tweets coded as *edification* linked followers to longer video or audio versions of sermons. No tweets in our sample were overtly controversial. Instead, these tweets appeared to encourage frequent, pleasant attention to the divine and to uplift, inform, and encourage. Three subcategories embodied this theme, namely, *positive thoughts*, *biblical concepts*, and *theological comments*.

Positive thoughts were defined as tweets that were inspirational in nature but did not reference a specific biblical passage or theological concept. For example, Jud Wilhite (2019) notes that "worry never fixes tomorrow, but it always ruins today." Similarly, Craig Groeschel (2019) asserts that "passion always follows purpose." *Biblical concepts* were also inspirational in nature but included a specific Bible quotation or discussion of any event, parable, or story within the biblical text. Several examples of *biblical concepts* are as follows:

> Steven Furtick (@stevenfurtick) on August 1, 2019, at 6:30 p.m.: You CAN survive whatever wilderness you may be facing right now. Here's how. (See Matthew 3:17) [Video of sermon snippet attached].

> Ed Young (@EdYoung) on September 14, 2019, at 11:30 a.m.: "My strength is made perfect in weakness."—Jesus We are only as strong as our weakest moment!

A *theological comment*, in contrast, was defined as a tweet about a religious concept that did not directly reference the Bible. For example:

> Craig Groeschel (@craiggroeschel) on August 27, 2019, at 9:43 p.m.: Fear doesn't come from God.

> Steven Furtick (@stevenfurtick) on August 6, 2019, at 7:00 p.m.: Jesus has already taken care of what's tormenting you. [Video of sermon snippet attached].

All of these forms of pastoral edification served to solidify the pastor as a SMI who is uniquely influenced by the divine, and who may thus legitimately influence his followers accordingly.

Variations in Pastoral SMI Communication Practices

In addition to examining the common themes that emerged *across* megachurch pastors in terms of their SMI Twitter communication, we also investigated the variations among ministers in the enactment of those practices. Although our investigation was primarily qualitative, we did quantify how often each of the pastors in the sample exhibited each of the identified themes and subthemes. The pastors demonstrated significant variation in which SMI Twitter communication practices they exhibited with the timeframe of our investigation, suggesting that megachurch pastors are not monolithic in their self-presentation strategies. Although almost all the pastors in our sample employed each of the previously discussed themes occasionally, each pastor made different choices in terms of the configuration of influencer practices they emphasized. As will be addressed in the discussion of our findings, these differences could be attributed to multiple factors; however, the trends we observed are briefly described here.

For example, some pastors emphasized Twitter as a promotional tool more heavily than did others. Andy Stanley was the pastor in the sample who demonstrated the highest proportion of *self-promotion* tweets. Another subset of pastors' communication practice clustered around *positive thoughts* and *theological comments*. This cluster of megachurch pastors, interestingly, tended to be from some of the largest churches in the sample and commanded "celebrity pastor" status (e.g., Joel Osteen, Craig Groeschel, Steven Furtick). Some pastors, like Robert Morris, focused on *church promotion*, while others (e.g., Kyle Idleman; Joseph Walker, III) participated more fully in *audience engagement*. Future research should further examine the variations within megachurch pastor communication practices. The implications of these findings are next discussed.

MEGACHURCH PASTORS AS EXEMPLARS AND CHALLENGERS OF SMI CONCEPTUALIZATION

This chapter examined megachurch pastors as SMIs through a qualitative content analysis of their Twitter communication. Our results indicated that megachurch pastors used many of the communication practices commercial SMIs employ, including self-branding through personal promotion and the construction of an approachable and ever-present online persona. Simultaneously, megachurch pastors expressed their clerical identity even as they engaged in these commercial SMI practices. We also observed differences in how individual megachurch pastors configured their online self-presentation. Each of these findings will be discussed in turn.

First, our findings affirmed the enthusiastic embrace of branding by the megachurch (Twitchell, 2004). Specifically, megachurch pastors appeared to accept and exploit social media as a contemporary means of amplifying influence. At the time of data collection, almost all megachurch pastors of the twenty largest megachurches in the United States possessed an active Twitter account. Our method of content analysis was unable to discern if a given pastor's Twitter account was managed by the pastor himself or a communication team. However, regardless of the source of Twitter management, the tweets posted typically displayed content-creation best practices. For example, the pastors often used hashtags, links, and professionally produced videos, graphics, and images in their tweets. Tweets were often published using commercial social media management software, which suggests a high level of social media strategy savvy. Of course, the use of communication teams to produce and publish content raises questions about the perceived authenticity the pastors seek to cultivate. Further, we found the megachurch pastors'

Twitter communication imbued with the marketing imperative to focus on a brand's unique value (e.g., Kapferer, 2012). As previously noted, ministers contextualized much of their communication—even promotional tweets—as satiating some felt need (whether physical, emotional, intellectual, or spiritual) of their online flock.

Second, our findings demonstrated how megachurch pastors functioned as SMIs while maintaining their clerical role. We found that, although pastors largely embraced branding and commercial SMI practices, each of these communication events was infused with a "Christian flavor," or, to be more specific, an essence of evangelical megachurch. For example, pastors promoted books that dealt with faith topics and engaged with their online community through the solicitation of prayer requests. Even the subtheme we identified that was not explicitly religious, *persona construction*, abstained from "off-color" content and promoted values in alignment with evangelical Christendom, such as a focus on marriage and family. Further, our findings related to the potentially unique challenges faced by megachurch pastors as SMIs largely corroborated earlier work on the construction of pastoral authority through online communication (e.g., Cheong, 2014; Cheong, 2016; Cheong et al., 2011). Specifically, as has been previously reported, the pastors in our sample also legitimized their authority by casting themselves as kind sages who could translate complex theological concepts into tweetable snippets.

Third, one of our most interesting findings involved the variations among megachurch pastors in terms of how they configured their adoption of SMI strategies, which suggests that megachurch pastors do not act as SMIs monolithically. As previously reported, some pastors more heavily emphasized a given theme (i.e., promotion, rapport building, edification) in their tweets than did others. These differences could be attributed to many factors. Possible factors may include, for instance, the timing of our cross-sectional sample. Because the study focused on one three-month period of tweets, a higher proportion of tweets for a given minister may be an artifact of a book release rather than a sustained practice in his SMI communication. Future longitudinal research would help to clarify this potential explanation.

The differences among pastors' SMI Twitter communication practices may also relate to their larger pastoral persona, which is constructed from a number of interconnected information systems, of which Twitter is typically only one component. For example, Cooke (2012) described Joel Osteen's brand as "the inspirational guy" (p. 28), which is carried across multiple media platforms and properties. Thus, the constellation of SMI Twitter communication practices observed for an individual pastor may be derived from and consistent with his larger personal brand image. Alternately or additively, pastors may also shape their social media communication in light of other markers of social identity, such as gender or race (e.g., Martin et al., 2011).

A final proposed potential explanation for our findings is that they reflect conscious or unconscious negotiations with the tensions associated with uploading the pastoral persona. For example, some pastors may find self-promotion distasteful, and therefore focus on the communication of church events, the teaching of biblical principles, or the intentional engagement of online audiences. In reality, all of the themes identified in our study integrate and interact in layered ways to position the pastor as an SMI. For instance, although *church promotion* does not explicitly focus on the pastor, it does so indirectly because the pastoral delivery of a religious message has long been a centerpiece of Protestant worship (Eagle, 2015).

Taken together, the findings from this investigation enrich and challenge current conceptualizations of SMIs. For example, this examination of mega-church pastors on Twitter encourages reflection on the boundary conditions of the SMI designation. Given the various conceptions of the SMI role previously reviewed, do all megachurch pastors automatically qualify as such? For example, is motivation or desire to influence a prerequisite for the designation? Presumably, megachurch pastors are fundamentally motivated to influence because they are directed by the Great Commission of Jesus to make and teach disciples. Alternatively, does the size of one's preexisting network solidify this distinction? Again, many megachurch pastors arguably exert considerable influence, given the size of their congregations and reach of their social and other media properties. Other possible boundary conditions may include technological skills, the extent and nature of SMI practices, and quantitative and qualitative characteristics of audience interaction. Future research should work to clarify the perimeters of the SMI role.

Another fruitful stream of future research could examine how followers respond to megachurch pastors' Twitter communication, and how this feedback iteratively shapes SMI practices. The current investigation focused on pastors, rather than their followers; however, preliminary results suggest that pastors face decisions between depth and breadth in audience engagement. Future comparisons between sacred and secular audience expectations, communication and behaviors could also be informative.

This investigation also revealed the unique challenges some influencers may face because of the real or perceived inconsistencies between their role and expectations for SMIs. For this particular investigation, the pastoral role was arguably unique in that it originated in the divine. Megachurch pastors demonstrated varying strategies for reconciling this potential discrepancy. However, it is plausible that this finding may extend to any kind of SMI who perceives such a disconnect. Future research can examine if this pattern emerges for other types of SMIs, and if and how they communicatively forge reconciliation.

In conclusion, this chapter examined the role of the megachurch pastor as SMI. The qualitative content analysis of megachurch pastors' tweets revealed patterns of communication that both aligned with and diverged from commercial SMI practices as documented in the literature to date. The unique clerical position both enhances and challenges traditional conceptions of the SMI role. We remain intrigued to observe how, going forward, megachurch pastors metaphorically amplify their voices in the temple of Twitter.

NOTE

1. Titles vary. Other monikers include *Lead Pastor*, *Lead Follower*, *Vision Pastor*, or *Lead Minister*.

REFERENCES

Abidin, C. (2017). #familygoals: Family influencers, calibrated amateurism, and justifying young digital labor. *Social Media + Society, 3*(2), 1–15. https://doi.org/10.1177/2056305117707191

Agonisto, D., Arnaboldi, M., & Calisanno, A. (2019). How to quantify social media influencers: An empirical application at the Teatro alla Scala. *Heliyon, 5*(5), e01677–e01677. https://doi.org/10.1016/j.heliyon.2019.e01677

Audrezet, A., de Kerviler, G., & Guidry Moulard, J. (2018). Authenticity under threat: When social media influencers need to go beyond self-presentation. *Journal of Business Research.* https://doi.org/10.1016/j.jbusres.2018.07.008

Baym, N. K. (2015). *Personal connections in the digital age* (2nd ed.). Malden, MA: Polity.

Baym, N. K. (2018). *Playing to the crowd: Musicians, audiences, and the intimate work of connection.* New York, NY: NYU Press.

Belch, G. E., & Belch, M. A. (2012). *Advertising and promotion: An integrated marketing communications perspective* (9th ed.). New York, NY: McGraw-Hill Irwin.

Boorstin, D. J. (1962). *The image: A guide to pseudo-events in America.* New York, NY: Penguin Random House.

Campbell, H. (2007). Who's got the power? Religious authority and the internet. *Journal of Computer-Mediated Communication, 12*(3), 1043–1062. https://doi.org/10.1111/j.1083-6101.2007.00362.x

Campbell, H. (2010). Bloggers and religious authority online. *Journal of Computer-Mediated Communication, 15*(2), 251–276. https://doi.org/10.1111/j.1083-6101.2010.01519.x

Campbell, H., & Garner, S. (2016). *Networked theology: Negotiating faith in digital culture.* Grand Rapids, MI: Baker Academic.

Cheong, P. H. (2014). Tweet the message? Religious authority and social media innovation. *Journal of Religion, Media and Digital Culture, 3*, 1–19. http://jrmdc.com/papers-archive/volume-3-issue-3-december-2014/

Cheong, P. H. (2016). Religious authority and social media branding in a culture of religious celebrification. In S. Hoover (Ed.), *The media and religious authority* (pp. 81–102). Penn State University Press.

Cheong, P. H., Huang, S., & Poon, J. P. H. (2011). Religious communication and epistemic authority of leaders in wired faith organizations. *Journal of Communication, 61*(5), 938–958. https://doi.org/10.1111/j.1460-2466.2011.01579.x

Cooke, P. (2012). *Unique: Telling your story in the age of brands and social media.* Grand Rapids, MI: Baker Books.

Corbin, J. M., & Strauss, A. L. (2008). *Basics of qualitative research: Techniques and procedures for developing grounded theory* (3rd ed.). Thousand Oaks, CA: Sage.

Eagle, D. E. (2015). Historicizing the megachurch. *Journal of Social History, 48*(3), 589–604. https://doi.org/10.1093/jsh/shu109

Einstein, M. (2008). *Brands of faith: Marketing religion in a commercial age.* New York, NY: Routledge.

Fox, J., & McEwan, B. (2019). Social media. In M. B. Oliver, A. Raney, & J. Bryant (Eds.), *Media effects: Advances in theory and research* (4th ed., pp. 373–389). New York, NY: Routledge.

Freberg, K., Graham, K., McGaughey, K., & Freberg, L. A. (2011). Who are the social media influencers? A study of public perceptions of personality. *Public Relations Review, 37*(1), 90–92. https://doi.org/10.1016/j.pubrev.2010.11.001

Furtick, S. (2019). [@stevenfurtick]. (2019, Aug 1). You CAN survive whatever wilderness you may be facing right now [Video attached]. [Tweet]. Twitter. https://twitter.com/stevenfurtick/status/1157056002400952321

Furtick, S. (2019). [@stevenfurtick]. (2019, Aug 6). Jesus has already taken care of what's tormenting you. [Video attached]. [Tweet]. [Twitter]. https://twitter.com/stevenfurtick/status/1158875499474706437

Gamson, J. (2011). The unwatched life is not worth living: The elevation of the ordinary in celebrity culture. *PMLA, 126*(4), 1061–1069. https://doi.org/10.1632/pmla.2011.126.4.1061

Gibson, J. J. (1979). *The ecological approach to visual perception.* Boston, MA: Houghton Mifflin.

Goffman, E. (1959). *The presentation of self in everyday life.* New York, NY: Doubleday.

Groeschel, C. [@craiggroeschel]. (2019, Aug 23). Passion always follows purpose. [Tweet]. Twitter. https://twitter.com/craiggroeschel/status/1164854817455529984

Groeschel, C. [@craiggroeschel]. (2019, Aug 27). Fear doesn't come from God. [Tweet]. Twitter. https://twitter.com/craiggroeschel/status/1166526563887830954

Hartford Institute for Religion Research. (2015). *Megachurch definition.* http://hirr.hartsem.edu/megachurch/definition.html

Hartford Institute for Religion Research. (2015). *Database of megachurches in the U.S.* http://hirr.hartsem.edu/cgi-bin/mega/db.pl?db=default&uid=default&view_records=1&ID=*&sb=3&so=descend

Hodges, C. [@Chris_Hodges]. (2019, Sep 3). Excited about this new book from my friend @pastorbrady. Check it out here: [Image with link attached]. [Tweet]. Twitter. https://twitter.com/Chris_Hodges/status/1168996760494182401

Horton, D., & Wohl, R. R. (1956). Mass communication and para-social interaction: Observations on intimacy at a distance. *Psychiatry, 19*(3), 215–229. https://doi.org/10.1080/00332747.1956.11023049

Hsieh, H.-F., & Shannon, S. E. (2005). Three approaches to qualitative content analysis. *Qualitative Health Research, 15*(9), 1277–1288. https://doi.org/10.1177/1049732305276687

Hwang, K., & Zhang, Q. (2018). Influence of parasocial relationship between digital celebrities and their followers on followers' purchase and electronic word-of-mouth intentions, and persuasion knowledge. *Computers in Human Behavior, 87*, 155–173. https://doi.org/10.1016/j.chb.2018.05.029

Idleman, K. [@Kyleidleman]. (2019, Jul 28). So sorry you are feeling that way and experiencing this - saying a prayer for you now. It's no accident [Tweet]. Twitter. https://twitter.com//KyleIdleman/status/1155461269639639040

Johnson, J. (2017). Megachurches, celebrity pastors, and the evangelical industrial complex. In B. Forbes & J. Mahan (Eds.), *Religion and popular culture in America* (3rd ed., pp. 159–176). Oakland, CA: University of California Press.

Kapferer, J. N. (2012). *The new strategic brand management: Advanced insights & strategic thinking* (5th ed.). New York, NY: Kogan Page.

Keller, K. L. (2009). Building strong brands in a modern marketing communications environment. *Journal of Marketing Communications, 15*(2–3), 139–155. https://doi.org/10.1080/13527260902757530

Kent, M. L., & Taylor, M. (1998). Building dialogic relationships through the world wide web. *Public Relations Review, 24*(3), 321–334. https://doi.org/10.1016/S0363-8111(99)80143-X

Khamis, S., Ang, L., & Welling, R. (2017). Self-branding, 'micro-celebrity' and the rise of social media influencers. *Celebrity Studies, 8*(2), 191–208. https://doi.org/10.1080/19392397.2016.1218292

Lee, S., & Sinitiere, P. L. (2009). *Holy mavericks: Evangelical innovators and the spiritual marketplace.* New York, NY: New York University Press.

Lou, C., & Yuan, S. (2019). Influencer marketing: How message value and credibility affect consumer trust of branded content on social media. *Journal of Interactive Advertising, 19*(1), 58–73. https://doi.org/10.1080/15252019.2018.1533501

Martin, P. P., Bowles, T. A., Adkins, L., & Leach, M. T. (2011). Black mega-churches in the internet age: Exploring theological teachings and social outreach efforts. *Journal of African American Studies, 15*. https://doi.org/10.1007/s12111-011-9181-2

Marwick, A. E. (2016). You may know me from YouTube: (Micro) celebrity in social media. In P. D. Marshall & S. Redmond (Eds.), *A companion to celebrity* (pp. 350–333). Wiley Blackwell.

Marwick, A. E., & boyd, danah. (2010). I tweet honestly, I tweet passionately: Twitter users, context collapse, and the imagined audience. *New Media & Society, 13*(1), 114–133. https://doi.org/10.1177/1461444810365313

Miller, V. J. (2003). *Consuming religion: Christian faith and practice in a consumer culture.* New York, NY: Continuum.

Morris, R. [@PsRobertMorris]. (2019, Sep 19). God is 100% grace all the time. I hope you'll join me at @gatewaypeople this weekend as I continue [Video attached]. [Tweet]. Twitter. https://twitter.com/PsRobertMorris/status/1175440967635218433

O'Leary, A. (2012, June 2). Christian leaders are powerhouses on Twitter. *The New York Times.* https://www.nytimes.com/2012/06/02/technology/christian-leaders-a re-powerhouses-on-twitter.html

Outreach 100. (2019). *Largest churches in America.* https://outreach100.com/largest -churches-in-america

Pew Research Center. (2019). Social media factsheet. https://www.pewresearch.org/ internet/fact-sheet/social-media/

Rasmussen, L. (2018). Parasocial interaction in the digital age: An examination of relationship building and the effectiveness of YouTube celebrities. *The Journal of Social Media in Society, 7*(1), 280–294. https://thejsms.org/tsmri/index.php/TSMR I/article/view/364

Rojas, R. (2019, April 17). Let he who is without Yeezys cast the first stone. *The New York Times.* https://www.nytimes.com/2019/04/17/nyregion/preachers-sneakers-in stagram-account.html

Schouten, A. P., Janssen, L., & Verspaget, M. (2019). Celebrity vs. influencer endorsements in advertising: The role of identification, credibility, and product-endorser fit. *International Journal of Advertising*, 1–24. https://doi.org/10.1080/0 2650487.2019.1634898

Stanley, A. [@AndyStanley]. (2019, Aug 13). Had an amazing day with Reggie Joiner, Joel Thomas, and the fine folks at Mission Community Church talking about Irresistible.[Link and image attached] [Tweet]. Twitter. https://twitter.com/ AndyStanley/status/1175428432836136963

Stanley, A. [@AndyStanley]. (2019, Sep 21). Don't have time to read Irresistible? How 'bout I read it to you? [Image attached] [Tweet]. Twitter. https://twitter.com/ AndyStanley/status/1161241913267298304

Twitchell, J. B. (2004). *Branded nation: The marketing of Megachurch, College, Inc., and Museumworld.* New York, NY: Simon & Schuster.

Twitter. (2019). *Getting started.* https://help.twitter.com/en/twitter-guide

Watkins, B., & Lewis, R. (2014). Initiating dialogue on social media: An investiga-tion of athletes' use of dialogic principles and structural features of Twitter. *Public Relations Review, 40*(5), 853–855. https://doi.org/10.1016/j.pubrev.2014.08.001

Wigg-Stevenson, T. (2009, January 2). Jesus is not a brand. *Christianity Today.* https ://www.christianitytoday.com/ct/2009/january/10.20.html

Wilhite, J. [@JudWilhite]. (2019, Sep 18). Worry never fixes tomorrow, but it always ruins today. [Tweet]. Twitter. https://twitter.com/JudWilhite/status/117434503822 4121861

Young, E. [@EdYoung]. (2019, Sep 3). We should never underestimate the power of prayer; it undeniably moves the heart of God. Our team here @fc wants [Tweet]. Twitter. https://twitter.com/EdYoung/status/1168939298089054212

Young, E. [@EdYoung]. (2019, Sep 14). "My strength is made perfect in weak-ness."—Jesus We are only as strong as our weakest moment! [Tweet]. Twitter. https://twitter.com/EdYoung/status/1172895322810593281

Chapter 4

Become an #AcademicInfluencer

A Blueprint for Building Bridges between the Classroom and Industry

Carolyn Kim, Karen Freberg,
Mitchell Friedman, and Amanda J. Weed

Influencers—whether they are journalists, bloggers, vloggers, public figures, industry analysts, or any individual with a highly engaged social media following—can help expand reach, increase awareness, boost reputation, and drive engagement among target audiences (Cole, 2018). In this chapter, the authors discuss benefits and best practices for developing influencer status for academics to burnish their credentials with a strategic focus grounded in tactics to realize their professional, institutional, and even personal goals.

Academics have received minimal attention in the discussion of influencers, in particular as scholars are summoned to make research more widely accessible through venues such as ResearchGate and Academia.edu, with an eye toward the reputational benefits of such endeavors in maintaining "scholarly identity" (Brigham, 2016; Chapman & Greenhow, 2019; Duffy & Pooley, 2017; Herman & Nicholas, 2019). Linder (2018) and Cabrera and Lloret (2016) offer a more granular approach to assist academics wary of immersing themselves in the often choppy waters of the social media ocean by considering a broad range of opportunities available to academics looking to share their work and expertise on social media.

Within each community, some individuals will have a dominant or prominent voice. In digital spaces, communities give rise to a variety of individuals who effectively create their own brand and media outlet and reach the point where they are deemed to be powerful and persuasive in nature. In other words, they are an *influencer* and they have the power to *shape culture*.

While most of the literature and mainstream media has focused on celebrity and micro-influencers who are working with brands, there has been little to no research that has explored the nature of influencers in an academic capacity (e.g., academic influencers). In addition, faculty members are a group of professionals who are a captive audience known not only for displaying their expertise but also for utilizing their presence on social media to help create a stronger bridge between practice and education. Faculty members use social media to facilitate relationships for students and professionals, as well as to gain insights on how to create new opportunities that extend their reach beyond the classroom.

Whether a newly minted Ph.D. in a first-time faculty role, a practitioner who teaches in addition to consulting, or a tenured professor who is well-known, educators from a variety of backgrounds can use guidance focused on this topic to enhance their expertise and career. This chapter highlights the current state of social media influencer research, discusses the conceptualization of an academic influencer, and examines the ways in which this can be addressed through research, teaching, and professional service. In addition, this chapter addresses a new influencer audience and element to consider in the higher education and professional space for educators.

CONCEPTUALIZATION OF SOCIAL MEDIA INFLUENCERS

Influencers have been on the rise among public relations, marketing, and social media campaigns over the years as a key strategy to amplify, support, and create engagement through their means to foster a strong connection with a brand (or entity and organization) and their key publics. Influencers have become a powerful third-party entity that helps change the way in which organizations, agencies, and other professional entities communicate with their key publics. Social media platforms empower social media influencers by giving them a platform to foster a community, formulate a brand voice, and connect followers with similar interests online. In other words, these new tools provide opportunities for new, expanded expression and promotion; prior to the emergence of the Internet, such efforts were more difficult to undertake, let alone master. As an influencer's community and brand voice grows, so does their influence. In the industry, influencer marketing has become a go-to strategy for marketing, public relations, and advertising professionals to engage and specialize in. In fact, according to a research report by Influencer Hub, there were around 320 new influencer-specific platforms that were created in the first part of 2019 alone to focus on this particular area in the social media industry ("The State of Influencer Marketing 2019," 2019)

The specialization of research dedicated to exploring the nature of influencer marketing has risen substantially over the last several years. Within this area of specialization, several focal points have emerged in the analysis and exploration of influencers in the digital space. For example, research has explored influencers in several ways, including based on their personality characteristics (Freberg et al., 2011), professional attributes and contributions (Enke & Borchers, 2019), community engagement (Himelboim & Golan, 2019; Smith et al., 2017), trust (Lou & Yuan, 2019), and paid media role in formulating partnerships (Luoma-aho et al., 2019).

There have been many ways in which social media influencers (SMIs) have been conceptualized, including as individuals who shape attitudes through blogs, tweets, and other social media updates (Freberg et al., 2011). This definition of *SMI* has been expanded by other scholars who have emphasized how their online digital presence equates with the strategic amplification and investment in the production of content, interaction, and formulating a strong personal brand on social media to build their influence in the industry (Enke & Borchers, 2019). Essentially, SMIs are individuals who have built up a community overtime through sustainable efforts in building their community, creating engaging content, and solidifying themselves as an expert or person who has a passion for a particular topic, issue, or area within society. SMIs come in all shapes, sizes, and types, which have evolved and changed as platforms changed. One of the areas that are attributed to SMIs is that they are the same as third-party endorsers or opinion leaders, who are cited in most academic literature, especially in public relations. However, SMIs are different from opinion leaders or third-party endorsers in a few ways. SMIs bring their experiences, unique perspectives, and brand voices to the table, which makes it difficult to categorize them. Some SMIs enjoy a strong standing based on their role and profession, such as sports figures, pop stars, and media professionals. For the most part, SMIs are regular people with a specific interest and passion, as well as the dedication to create a name for themselves within their industry and community.

While previous definitions have focused on the overall attributes of a social media influencer, others have looked at their role in the traditional marketing sphere. For example, some scholars have viewed SMIs as a paid media entity that serves an intermediate function to promote engagement between followers and the brand they are collaborating with (Himelboim & Golan, 2019). SMIs have direct communication with their audience due to the trust and consistent engagement they have created through their online community (Childers et al., 2019). SMIs have also been impactful in brand campaigns due to the perception of trust and source credibility they establish with their communities (Lou & Yuan, 2019).

Characteristics of SMIs

There are certainly key characteristics of successful and sustainable SMIs in the marketplace. *Authenticity* is a key characteristic influencers need to embrace as well as showcase on their various platforms (Charlton & Cornwell, 2019). Influencers have to be true to who they are as a brand but also be strategic in the brand partnerships they engage in (Luoma-aho et al., 2019). If followers view a partnership with an SMI to be true to the influencer's overall brand, they will be viewed as more trustworthy and authentic to their own brand, but if the partnership is not aligned, then this raises authenticity and trust issues with the SMI among their followers (Luoma-aho et al., 2019). Community members and followers of SMIs are more likely to trust the SMI versus a paid spokesperson due to the relationship they have with the influencer (Jiménez-Castillo & Sánchez-Fernández, 2019).

Expertise, specialization, or focus in a particular area has to be presented and accounted for by the SMI (Zhao et al., 2018). An SMI is able to build a community, which is based not only on similar interests but also a presence in establishing themselves as a voice of authority on the subject. Expertise can come from the particular role or position the influencer is in (such as a journalist or scientist), or it could be formulated over time via fame and celebrity status (e.g., Dwayne Johnson aka "The Rock" or Ninja).

Communication or *engagement* is another factor that separates SMIs by other means for brands and organizations (Smith et al., 2017). Engagement focuses on the interactivity between SMI and followers either within the community they are a part of or have created, or with the client with which they are working. Passing along advice, insights, recommendations, and perspectives through word-of-mouth communications is a powerful way to foster strong engagement with followers (Jiménez-Castillo & Sánchez-Fernández, 2019).

In essence, the study of SMIs will continue to grow in the public relations, advertising, and marketing spaces. Yet, while this research continues to evolve, it is important to understand the need to explore specific niche or specialized industry-oriented influencers to determine their overall impact on their communities and branding. One of these areas that has been overlooked and understudied has been academic influencers, which will be discussed in the next section.

CONCEPTUALIZATION OF ACADEMIC INFLUENCERS

As mentioned in the previous section, most of the research that has explored SMIs has focused on either established marketing influencers such as Brian Solis and Deirdre Breakenridge in the social media industry (Freberg et al.,

2011) or others from particular industries such as fashion (Jin et al., 2019), fitness and sports ("Analyzing Sentiment and Themes in Fitness Influencers' Twitter Dialogue," n.d.), celebrities and entertainment (Schouten et al., 2019), and more. Education has yet to be explored in terms of the nature of educators and their presence on social media platforms.

Academic influencers are individuals who have built a community and brand for themselves based on their research, teaching, service, and professional activities in and out of the classroom. Academics can use their influencer status to foster enhanced collaboration between students and industry communities. More specifically, professors commonly connect with industry professionals and organizations in the local community for guest speaking (Glenwick & Chabot, 1991; Payne et al., 2003) or experiential learning projects (Bush et al., 2017; Hopkins et al., 2011; Todd, 2009), which students across diverse fields of study perceive as a valuable addition to the educational experience (Agha-Jaffar, 2000; Metrejean et al., 2002; Roush, 2013). Prior research extolls the benefits of integrating real-world experiences in the classroom to prepare students for the expectations of their career field (Glenwick & Chabot, 1991; Payne et al., 2003). Moreover, Merle and Craig (2017) found that students have a strong preference to connect with industry professionals, rather than academics, to learn from their personal experience in the field. The academic influencer has great potential to increase student opportunities for industry networking, exposure to professional tools, access to internships, and experiential learning through company collaborations. Academic influence through social media can expand the breadth of the student experience beyond the confines of the university and local community, which instills a greater understanding of their chosen field of study in the national and global perspectives.

There has been some research exploring the impact and influence academics have on social media, particularly if they are sharing their research and articles in the online community (Li & Gillet, 2013). However, Freberg and Merle (2016) explored the perception of students when they saw their professor was on social media, which focused on the overall perception of an educator and academic being on social media. In this study, the students were more inclined to register for a class if they knew the professor was engaged and active on social media (Merle & Freberg, 2016). As noted, influencers can come from all spectrums and industries, and higher education and academics are not the exception. In fact, academics are increasingly expected to not only showcase their expertise to the digital world but formulate strong partnerships with brands, organizations, and industry to foster strong connections for their students, program, university, and academic community. Embracing the nature of influence for an academic is an opportunity to utilize new channels and media to make an impact in and out of the classroom for their students.

As discussed in later sections of this chapter, there are different ways in which academic influencers could amplify and use their influence based on some of the expectations and duties they are already doing as part of their job. Academic influencers can use and embrace their work as a key component to their influence, enabling them to have an impact in a particular area within the academic field. For research-focused academic influencers, these are individuals who embark on advocating, promoting, and sharing their insights on research not only they have done but from those who are in their community. Texas Tech associate professor Nick Bowman is one example of a research-based academic influencer who focuses and shares ideas for research and perspectives from working on teams, as well as sharing his journey on fellowships around the world where he is collaborating on various teams. Likewise, there are those who specialize in sharing and creating content that can be used within the classroom for teaching and have built a community and brand for themselves this way. Teaching-focused academic influencers, like Shephard University associate professor Matt Kushin, have done this very well. Kushin has created a name for himself in his published blog posts, assignments, and social media assignment book *Teach Social Media*. On the other hand, there are other academic influencers who have bridged the barrier between academia and industry not by virtue of their research and teaching, but more so by their work as practitioners. University of the Sunshine Coast lecturer Karen Sutherland fits this description perfectly with her social media consulting work, her two books on public relations and social media, research, and teaching courses where she uses client work for her students. All three types of academic influencers have a significant impact on the field moving forward in the modern age. In addition, these academic influencers are adding to the list of expectations universities and others are now expecting academics to have when they start their tenure track jobs.

For the purpose of this chapter, we define and conceptualize academic influencers as individuals who have established an authentic voice and authority within the community based on their expertise, mentorship, and relationship building with academia and industry.

COMPONENTS OF ACADEMIC INFLUENCERS

There are many different areas for academic influencers to consider in their role not only as educators but as an online force to bridge the gap of knowledge, skills, and relationships between academia and industry. In this section, we discuss some of the traditional (teaching, research, and service) components that make up academic influencers, while also introducing new areas (personal learning environments) to be evaluated on for future promotional efforts at universities.

Benefits of Research

Research is at the core of what many faculty members work on throughout their careers. The phrase "publish or perish" is all too common for educators and young faculty to hear as they enter the tenure track roles. Publishing in academic journals has been the standard for universities to acknowledge faculty research. However, academic research is also not black and white. It is a mixture of grays following a long continuum of different attributes that can make an impact on both theory building and development but also can be applied to industry insights and strategies. Applied research can help industry professionals improve sales, foster stronger bonds to help in community building, and even adapt messaging in handling crises. In many ways, the work that is being done in social media is both an applied and a theoretical discipline.

One of the primary challenges for the faculty member to embrace is balancing theory and application of theories in our research as well as in our classroom activities. Researchers and practitioners alike benefit from understanding how relevant theories evolved scientifically and also need to understand how theories can be applied in strategies, tactics, and communication campaigns. This is where the bridging role of the academic influencer can come into play. Most of the time, a faculty member is classified in one group or another, but there is a growing expectation that faculty members need to balance these two worlds.

Here are some ways in which an academic influencer can foster a stronger connection with their community through their research:

- *Explore questions that need to be answered both in academia and in the industry.* Identify the gaps in academic literature and trade publications. In order to influence change in both sectors, the gaps in each sector need to be considered. Academic influencers are able to detect these gaps as potential opportunities to promote and market their expertise in the industry.
- *Consider both theoretical and applicable contributions.* Academic research not just is limited to theoretical contributions but can also help in formulating stronger best practices that could be used in the industry. Before embarking on such research, consider identifying the contributions to aim for in the research and set objectives in place for the research to accomplish for academia and industry.
- *Become the best advocate for your research.* Translate the work that has been done in the research study into actionable and applicable insights.

Academic influencers are able to navigate these insights to position their work in front of industry professionals and brands. Summarizing the major points pertaining to the "so what" factor of the research is a top priority.

Benefits of Teaching

In academia, the three areas most faculty members are evaluated on for tenure purposes are research, teaching, and service. As described above, research focuses on the contribution the faculty makes to the body of knowledge in academia (research) that is published in academic-oriented publications and scholarly journals. Teaching focuses on the evaluation of effectiveness in and out of the classroom by students, professionals, and colleagues. Service duties involve those efforts that are aligned with giving back to the university, department, and even profession by serving on various committees as an advisor (theses and dissertations), holding leadership positions, or reviewing submissions to conferences and academic publications.

One of the unstated but expected requirements for academic influencers is to have not only knowledge about how to use social media for their classes but for their own personal brand as well. That means academics need to walk the walk and talk the talk. When hired to teach social media courses, many educators have not been trained to teach social media since there were no social media classes offered during the time these educators were in school. In addition, the overall focus on teaching has often taken a back seat to research. Research has been at the forefront of most university expectations of faculty due to the grant and financial support research can bring to the university. Teaching gives short shrift to what might best be described as promotional efforts available to instructors seeking to improve by looking outside the boundaries of the classroom. With that being said, teaching has attracted some attention in the domain of peer-reviewed publications. Faculty do focus largely on the academic research responsibilities and the need to share the fruits of their labor (Brigham, 2016; Chapman & Greenhow, 2019; Duffy & Pooley, 2017; Herman & Nicholas, 2019).

Teaching is one activity an academic influencer can capitalize on and amplify in their network to build on their influence. Teaching offers many benefits since it brings forward insights from outside the classroom environment to better serve the needs of multiple stakeholders—students, institutions, and, yes, even the instructors themselves. Faculty may be hesitant to identify themselves as an academic influencer, since it involves promoting oneself on social media to become their own best advocate. Such "self-promotion" still seems to be a dirty word in many of the hallowed halls of academia, yet the emergence of social media within the marketing arena empowers every-one—academics included—to initiate more strategic efforts to further their goals. The focus is more modest: to identify ways the academic can achieve even a modicum of influence based solely on their efforts to meld the classroom and industry.

The overall goal of teaching is to create interesting and engaging learning experiences for students. The conception of "teacher as #academicinfluencer" is reflected in three actions that can guide instruction: (1) sharing your teaching experiences with non-students; (2) celebrating student achievements; and (3) inviting the outside world into the classroom. Each of these actions is described below in further detail.

- *Share teaching experiences with non-students.* Sharing different aspects of the classroom experience with stakeholders outside the university highlights for them the nature of instruction and the student experience in the classroom. More specifically, individual session contents; pictures of students engaged in different activities; student work products; and observations/assessments of individual classes often make up the majority of what is shared with the world outside the classroom. The content produced on these topics, and thus that could be shared, is unlimited. The form such content takes, whether it is text, audio, video, or some combination of them, likewise seems open to use based on individual skill sets, preferences, and time. To that end, blogs, websites, and accounts on Facebook, LinkedIn, Twitter, Instagram, and YouTube represent some of the social media tools academic influencers can use to tell the story of what is happening in the classroom to those outside of the classroom. Academic influencers may also employ more traditional communications vehicles, such as newsletters, in their effort to share the classroom experiences with the world outside the university.
- *Celebrating student achievement.* Effective teaching is rigorously student-centered. In other words, the students take center stage in the process. It is about them, what they do in classes, how they apply their learning, and, in the longer term, how they transform their new insight and understanding into professional (and even personal) opportunities long after the class has ended. Without students, none of us have a job. This recognition can serve as the ongoing motivation for efforts to become academic influencers.
- *Inviting the outside world into classroom.* In this domain, professors have long connected with industry professionals and organizations in the local community to secure guest speakers (Glenwick & Chabot, 1991) and/or to recruit sponsors for capstone, experiential learning, and thesis projects (Bush et al., 2017; Hopkins et al., 2011). Thus, organizations are constantly solicited to work with students, which requires ongoing effort using all the social media and communications tools available. It is imperative to acknowledge industry participants, which, in turn, often leads to their ongoing participation—and

in some instances has even generated other inquiries from individuals inside and outside an educator's network to see how they can work with students to support their learning and as a result secure from them substantive information and insight to help achieve core organizational objectives.

Benefits of Personal Learning Environments for Academic Influencers

Academic influencers can leverage digital media in dynamic ways that allow for the enhancement of their professional brands while also building their expertise. This is accomplished through the use of a Personal Learning Environment (PLE) that develops as a result of social and digital technologies. Debbagh and Katsantas (2012) operationalized a PLE as a platform that serves "for both integrating formal and informal learning and fostering self-regulated learning in higher education contexts" (p. 3). In other words, academic influencers are able to leverage any number of digital platforms (personal websites, social media, etc.) as an opportunity to create PLEs. It is about the use of the digital space—academic influencers craft their digital interaction in a way that allows them to share in meaning-making activities, serve as connections to curate content and information, and, ultimately, help shape their own knowledge and that of others through their online presence.

As the digital landscape has grown, the opportunity to engage in formal and informal learning has expanded well beyond the confines of higher education. Examples include the original Lynda.com, LinkedIn Learning, industry and academic learning communities through Facebook groups and Twitter chats, and YouTube channels dedicated to particular areas of expertise. These digital platforms share a few commonalities that foster the potential for individuals to create a PLE.

First, PLEs provide an opportunity for formal education or learning that is designed and presented. This is true of any online course, video, or content that is created to deliver educational information. Second, a PLE has an informal learning component related to peer interaction. These digital learning platforms allow people to comment, share, respond, and engage with not only the content creator but also others who are interacting with the content in order to learn. Finally, a key component to a PLE is the capacity for someone to pursue knowledge that interests him or her. This trifecta of receiving content, interacting, and pursuing areas of interest make a PLE particularly salient on social media. Dabbagh and Kitsantas (2012) pointed out that "there is strong evidence that social media can facilitate the creation of PLEs that help learners aggregate and share the results of learning achievements, participate in collective knowledge generation, and manage their own meaning making" (p. 3).

Faculty Creation and Use of a PLE

A PLE provides an opportunity for faculty to demonstrate academic influence in several ways. First, it allows a faculty member to continue to hone expertise in new and developing areas of interests by learning from others within digital spaces about emerging trends, best practices, and emerging technology. Second, it connects faculty members with others, both within and outside the academic community, around areas of common interest. Third, it facilitates the opportunity for the faculty member to provide contributions to these conversations in a way that positions them as a leading voice of influence or insight.

The first step for an academic influencer is to identify where to develop a PLE. Some faculty have found specific platforms, such as LinkedIn or Facebook, to be dynamic for their particular discipline or expertise. Others may find that a platform such as Medium, a personal website or blog, or a YouTube channel will be best. It may be helpful to consider where conversations are taking place that relate to the academic influencer's areas of interest. It is likely that, once a faculty member is committed to using digital media to generate a PLE, multiple platforms will comprise the overall landscape of their personal PLE.

Second, faculty should identify where they will engage in learning, both formally and informally. Specific online communities are dedicated to particular topics. Thus, the topic or the source of the content may be a formalized way of learning. For example, a faculty member may choose to be part of a group that is dedicated to discussing social media in higher education or changes to the non-profit sector as a result of communication technology. The sponsor of the group, or the individual running it, will likely be providing information around the topic. However, faculty also engage in informal learning through sharing and engagement by those *within* the group. This effort will allow an educator to bridge the gap between the academy and other sectors, creating relationships with industry professionals and other academics.

Third, faculty who wish to be influencers must move beyond only identifying and joining communities—they must contribute in meaningful ways. This step involves more than curating or aggregating information from others. It requires an academic influencer to integrate the information in meaningful ways that allow them to become a content creator, someone who responds to questions from within the community, and an individual who begins sharing new ideas or insights.

The process of a PLE facilitates the advancement and creation of personal learning environments for others. When considering the first two steps of the process (joining and interacting), it becomes apparent that they are really about *receiving* information. The third step, which involves participating with new content, is about *giving* information. This third step is precisely why a PLE is so powerful for academic influencers—the academic influencer moves from consuming to producing. This production is influential since it takes shape and flourishes within a community of people interested in the same concepts, who are looking to gain new insights and will then, potentially, produce new ideas as well.

In conclusion, using a PLE allows faculty an opportunity to learn and stay up to date on the most recent trends or insights. It also bridges new relationships with individuals who share common interests but may be outside the typical social or professional circles in an offline world. Finally, an academic influencer can use a PLE to expand the way they contribute to areas of expertise, leading to potential other online and offline opportunities to speak, write, and present.

Through the integration of PLEs in the service element of academic job duties, faculty have the opportunity to serve three distinct communities, including students, other faculty, and industry practitioners.

- *Facilitating networking between students and professionals.* PLEs serve students by offering extracurricular opportunities that facilitate learning and networking with professionals already working in the field. While pre-professional student organizations offer those learning and networking opportunities, there are often limitations based on geographic boundaries and time availability of industry professionals. Digital PLEs offer a unique path to connect students with professionals for advanced learning related to emerging knowledge and skills, and build long-term networking relationships. Specific Twitter chats, such as #PRStudChat and #SMStudentChat, were created for this unique purpose by hosting interactive conversations between students and industry professionals
- *Develop a support network between faculty.* Outside the conference environment, faculty have few opportunities to collaborate and share knowledge with faculty beyond those at their home university network. PLEs offer a year-round outlet for faculty to share best teaching practices, pursue interdisciplinary and/or interuniversity research collaborations, and connect with a general support community. Digital communities such as the Social Media Professors Community Group and the Student-Run Agency Advisors Facebook groups offer year-round support to serve faculty in unique aspects of teaching.
- *Collaborating with industry professionals.* There are noted benefits of collaboration between faculty and industry professionals for teaching in the classroom (Bush et al., 2017; Hopkins et al., 2011; Glenwick & Chabot, 1991), and those benefits also hold the potential to expand in service to university and industry organizations. PLEs that serve industry professionals

within the network open opportunities for reciprocal collaboration that might include access to proprietary products and services often outside the financial means of university departmental budgets. In turn, industry professionals have the opportunity to "beta test" products or programs to gain valuable feedback before launching to the general public. In addition, PLEs that integrate academic and industry networks offer channels for meaningful exchanges of information that can lead to research and/or teaching collaborations that best address the objectives of higher education while advancing training of students to best meet the needs of their chosen industry.

FUTURE DIRECTIONS

While influencers in other fields continue to grow their brand partnerships and areas of expertise, academic influencers still have a long way to go in not only establishing their place in the education space but gaining the respect and recognition from the industry as well. One of the biggest challenges moving forward is adapting to a new model of evaluation to encourage university administration to value online activities such as blogging, social media engagement, and influencing online as valuable assets to be accounted for in promotion cases. This is why in this chapter, we hope to propose a new format for what faculty, including academic influencers, should be accounted for and evaluated on for their promotion and review cases.

As shown in figure 4.1, there are three traditional areas that most educators are evaluated on: research, teaching, and service. Yet, there are some new areas such as consulting (providing insights to businesses, non-profits, agencies, and brands based on the expertise), personal branding (any person, brand, or community can create an image online, but it does not mean a thing when the personality, voice, and person behind the screen do not match the person or brand you see in front of you), connecting (extending the presence of personal learning environments and the role the educators play in these environments), and social connecting (or, in other words, becoming a social connector). A social connector creates and leverages personal learning networks—or dynamic connections with established mentors across multiple industries and organizational types—to help catalyze student leadership development before they enter the workforce (Remund & Freberg, 2013). They understand how valuable professional mentors can be to students and embrace the use of technology and other means to connect students with such role models.

In addition, developing a personal brand for professionals in academia can benefit their students and work in the classroom, but the status as an academic

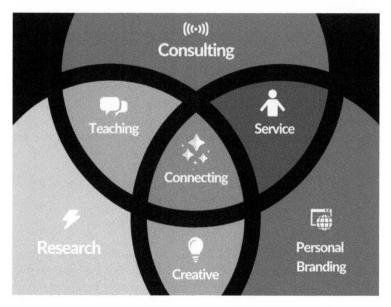

Figure 4.1 Proposed Model for Academic Influencers. Graphic created by author.

influencer can also boost opportunities for achievements that are viewed favorably in the tenure and/or promotion review. The road to becoming an academic influencer can take many paths, and the authors will demonstrate how several educators have built their role as influencers to elevate the educational experience and professional development of students on a global scale.

While this proposed model is still in the exploratory stage, more research and discussion on the topic is encouraged to determine if there are more components to consider when it comes to academic influencers. In addition, more research is needed to understand how academic influencers, in general, become influential and what additional factors play a part in establishing their presence. Further, practitioner academics demand further exploration in terms of how they use social media to establish their influence and, in so doing, become a new, vibrant entity within the broader faculty community.

REFERENCES

Agha-Jaffar, T. (2000). From theory to praxis in women's studies: Guest speakers and service-learning as pedagogy. *Feminist Teacher, 13*(1), 1–11. www.jstor.org/stable/40545928

Auxier, B., Golbeck, J., & Buntain, C. (2019). Analyzing sentiment and themes in fitness influencers' Twitter dialogue. Information in Contemporary Society—14th

International Conference, iConference 2019, Proceedings, 11420, 429–435. https://doi.org/10.1007/978-3-030-15742-5_41

Brigham, T. J. (2016). Online professional profiles: Health care and library researchers show off their work. *Medical Reference Services Quarterly, 35*(4), 440–448. https://doi.org/10.1080/02763869.2016.1220760

Bush, L., Haygood, D., & Vincent, H. (2017). Student-run communications agencies: Providing students with real-world experiences that impact their careers. *Journalism & Mass Communication Educator, 72*(4), 410–424. https://doi.org/10.1177/1077695816673254

Cabrera, M., & Lloret, N. (2016). Digital tools for academic branding and self-promotion. *Information Science Reference*. https://doi.org/10.4018/978-1-5225-0917-2

Chapman, A. L., & Greenhow, C. (2019). Citizen-scholars: Social media and the changing nature of scholarship. *Publications, 7*(1), 11. https://doi.org/10.3390/publications7010011

Charlton, A. B., & Cornwell, T. B. (2019). Authenticity in horizontal marketing partnerships: A better measure of brand compatibility. *Journal of Business Research, 100*, 279–298. https://doi.org/10.1016/j.jbusres.2019.03.054

Childers, C. C., Lemon, L. L., & Hoy, M. G. (2019). #Sponsored #Ad: Agency perspective on influencer marketing campaigns. *Journal of Current Issues & Research in Advertising, 40*(3), 258–274. https://doi.org/10.1080/10641734.2018.1521113

Dabbagh, N., & Kitsantas, A. (2012). Personal Learning Environments, social media, and self-regulated learning: A natural formula for connecting formal and informal learning. *Internet and Higher Education, 15*, 3–8. https://doi.org/10.1016/j.iheduc.2011.06.002

Davis, B. G. (2009). *Tools for teaching*. San Francisco, CA: John Wiley & Sons.

Duffy, B. E., & Pooley, J. D. (2017). "Facebook for academics": The convergence of self-branding and social media logic on Academia.edu. *Social Media+ Society, 3*(1), https://doi.org/10.1177/2056305117696523

Enke, N., & Borchers, N. S. (2019). Social media influencers in strategic communication: A conceptual framework for strategic social media influencer communication. *International Journal of Strategic Communication, 13*(4), 261–277. https://doi.org/10.1080/1553118X.2019.1620234

Freberg, K., Graham, K., McGaughey, K., & Freberg, L. A. (2011). Who are the social media influencers? A study of public perceptions of personality. *Public Relations Review, 37*(1), 90–92. https://doi.org/10.1016/j.pubrev.2010.11.001

Glenwick, D. S., & Chabot, D. R. (1991). The undergraduate clinical child psychology course: Bringing students to the real world and the real world to students. *Teaching of Psychology, 18*(1), 21–24. https://doi.org/10.1207/s15328023top1801_5

Herman, E., & Nicholas, D. (2019). Scholarly reputation building in the digital age: An activity-specific approach. *El Profesional de la Información, 28*(1). https://doi.org/10.3145/epi.2019.ene.02

Himelboim, I., & Golan, G. J. (2019). A social networks approach to viral advertising: The role of primary, contextual, and low influencers. *Social Media + Society, 5*(3), 1–31. https://doi.org/10.1177/2056305119847516

Hopkins, C. D., Raymond, M. A., & Carlson, L. (2011). Educating students to give them a sustainable competitive advantage. *Journal of Marketing Education, 33,* 337–347. https://doi.org/10.1177/0273475311420241

Influencer Marketing Hub. (2020). *Influencer marketing benchmark report: 2020.* https://influencermarketinghub.com/influencer-marketing-2019-benchmark-report/

Jiménez-Castillo, D., & Sánchez-Fernández, R. (2019). The role of digital influencers in brand recommendation: Examining their impact on engagement, expected value and purchase intention. *International Journal of Information Management, 49,* 366–376. https://doi.org/10.1016/j.ijinfomgt.2019.07.009

Jin, S. V., Muqaddam, A., & Ryu, E. (2019). Instafamous and social media influencer marketing. *Marketing Intelligence & Planning, 37*(5), 567–579. https://doi.org/10.1108/MIP-09-2018-0375

Lang, J. M. (2016). *Small teaching: Everyday lessons from the science of learning.* John Wiley & Sons.

Li, N., & Gillet, D. (2013). Identifying influential scholars in academic social media platforms. 2013 IEEE/ACM International Conference on Advances in Social Networks Analysis and Mining (ASONAM 2013), 608–614. https://ieeexplore.ieee.org/document/6785765

Linder, K. E. (2018). *Managing your professional identity online: A guide for faculty, staff, and administrators.* Sterling, VA: Stylus Publishing, LLC.

Lou, C., & Yuan, S. (2019). Influencer marketing: How message value and credibility affect consumer trust of branded content on social media. *Journal of Interactive Advertising, 19*(1), 58–73. https://doi.org/10.1080/15252019.2018.1533501

Luoma-aho, V., Pirttimäki, T., Maity, D., Munnukka, J., & Reinikainen, H. (2019). Primed authenticity: How priming impacts authenticity perception of social media influencers. *International Journal of Strategic Communication, 13*(4), 352–365. https://doi.org/10.1080/1553118X.2019.1617716

McKeachie, W. (1999). *McKeachie's teaching tips.* Boston, MA: Cengage Learning.

Merle, P., & Freberg, K. (2016). All about that tweet: Student perceptions of professors' social media use in the classroom. *Journal of Research in Interactive Marketing, 10*(2), 124–136. https://doi.org/10.1108/JRIM-01-2015-0008

Merle, P. F., & Craig, C. (2017). Be my guest: A survey of mass communication students' perception of guest speakers. *College Teaching, 65*(2), 41–49. https://doi.org/10.1080/87567555.2016.1232691

Metrejean, C., Pittman, J., & Zarzeski, M. T. (2002). Guest speakers: Reflections on the role of accountants in classroom. *Accounting Education: An International Journal, 11*(4), 347–43. https://doi.org/10.1080/0963928021000031466

Palmer, P. J. (2017). *The courage to teach: Exploring the inner landscape of a teacher's life.* San Francisco, CA: John Wiley & Sons.

Payne, B. K., Sumter, M., & Sun, I. (2003). Bringing the field into the criminal justice classroom: Field trips, ride-alongs, and guest speakers. *Journal of Criminal Justice Education, 14*(2), 327–344. https://doi.org/10.1080/10511250300085821

Remund, D., & Freberg, K. (2013). Scholar as social curator and social connector: The escalating need for public relations professors who successfully link theory and practice in a fast-changing digital world. *Teaching Public Relations*, 1–5. https ://aejmc.us/prd/wp-content/uploads/sites/23/2014/11/tpr86su13.pdf

Roush, C. (2013). The effective use of guest speakers. *AEJMC News*. http://www .aejmc.org/home/2013/03/guest-speakers/

Schouten, A. P., Janssen, L., & Verspaget, M. (2019). Celebrity vs. Influencer endorsements in advertising: The role of identification, credibility, and product-endorser fit. *International Journal of Advertising, 39*(2), 1–24. https://doi.org/10.1 080/02650487.2019.1634898

Smith, B. G., Stumberger, N., Guild, J., & Dugan, A. (2017). What's at stake? An analysis of employee social media engagement and the influence of power and social stake. *Public Relations Review, 43*(5), 978–988. https://doi.org/10.1016/j .pubrev.2017.04.010

Todd, V. (2009). PRSSA faculty and professional advisors' perceptions of pub-lic relations curriculum, assessment of students' learning, and faculty per-formance. *Journalism & Mass Communication Educator, 64*(1), 71–90. 10.1177/107769580906400106

Zhao, X., Zhan, M., & Liu, B. F. (2018). Disentangling social media influence in crises: Testing a four-factor model of social media influence with large data. *Public Relations Review, 44*(4), 549–561. https://doi.org/10.1016/j.pubrev.2018.08.002

Chapter 5

Social Media Influencers in Africa

An Analysis of Instagram Content and Brand Endorsements

Anne W. Njathi and Nicole M. Lee

Social media influencers (SMIs) have significant implications for modern-day public relations and marketing. The proliferation of the Internet has brought about a complete transformation of brand communication with social media platforms taking center stage. As Hearn and Schoenhoff (2015) traced the growing influence of SMIs, they note that "businesses have begun to rely on SMIs due to the sheer volume of advertising online, which drives down actual click-through rates and individual engagement levels" (p. 203). As such, influencer marketing—arguably the new form of celebrity endorsement—has seen more and more brands augmenting their visibility, brand positioning, sales, and market share through SMI partnerships.

Although several studies (Audrezet et al., 2018; Hudson et al., 2016; Djafarova & Rushworth, 2017; Booth & Matic, 2011; De Veirman et al., 2017; Chu & Choi, 2011; Lazazzera, 2018; Kádeková & Holienčinová, 2018) have demonstrated how developed countries have adopted this digitally mediated communication strategy, the continent of Africa still remains understudied. As such, the purpose of this study is to interrogate, analyze, and understand how public relations and marketing professionals are leveraging SMIs across Africa to push relevant brand experiences in these fast-growing consumer markets. This is fundamental to understanding the interrelations between the brand communication landscape in Africa, the relatively young proliferation of the Internet, and the ubiquity of smartphones, especially in the age of the digital revolution and its overall contribution to the African economy. Specifically, we analyzed SMI Instagram posts from fifty SMIs across five countries: Nigeria, Kenya, South Africa, Tanzania, and Ethiopia.

Due to the paucity of research examining brand communication in Africa, we hope this study will serve as a basis for further investigation.

TECHNOLOGICAL DEVELOPMENT ON THE AFRICAN CONTINENT

As previously mentioned, the content of Africa is largely understudied when it comes to understanding how developing countries adopt digital communication strategies. This is despite the fact that Africa is home to four of the five fastest-growing economies in the world (Robertson, 2019) and has witnessed the fastest growth rates in Internet penetration with an increase from 2.1 percent in 2005 to 24.4 percent in 2018 (ITU, 2018). Today, the African continent has around 39.8 percent Internet penetration from an estimated population of 1.2 billion (Internet World Statistics, 2019).

Mobile Internet has also drastically increased globally, and particularly in Africa. By the year 2016, the adoption of smartphones in Africa was on an upward trajectory with countries such as South Africa, Nigeria, Senegal, and Kenya leading the way (GSMA, 2016). Indeed, by the end of 2018, there were around 456 million unique mobile subscribers in Sub-Saharan Africa, which was an increase of 20 million over the previous year and represented a subscriber penetration rate of 44 percent (GSMA, 2019). Around 239 million people, equivalent to 23 percent of the population, also use mobile Internet on a regular basis.

The rate of smartphone adoption is particularly surprising for Sub-Saharan Africa, where the increase in the use of mobile phones is remarkably high compared to the cost of the devices and the prevalence of poverty (Aker & Mbiti, 2010). This can be partly understood through Castells et al. (2006), who argued over a decade ago that mobile telephony moved from being a technology of privilege to that of mainstream necessity. To this effect, there is an estimated 5.5 billion smartphones in use across the world today, now accounting for two-thirds of the global mobile connections (Kemp, 2019). Donner (2015) attributes these figures to the fact that "mobile devices can appeal to near universal human needs and desires" (p. 59).

According to the 2015 Internet Society Report, "Africa's significant growth in mobile communications and steady growth in Internet penetration are in large part attributable to efforts by African governments working in partnership with other stakeholders to create an enabling environment, fostering the development of Internet infrastructure" (p. 2). For example, the adoption of fiber cable technology through submarine infrastructure in 2009 increased Africa's international bandwidth twenty-fold, while its terrestrial network increased by more than 100 percent within five years (*Internet Society Report*, 2015).

However, since cable Internet is not evenly distributed across Africa mobile Internet has helped fill the void in many places. Indeed, mobile phones have opened up new avenues for individuals and groups to transform and improve social, human, and economic situations they find themselves in (Svensson & Wamala, 2012). Social media is one of the main uses of the Internet on mobile devices among Africans, particularly millennials (Wangari, 2017; Silver & Johnson, 2018). Adults under the age of thirty are more likely than older generations to go online and the most popular online activities are keeping in touch with family and friends and using social media. Entertainment (61%) and sports (57%) are ranked as the most popular topics of discussion on social media across Sub-Saharan Africa. These interests are closely followed by religion (45%), politics (37%), and the products they use (37%) (Silver & Johnson, 2018). These topics shed light on what content people in Sub-Saharan Africa are interacting with on social media platforms and present an opportunity for businesses to develop strategies that engage Africa's young, connected, and fast-growing consumer base (Afolabi, 2016; Agyenim-Boateng et al., 2015).

BRAND COMMUNICATION
STRATEGIES ACROSS AFRICA

Africa, and Sub-Saharan Africa in particular, is going through an immense shift—just like the rest of the world—from traditional marketing to marketing that not only focuses on online interactions and conversations on popular social media platforms such as Facebook and YouTube, but also market engagement and brand advocacy (Afolabi, 2016). With Web 3.0 focusing on "user's cooperation" (Barassi & Trere, 2012) and participatory culture (Jenkins et al., 2006; Gil de Zuniga et al., 2012), digital marketing has developed dramatically in recent years. This evolution, coupled with the proliferation of the Internet and the ubiquity of smartphones, has seen millions of Africans become more connected than ever before. Increasingly, these factors have led to moving advertising budgets to online platforms in Africa as brands continuously look for new ways to present their messages to online consumers who follow major SMIs (Toesland, 2017). According to Toesland (2017):

> Sponsored posts, where a brand might pay an influencer for featuring their product or service in a tweet on Twitter, or a picture on Instagram, are growing in popularity as African businesses of all sizes begin to recognize the importance of reaching this customer base. If a business effectively collaborates with an influencer, this advertising method can generate interest around their brand and attract new customers. (p. 5)

Industry publications suggest that SMIs are capitalizing on their captive follower base to sign advertising deals with high-profile brands. Orange et al. (2019) note the emergence of young African SMIs entering the world of fashion, music, arts, and food as new products are being introduced in Africa. Consequently, "with new products and services being consistently introduced in Africa, there is a myriad of opportunities for influencers to introduce new brands or products to a wider market" (p. 5). Despite these observations from industry leaders (e.g., Afolabi, 2016; Toesland, 2017; Orange et al., 2019), there is little to no academic research on influencer marketing in different parts of Africa. Indeed, there are only a handful of case studies (e.g., Backaler, 2018; Otiende, 2018) showcasing how businesses in Africa are taking advantage of the influencer marketing approach in particular and social media marketing in general.

Some global brands such as Huawei, a Chinese multinational technology company, have SMIs across the world, including in African countries such as South Africa and Nigeria as part of their global marketing strategies (Backaler, 2018). Similarly, U.S.-based technology company, Intel, used African SMIs to launch its 2-in-1 laptop/tablet. According to Backaler (2018):

> The local Intel African team recruited eight social, photography, tech, music and entertainment influencers to participate in a campaign called #InsideOut. The influencers developed original content to build awareness around the product launch with three main influencers developing their own YouTube series related to the campaign that generated approximately 150K local views on Intel Africa YouTube channel. (p. 182)

A recent industry study conducted by Humanz (2019), an influencer marketing firm based in South Africa, agrees that influencer marketing is indeed on an upward rise with 152,791 SMIs on Instagram and 69,488 on Twitter in South Africa alone. Instagram is the most popular platform with most the most SMIs in categories such as fitness (4,514), lifestyle (4,208), and fashion (3,811). According to Media Update (2019), the average engagement rate for South African SMIs is 7.83 percent on Instagram and 1.48 percent on Twitter, which exceeds the global averages (Media Update, 2019). Thus, it is not surprising to see Absolut, the Swedish vodka, launch a seventeen-week-long Instagram campaign and brand ambassador program dubbed #AbsolutNights, including South African SMIs. Overall, across eight countries participating globally, this awareness campaign surpassed its original targets hitting 243 posts and 340,884 interactions recorded as likes, comments, and mentions (Backaler, 2018). Another successful campaign was the #DearSouthAfrica campaign by Zara that used sixty micro-influencers with less than 100,000 followers to spread the word online of its official online store in South Africa (Ntloko, 2019).

SMI marketing is also thriving in Kenya with brands seeking novel ways to connect with consumers (Dotsavvy, 2016; *Business Today*, 2018). The most popular SMIs leverage Facebook, YouTube, Twitter, and Instagram to publish their content while amplifying their visibility. According to Otiende (2018), companies such as Safaricom, Tecno Kenya, and Airtel are increasingly using popular SMIs for brand communication. Such campaigns include *#GloUpWithCX* by Tecno in 2017, which leveraged renowned SMIs on Instagram to launch a new mobile device. Similarly, Airtel Kenya used established personalities for its *AirtelTubonge #WachaNikupigie* 2017 campaign.

Since 2015, the state of influencer marketing in Nigeria has increased with brands and the general public coming to terms with influencer marketing being the future of digital brand communication. A survey conducted in 2018 revealed top brands that delivered high-impact SMI marketing campaigns, including Pepsi Nigeria, Taxify, H2O, Tecno, and Indomie (Dotts Media House, 2018). Pepsi's *#NaijaAllTheWay* campaign was singled out as particularly successful with high reach and engagement.

Influencer marketing is also on the rise in Tanzania, which has around 1.9 million users on Instagram, 90 percent of which are younger than forty-five (Kowalczyk, 2017). Boshe (2017) noted successful campaigns such as Coca-Cola's *Coke Studio* and NBC bank's *Wajibika*. Boshe (2017) claimed that the success of these campaigns could be attributed to setting appropriate and realistic objectives, creating unique content, and conducting comprehensive influencer research.

Unlike South Africa, Nigeria, Kenya, and Tanzania, Ethiopia has a general lack of online information on Instagram use by SMIs and brands. In fact, Gizat (2016) explains that multinational companies in Ethiopia such as Diageo, Heineken, Coca-Cola, and Pepsi may be missing social media marketing opportunities because they do not localize content for an Ethiopian market. This is surprising for a country like Ethiopia that has been growing economically in recent years (World Bank, 2019) and has high rates of Internet penetration.

Despite variation from country to country, Okike (2019) claims brands in Africa are integrating strategies such as SMI marketing into every major marketing campaign. Media outlets have indicated an increase in young African SMIs in areas such as fashion, music, arts, food, and health care (e.g., Medium, 2018). Unfortunately, there is not currently substantive academic research to further support the observations made by blogs and other media sources. Further, while the case study approach offers valuable insights, it does not tell the whole story. There is still a question about who SMIs in Africa are, the extent to which they are using their influence to build brands and increase brand value, and whether disclosing partnerships is common practice. Further, it is important to understand how brands, in general, communicate with their customers through SMI marketing. This research gap led to the following research questions:

RQ1: What are the attributes of the top African SMIs?

RQ2: How often are African SMIs sharing brand content and what is the nature of the content being shared? What types of brands are featured?

RQ3: How often do posts featuring brands indicate a partnership or sponsorship? How are partnerships identified?

RQ4: Which types of posts receive the most follower engagement?

METHODOLOGY

To answer the aforementioned research questions, we conducted a content analysis of African SMIs' Instagram profiles and posts. Instagram is a photo and video sharing social network, which was founded in 2010 by software engineer Michel Krieger and computer programmer and former Google employee Kevin Systrom. Instagram was chosen because it is arguably the fastest-growing social media platform with around one billion monthly active users as of June 2018 (Instagram Statistics, 2019; Iqbal, 2019) and is among the most popular platforms among SMIs.

Sample

Fifty SMIs were chosen for the study. Ten SMIs were each selected from five countries (Nigeria, Kenya, South Africa, Tanzania, and Ethiopia). The five countries were determined because they represent the top five Sub-Saharan countries in terms of Internet penetration and are all within the top ten economies in Africa. The top Instagram SMIs from each country were selected for analysis using a variety of online media articles, blogs, and industry professionals. First, a combination of search terms was used to search on Google. They included "top African Instagram influencers," "leading African Instagram influencers," or "most influential Instagrammers in Africa" along with replacing "Africa" with each individual country. To be included in this study, SMIs had to be people who are primarily influencers and not celebrities who also have an Instagram account. This approach was adopted to distinguish between SMIs as people who have built their influence on social media versus celebrities who have earned their celebrity status through talents in their respective fields or other traditional means. Utilizing media provided a way to identify those who are considered SMIs.

In total, sixty-eight articles or lists were used to identify SMIs. From each article or list, all SMIs' Instagram handles were recorded and the number of followers and the SMI country of origin were cross-verified from Instagram and recorded. Each SMI that appeared more than once in an article or list was included in the analysis. Forty-two SMIs appeared in two or more articles or lists. In order to complete the lists of ten from each country, SMIs were chosen based on their number of followers. This process worked well for Nigeria, Kenya, and South Africa, but gaps still existed for Tanzania and Ethiopia. In addition to online searches, public relations and advertising professionals in these two countries were asked to share lists of top SMIs. Like the lists in the media, these were compared and the top SMIs were chosen based on follower count.

Prior to sampling individual posts, the SMIs' profiles were analyzed in order to determine the types of SMIs that have gained prominence in Africa. This included looking at which accounts were verified, their total following, and the main type of brand topic each one focused on (see table 5.1 for the final list of SMIs). The main topic was primarily determined by an SMI's own self-identification in their handle or biography section. For instance, some explicitly mentioned fashion or cooking. If there was no self-iden-tification, we looked through the sample to see what types of brands were featured. If there were multiple types of brands, they were categorized as Lifestyle/Other.

From each SMI, eighteen posts were selected for analysis using a stratified random sampling method. One post was selected for each month between January 2018 and June 2019. To select the individual post, a random number was generated that corresponded with a day of the month. For instance, for January, a number between one and thirty-one would be generated. If the number was four, the first post on January 4 was included in the sample. If there were no posts on a date, the first post following the date was selected. If there were no posts following that date for the rest of a given month, the last post in that month was selected. On the few occasions that an SMI did not post at all in a month, the first post from the following month was selected. In total, 900 posts were included in the content analysis.

Variables

Posts were analyzed for various message and content features related to brand presence and sponsorship. The unit of analysis was each individual post regardless of the post format.

Table 5.1 Final Sample of SMIs

Handle	Country	Followers	Verified Badge	Main Topic
@ebuka	Nigeria	2,246,420	Yes	Fashion/Accessories
@2lauraikeji	Nigeria	1,899,951	Yes	Lifestyle/Other
@thepatriciabright	Nigeria	1,114,722	Yes	Lifestyle/Other
@9jafoodie	Nigeria	282,690	No	Food/Cooking
@noble_igwe	Nigeria	218,570	Yes	Fashion/Accessories
@dimmaumeh	Nigeria	129,008	Yes	Lifestyle/Other
@toniolaoye1	Nigeria	127,858	No	Lifestyle/Other
@sisi_yemmie	Nigeria	124,138	Yes	Lifestyle/Other
@akinfaminu	Nigeria	79,217	Yes	Fashion/Accessories
@hadizaalawal	Nigeria	24,953	Yes	Lifestyle/Other
@queenveebosset	Kenya	1,604,249	Yes	Beauty/Makeup
@anerlisa	Kenya	793,681	No	Lifestyle/Other
@this_is_ess	Kenya	324,753	Yes	Lifestyle/Other
@justjoykendi	Kenya	188,731	Yes	Lifestyle/Other
@seth_gor	Kenya	154,652	Yes	Lifestyle/Other
@nanciemwai	Kenya	110,306	Yes	Lifestyle/Other
@silvianjoki	Kenya	108,905	No	Lifestyle/Other
@luciamusau	Kenya	98,258	No	Lifestyle/Other
@kaluhiskitchen	Kenya	79,020	Yes	Food/Cooking
@joannakinuthia	Kenya	78,242	Yes	Beauty/Makeup
@mihlalii_n	South Africa	916,992	No	Lifestyle/Other
@thickleeyonce	South Africa	477,950	Yes	Lifestyle/Other
@sarahlanga	South Africa	293,581	No	Lifestyle/Other
@shaunstylist	South Africa	196,698	No	Fashion/Accessories
@trevor_stuurman	South Africa	156,138	Yes	Fashion/Accessories
@snimhlongo	South Africa	137,404	No	Fashion/Accessories
@bakedonline	South Africa	136,541	No	Lifestyle/Other
@fashionbreed	South Africa	62,923	Yes	Fashion/Accessories
@crystal_kasper	South Africa	54,049	Yes	Lifestyle/Other
@aishaandlife	South Africa	19,578	No	Lifestyle/Other
@hajismanara	Tanzania	1,763,217	No	Lifestyle/Other
@flavianamatata	Tanzania	1,501,401	Yes	Lifestyle/Other
@open_kitchen2014	Tanzania	659,044	No	Food/Cooking
@lilommy	Tanzania	614,860	No	Lifestyle/Other
@poshyqueeen	Tanzania	580,364	No	Fashion/Accessories
@allyrehmtullah	Tanzania	72,311	No	Lifestyle/Other
@ossegrecasinare	Tanzania	58,145	No	Travel
@lavidoz	Tanzania	45,477	No	Fashion/Accessories
@drudysseus	Tanzania	14,558	No	Lifestyle/Other
@that_tanzanianguy	Tanzania	13,563	No	Travel
@addisalem_getaneh	Ethiopia	590,936	No	Lifestyle/Other
@touch_by_marzel	Ethiopia	363,990	No	Beauty/Makeup
@redeat_hable	Ethiopia	216,757	Yes	Lifestyle/Other
@dopeethiopian	Ethiopia	154,022	No	Lifestyle/Other
@bloom_chaka	Ethiopia	31,361	No	Lifestyle/Other
@chef_yohanis	Ethiopia	23,271	Yes	Food/Cooking
@calebmeakins	Ethiopia	13,634	No	Lifestyle/Other
@hannahjoytv	Ethiopia	12,443	Yes	Lifestyle/Other
@ethiopienne	Ethiopia	9,260	Yes	Lifestyle/Other
@mahletkelel	Ethiopia	6,887	Yes	Beauty/Makeup

General post attributes. Posts were coded for general attributes, including the type of post (photo, video, carousel/multiple photos), the number of likes, and the number of comments.

Brand presence. Whether or not a brand was present was also assessed. This included whether a brand was featured in the photo or video by name or logo, whether a brand was mentioned in the caption, whether the post linked to a sales page, and whether a brand was tagged in the photo or video. Each of these was coded as present or absent. The brand category was also coded. The categories were (1) clothing/jewelry/shoes, (2) makeup/beauty/hair, (3) travel, (4) food/beverage, (5) fitness/sport, (6) non-profit/cause-related, and (7) other/combination. The seven categories were mutually exclusive, and any post falling into more than one was coded other/combination. Finally, coders also noted if the brand in question was owned or created by the SMI. This variable was coded as present or absent.

Sponsorship. The third group of variables captured direct promotions or sponsorships. This consisted of coding whether the post was sponsored, whether the caption shared a promo code with followers, whether the caption specifically mentioned a sponsorship, partnership, or gifted products/services, and whether a hashtag was used to indicate paid content (e.g., #sponsored, #ad). Each of these was coded as present or absent.

Coding and Reliability

Both researchers served as coders for the study. Most SMIs from the five countries post in English. However, a minority in Tanzania also post in Swahili and a few in Ethiopia included both Amharic and English translations in single posts. Posts were coded the same regardless of the language. One coder was fluent in both English and Swahili, which allowed us to include posts in both languages. All posts in Amharic also included English translations and therefore were available for coding. To establish initial reliability, pilot coding was conducted on posts from SMIs outside the final sample. Once satisfactory reliability was reached, coders independently analyzed separate portions of the sample. Final reliability was computed based on 15 percent of the sample that was coded by both researchers. Intercoder reliability was assessed using Krippendorf's alpha.

Coders reached 100 percent agreement ($\alpha = 1$) on the type of post, whether the post was sponsored, and whether there was a promo code, sponsorship hashtag, or link to a sales code included. Good or acceptable reliability was reached for the remaining variables: whether a brand was visible in the photo or video ($\alpha = .94$), mentioned in the caption ($\alpha = .85$), or tagged in a photo ($\alpha = .92$), whether there was a direct mention of sponsorship in the caption ($\alpha = .79$), whether the brand was owned by the SMI ($\alpha = .79$), and the type of product or service featured ($\alpha = .82$).

RESULTS

Attributes of SMIs

The first research question asked about the attributes of the top SMIs in the five countries included in the study. Because the sample size for the profiles was fifty and not conducive to content analysis or intercoder reliability, both authors looked at all the profiles and recorded various attributes. We compared observations and discussed any conflicts in order to come to a consensus. The fifty SMIs had an average follower count of 379,713.58 (*SD* = 546,388.22) consisted of fifteen men and thirty-five women, and a half (*n* = 25) had a verified account. A majority of SMIs (62%, *n* = 31) identified as general lifestyle influencers and/or posted about a variety of topics, including fashion, beauty, travel, and food. However, some identified themselves more specifically, including nine (18.0%) fashion SMIs, four (8.0%) beauty SMIs, four (8.0%) food or cooking SMIs, and two (4.0%) travel SMIs. Interestingly, there were nine who indicated they no longer lived in their identified country or were in between countries but still posted content specific to the country, included their country in their bio, and were identified in blog posts as SMIs to follow for that country. Nigeria, for example, had four SMIs living in other countries abroad but posting Nigerian content including paid partnerships, identifying themselves as Nigerian, and being identified as such in online media about top SMIs.

Comparisons were also made between countries. Although the differences were not significant, the average follower count for each country ranged from 142,256.01 (*SD* = 197,774.12) for Ethiopia to 624,752.70 (*SD* = 828,562.87) for Nigeria. There were no significant differences between countries when it came to the type of SMIs in terms of topic. General lifestyle SMIs were the most common across all five countries. A Chi-Square Test of Association was conducted to determine if there were significant differences in the number of SMIs who were verified on Instagram. Results indicated that there were differences, $\chi^2(4) = 12.8$, $p = .01$, $\phi = .01$. Nigeria and Kenya each had eight verified SMIs, South Africa had four, Tanzania had three, and Ethiopia had two.

African SMIs and Branded Content

The second research question focused on the post-level content analysis and asked how often African SMIs shared brand content, the nature of the content being shared, and the types of brands being promoted. Descriptive statistics were used to answer these questions. In terms of how often brands are featured in SMI posts, 24.2 percent (*n* = 218) feature a brand name or logo in the photo(s) or video(s), 43.9 percent ($n = 395$) mention a brand in the caption, 29.0 percent ($n = 261$) have a brand tagged in the photo(s) or video(s), and 1.8 percent ($n = 16$) included a link to buy the product or service. In total, 58.2 percent ($n = 524$) feature a brand in some way. Of the posts that included brands, 24.8 percent ($n = 130$) featured clothing or accessory brands, 20.6 percent ($n = 108$) featured beauty or hair brands, 5.3 percent ($n = 28$) featured travel-related brands, and 11.1 percent ($n = 58$) featured food-, beverage-, or cooking-related brands. The rest of the posts (38.3%, $n = 200$) featured a combination of brand types or a brand that did not fit the other categories. A minority of posts (3.2%, $n = 17$) featured a brand that the influencer owned or created. Of the posts featuring a brand, 70.0 percent ($n = 367$) were photos, 12.2 percent ($n = 64$) were videos, and 17.7 percent ($n = 93$) were in carousel format.

African SMIs and Brand Partnerships

The third research question asked how often posts featuring brands indicate a partnership or sponsorship, and how partnerships are identified. Results indicated that only 8.4 percent ($n = 44$) of posts by African SMIs that feature a brand indicate sponsorship in some way. This is 4.9 percent of the total sample. We measured several ways in which an SMI could indicate to followers that the content was sponsored. Of the posts that indicated sponsorship, 50.0 percent ($n = 22$) directly mentioned it in the caption, 34.1 percent ($n = 15$) used Instagram's sponsored post feature, 13.6 percent ($n = 6$) included a promo code, and 27.3 percent ($n = 12$) used a hashtag such as #ad, #sp, or #sponsored. As indicated by the percentages, some posts used multiple methods to communicate sponsorship.

Eliciting Follower Engagement

The final research question focused on which types of posts garnered the most follower engagement. Indicators of engagement were the number of likes and the number of comments posts received. Kolmogorov-Smirnov, Shapiro-Wilk, and Levene's tests were used to choose between parametric and non-parametric statistics. Because the data violated the assumptions of normality and homogeneity of variances, non-parametric tests were conducted. A Kruskal-Wallis H test with Dunn's post-hoc pairwise comparisons was conducted to compare the three post formats. Results indicated that there was no significant difference in likes between the post formats, $\chi^2(2) = 2.49$, $p = .29$. However, there was a significant difference in comments between the post formats, $\chi^2(2) = 10.45$, $p = .005$, with a mean comment numbers of 217.84 ($SD = 409.14$) for videos, 152.08 ($SD = 271.66$)

for carousels, and 139.43 (SD = 332.05) for photos. Pairwise comparisons indicated that videos received significantly (p = 002) more comments than photos, but the difference between videos and carousel posts was not significant.

To compare posts that featured a brand with those that did not, a Mann-Whitney test was conducted. Results indicated there was no significant difference between posts that featured a brand and those that did not in terms of likes (U = 94,028.00, p = .24) or comments (U = 96,868.50, p = .78). Among the posts that featured a brand, there was no significant difference in likes between those that indicated a sponsorship or partnership and those that did not (U = 13,207.00, p = .26). However, sponsorship posts (M = 187.39, SD = 491.96) received significantly more comments than those that did not indicate sponsorship (M = 129.55, SD = 254.34), U = 11,625.50, p = .006.

DISCUSSION

Taken together, our results provide valuable insights into the status of SMI marketing in Africa. According to Ogilvy public relations Cape Town managing director Nicky Schermer, across the continent, influencer marketing "remains to a degree immature, largely due technical constraints. As those barriers lift, there are huge opportunities for brands" (as quoted in Toesland, 2017, para. 4). Our findings align with this notion. Although the countries examined represented five of the leading economies in Africa and those with extensive broadband penetration in the continent, there were differences from country to country. Influencer marketing appears particularly underdeveloped in Ethiopia and Tanzania, where it was challenging to even find SMIs to include in the study.

When it comes to SMI attributes, two factors lend insight into their online share of voice and level of influence. First, receiving verification indicates that the account has met Instagram's requirement of being in the public's interest, representing a real or authentic person or organization, being the only account for that person or business that is verified, having a complete profile, and representing a notable or well-known person or organization (Instagram, 2019). In addition to being difficult to find SMIs at all, Ethiopia and Tanzania had far fewer verified SMIs (with two and three, respectively) than other countries, such as Nigeria and Kenya, which had eight each. This may indicate a lack of development in the influencer industry in those countries.

The other factor that lends insight into the relative power of SMIs is their number of followers. The average number of followers for SMIs in this study suggests they fall under all categories of influencers as described by the

Association of National Advertisers (2018): micro (50 to 25,000 followers), mid-level (25,001 to 100,000 followers), and macro influencer (more than 100,000 followers). However, only a minority had over one million followers (Nigeria, $n = 3$; Kenya, $n = 2$; and Tanzania, $n = 3$), which would fall under the mega and celebrity categories. While various popular press articles define influencers with over one million followers as mega or celebrity influencers, this is subjective if looked at along with other variables such as an individual country's population, gross domestic product (GDP), and gross domestic income (GDI). We would also caution against generalizing based on the sample included in this study because each SMI is unique. Although we sought to include only those who were primarily influencers and not celebrities who happened to have an Instagram account, some of the SMIs may have also gained prominence through other means or leveraged their influence to create their own companies, start TV shows, or write books, thus blurring the lines between SMI and traditional celebrity. For instance, the most followed SMI was Ebuka Obi-Uchendu, a Nigerian influencer who first gained prominence after appearing on a reality show, much like the Kardashian family in the United States.

Although many SMIs had a singular focus, such as fashion bloggers, more often than not, they posted content that seemed extended beyond their claimed focus or, perhaps, original intent. This poses a challenge to brands whose intention is to work with a particular SMI who aligns with their brand attributes when it comes to identifying influencers with a consistently strong value proposition. To some extent, even identifying SMIs was a difficult task. Thus, it is no surprise to see brands using the same faces time and again as Moroe (2019) noted while commending Zara's #DearSouthAfrica campaign that incorporated new faces through partnering with micro-influencers.

In terms of direct sales tactics, we found that 1.8 percent ($n = 16$) of posts with a link to a sales page and 0.7 percent ($n = 6$) included a promotional code. African SMIs often feature brands in their posts but rarely explicitly try to sell those products or services. This is consistent with past research that indicates that despite increasing purchasing power and Internet access, African shoppers tend to not trust the online market for making purchases (UNCTAD, 2018). Although Sub-Saharan African consumers who engage in social networking are educated, young, and have high income (Silver & Johnson, 2018), they are willing to spend (Agyenim-Boateng et al., 2015), a minority purchase products and services online and most only use the Internet and mobile devices for social and entertainment purposes (Silver & Johnson, 2018).

Relatedly, we found that 8.4 percent ($n = 44$) of posts that feature a brand disclose any type of partnership with the brand. This could be because the SMIs post about brands without solicitation. However, in some cases, they may have received payment or goods or services without disclosing that to their followers. The countries included in the study vary in their disclosure laws and guidelines. Much like the Federal Trade Commission in the United States, the South African Advertising Regulatory Board (ARB) requires all SMIs to clearly disclose their terms of engagement with brands whether it is monetary rewards or payment in kind through free goods or services or give-aways of branded merchandise. In Kenya, Nigeria, and Tanzania, regulations exist but are less explicit when considering disclosing sponsorships specifi-cally. For instance, Kenya and Tanzania both require bloggers to be licensed, which includes a registration fee.

These relatively new and controversial regulations are a source of anger and confusion as bloggers, influencers, and general social media users strive to understand what policies apply to whom. Indeed, the fear of fines or even jail time has driven some social media content creators to abandon their pages completely (Dark, 2018). In Nigeria, the regulatory body, the Advertising Practitioners Council of Nigeria (APCON) must approve all advertisements before they are published. This has always applied to tradi-tional media, but the Council plans to more closely regulate online advertis-ing as well (Idris, 2019). Currently, however, it is unclear how and if that will apply to SMIs, especially those not receiving monetary incentives, or what disclosures will be required. Underlying these regulations are concerns about serious problems such as hate speech, misinformation, and extremism. However, critics raise concerns about censorship by the government and the digital divide (e.g., Mumbere, 2018; Ogola, 2018). This is especially potent in Ethiopia due to its history of frequent Internet shutdowns and the block-ing of social media platforms (Freedom House, 2018). The Ethiopian Media Council is still in its infancy and lacks the capability to regulate the digital space, let alone user-generated content on social media platforms (Abraha, 2017). Its mandate is currently limited to the traditional media industry. Indeed, none of these countries lack advertising laws when it comes to conventional advertising, but, with the exception of South Africa, they are lagging in the digital realm.

When examining engagement, there were significant differences in the number of comments based on the type of post (with video posts receiving the most comments) and whether the post indicated a partnership in any way (with those that did receiving more comments). The same pattern did not emerge for the number of likes a post received. One explanation for this is that comments require a higher level of engagement, so although less engag-ing content may receive likes, it is harder to earn comments. These findings also suggest that followers of African SMIs are not averse to brand sponsor-ships as disclosed partnerships had no impact on likes but a positive impact on the number of comments.

Implications

This chapter suggests several implications for public relations and marketing practitioners looking to reach consumers in African markets. The aforementioned findings highlight opportunities for brands wishing to work with SMIs in Africa. However, practitioners must recognize that each country has its own opportunities and challenges. For some countries, there are limited numbers of influencers with broad reach. This is true of Ethiopia and likely more so for many countries not included in the present study. Even where SMIs are present, online shopping is less of a norm and African consumers are less likely to purchase an item online immediately after seeing it on social media.

Besides the challenges of e-commerce and infrastructure, brands seeking a strong digital footprint in Africa are occupied by other challenges that, according to Agyenim-Boateng et al. (2015), include linguistic diversity, differences in consumer behavior, a fragmented retail market, low data availability and quality, and political instability and conflict. Backaler (2018) adds that these particularly concern multinational companies seeking to enter diverse emerging markets but fail as a result of replicating strategies used in their home markets. To succeed in acquiring the new emerging consumer class in many African countries, Bhan (2014) calls for understanding the values and customs of each particular culture.

Although SMIs from the countries chosen for this study happened to post primarily in English followed by Swahili, there is much greater linguistic diversity across Africa, especially if Northern Africa is included. Platforms such as Facebook are making it easier to engage with diverse audiences by adopting local native languages such as Swahili, Hausa, and Zulu (Afolabi, 2016), but brands must hire practitioners fluent in these languages.

Limitations and Future Research

The five countries studied in this chapter give a glimpse of the influencer marketing landscape in Africa, but they cannot be considered a full representation of the continent. To reiterate, Nigeria, Kenya, South Africa, Tanzania, and Ethiopia represent the five of the leading economies in Sub-Saharan Africa that also have high Internet penetration. However, they do not represent the linguistic or cultural diversity of the continent. Arguably, they also have less political instability and conflict than many other countries in Africa. Future research may seek to incorporate additional countries for comparison. Likewise, this study focused exclusively on African countries and did not make direct comparisons to other countries around the world, which may be of interest to future scholars.

As with traditional marketing, most brands in Sub-Saharan Africa still use well-known celebrities, such as actors and athletes, who command a huge following both online and offline. Thus, generating a pool of SMIs presented a set of challenges such as inconsistent posting, unclear brand partnerships, and SMIs doubling as entrepreneurs with their own brands. This content analysis is limited in that it does not fully capture the distinctions and complexities of self-promotion and brand promotion or the full spectrum of celebrity status.

Finally, the scope of the current study was limited to content created by SMIs. Although we recorded the number of likes and comments on each post, we did not analyze the substance or the nature of the comments, which provides an additional avenue for future study.

Results from this study suggest directions for future research and provide a basis for future studies on SMIs in Africa and other growing markets around the world. As the global economic landscape changes in the coming years and decades, this will be an important topic of study and of great interest to communication practitioners working for international brands.

REFERENCES

Abraha, H. (2017). Examining approaches to internet regulation in Ethiopia. *Information & Communications Technology Law*, 1–19. doi:10.1080/13600834.2 017.1374057

Agyenim-Boateng, Y., Benson-Armer, R., & Russo, B. (2015, July). Winning in Africa's consumer market. https://www.mckinsey.com/industries/consumer-packa ged-goods/our-insights/winning-in-africas-consumer-market

Afolabi, A. (2016). Social media marketing; The case of Africa. doi:10.13140/ RG.2.2.20612.73609

Aker, J. C., & Mbiti, I. M. (2010). Mobile phones and economic development in Africa. *Journal of Economic Perspectives, 24*, 207–232. doi: 10.1257/jep.24.3.207

Ana. (2018). How Ana members are using influencer marketing. https://www.ana.net/ miccontent/show/id/ii-2018-members-using-influencer

ARB. (2019, July 4). Appendix K- social media code. http://arb.org.za/assets/appen-dix-k.pdf

Audrezet, A., de Kerviler, G., & Guidry Moulard, J. (2018). Authenticity under threat: When social media influencers need to go beyond self-presentation. *Journal of Business Research*. Advance online publication. doi: 10.1016/j.jbusres.2018.07.008

Backaler, J. (2018). *Digital influence: Unleash the power of influencer marketing to accelerate your global business*. PA: Palgrave Macmillan (Springer International Publishing with rights).

Barassi, V., & Treré, E. (2012). Does Web 3.0 come after Web 2.0? Deconstructing theoretical assumptions through practice. *New Media & Society, 14*(8), 1269–1285. https://doi.org/10.1177/1461444812445878

Bhan, N. (2014, June 27). How Africa is challenging marketing. https://hbr.org/2014/06/how-africa-is-challenging-marketing

Booth, N., & Matic, J. A. (2011). Mapping and leveraging influencers in social media to shape corporate brand perceptions. *Corporate Communications: An International Journal, 16*, 184–191. doi:10.1108/13563281111156853

Boshe, F. (2017, September 4). Influencer Marketing is growing in Tanzania, but is your brand doing it right? https://www.linkedin.com/pulse/influencer-marketing-growing-tanzania-your-brand-doing-fredrick-boshe

Businesstech. (2019, July 4). South African "influencers" have to mark all sponsored posts as adverts: watchdog. https://businesstech.co.za/news/internet/327465/south-african-influencers-have-to-mark-all-sponsored-posts-as-adverts-watchdog/

Business Today. (2018, February 9). Top social media influencers in Kenya. https://businesstoday.co.ke/top-social-media-influencers-kenya/

Castells, M., Fernandez-Ardevol, M., Linchhuan-Qui, J., and Sey, A. (2006). *Mobile communication and society: A global perspective.* MIT Press.

Chu, S., & Choi, S. M. (2011). Electronic word-of-mouth in social networking sites: A cross-cultural study of the United States and China. *Journal of Global Marketing, 24*, 263–281. doi:10.1080/08911762.2011.592461

Dark, S. (2018, July 6). Strict new internet laws in Tanzania are driving bloggers and content creators offline. https://www.theverge.com/2018/7/6/17536686/tanzania-internet-laws-censorship-uganda-social-media-tax

De Veirman, M., Cauberghe, V., & Hudders, L. (2017). Marketing through Instagram influencers: The impact of number of followers and product divergence on brand attitude. *International Journal of Advertising, 36*, 798–828. doi:10.1080/02650487.2017.1348035

Donner, J. (2015). *After access: Inclusion, development, and a more mobile internet.* MIT Press.

Dotsavvyafrica. (2016, September 10). The art (&science) of digital influencer marketing in Kenya. https://www.dotsavvyafrica.com/the-art-science-of-digital-influencer-marketing-in-kenya

Dotts Media House. (2018). The state of influencer marketing in Nigeria report. https://africanbusinessmagazine.com/sectors/technology/africas-new-media-influencers/

Djafarova, E., & Rushworth, C. (2017). Exploring the credibility of online celebrities' Instagram profiles in influencing the purchase decisions of young female users. *Computers in Human Behavior, 68*, 1–7. doi: 10.1016/j.chb.2016.11.009

Freedom House. (2018). Freedom on the net. https://freedomhouse.org/report/freedom-net/2018/ethiopia

Gil de Zúñiga, H., Jung, N., & Valenzuela, S. (2012). Social media use for news and individuals' social capital, civic engagement and political participation. *Journal of Computer-Mediated Communication, 17*(3), 319–336.

GSMA. (2016). *State of industry report on mobile money.* https://www.gsma.com/mobilefordevelopment/wp-content/uploads/2017/03/GSMA_State-of-the-Industry-Report-on-Mobile-Money_2016.pdf

GSMA. (2019). The mobile economy sub Saharan Africa 2019. https://www.gsma.com/r/mobileeconomy/sub-saharan-africa/

Hearn, A., & Schoenhoff, S. (2015). From celebrity to influencer: Tracing the diffusion of celebrity value across the data stream. In P. D. Marshall & S. Redmond (Eds.), *A companion to celebrity*. doi:10.1002/9781118475089.ch11

How many people use Instagram? (2017, March 23). http://mediakix.com/2017/03/how-many-people-use-instagram/#gs.d2jwgf

Hudson, S., Huang, L., Roth, M. S., & Madden, T. J. (2016). The influence of social media interactions on consumer–brand relationships: A three-country study of brand perceptions and marketing behaviors. *International Journal of Research in Marketing, 33*, 27–41. doi: 10.1016/j.ijresmar.2015.06.004

Humanz. (2019, August 29). Influencer marketing statistics & benchmarks South Africa 2019. https://home.humanz.ai/wp-content/uploads/2019/10/2019-Q3-ZA-Humanz-market-report-Web.pdf

Idris, A. (2019, September 3). Nigeria's advertising regulator, APCON, wants to regulate online adverts. https://techcabal.com/2019/09/03/nigerias-advertising-regulator-apcon-wants-to-regulate-online-adverts/

Instagram. (2019). Verified Badges. https://help.instagram.com/854227311295302

Internet Society. (2015). Internet development and Internet governance in Africa. https://www.internetsociety.org/resources/doc/2015/internet-development-and-internet-governance-in-africa/

Iqani, M. (2019). Picturing luxury, producing value: The cultural labour of social media brand influencers in South Africa. *International Journal of Cultural Studies, 22*(2), 229–247. https://doi.org/10.1177/1367877918821237

Jenkins, H., Clinton, K., Purushotma, R., Robison, A. J., & Weigel, M. (2006). *Confronting the challenges of participatory culture*. The MacArthur Foundation http://digitallearning.macfound.org

Kádeková, Z., & Holienčinová, M. (2018). Influencer marketing as a modern phenomenon creating a new frontier of virtual opportunities. *Communication Today, 9*, 90–105.

Kemp, S. (2019, January 30). Digital 2019: Global Internet use accelerates. https://wearesocial.com/blog/2019/01/digital-2019-global-internet-use-accelerates

Kowalczyk, K. (2017, May). Instagram user demographics in Tanzania—May 2017. https://napoleoncat.com/blog/instagram-users-in-tanzania/

Lazazzera, M. (2018, January 14). How Instagram influencers turn followers into dollars. https://www.ft.com/content/fc964254-155f-11e7-b0c1-37e417ee6c76

Moroe, K. (2019, September 20). Key take-outs from Zara's #DearSouthAfrica campaign. https://10and5.com/2019/09/20/key-take-outs%E2%80%8B-from-zaras-dearsouthafrica-campaign%E2%80%8B/

Mumbere, D. (2018, December 4). Tanzania cyber law introduces $900 fees for bloggers, compulsory passwords. https://www.africanews.com/2018/04/12/tanzania-cyber-law-introduces-900-fees-for-bloggers-compulsory-passwords/

Ntloko, K. (2019, October 3). Micro-influencer marketing: How Zara saw success. https://www.meltwater.com/za/blog/micro-influencer-marketing-how-zara-saw-success/

Ogola, G. (2018, October 4). The threats to media freedom are getting more sophisticated in Africa's digital age. https://qz.com/africa/1412973/african-governments-are-blocking-social-media-or-taxing-it/

Okike, S. (2019, July 17). The rise of micro-influencers in Africa. https://techpoint.af rica/2019/07/17/the-rise-of-micro-influencers-in-africa/

Orange, E., Weiner, J., & Ranasinghe, E. (2019). The rise- and fall-? of the social media influence. https://medium.com/positive-returns/the-rise-and-fall-of-the-soci al-media-influence-28ee82eabf5d

Otiende, L. N. (2018). Impact of social media influencers on social brand communi-cation for Kenyan tech brands on Instagram. http://erepo.usiu.ac.ke/handle/11732 /4177;jsessionid=EAB40B56295BCDA5123B88AF64B414DF

Parliament Act. (2019). Kenya-information-and-communication-amendment-bill -2019. http://www.parliament.go.ke/sites/default/files/2019-06/Kenya%20Inform ation%20and%20Communications%20%28Amendment%29%20Bill%2C%202 019.pdf

Robertson, C. (2019, April 10). This African nation has the fastest growing economy in the world. *CNBC Africa*. https://www.cnbcafrica.com/news/west-africa/2019/04 /10/this-african-nation-has-the-fastest-growing-economy-in-the-world/

Silver, L., & Johnson, Courtney. (2018, October 9). Internet use is growing across much of sub-Saharan Africa, but most are still offline. https://www.pewresearch.o rg/global/2018/10/09/internet-use-is-growing-across-much-of-sub-saharan-africa -but-most-are-still-offline/

Svensson, J., & Wamala, C. (2012, June 6–7). M4D: Mobile communication for development. Paper presented at 3rd Sanord International Symposium, Aarhus University, Denmark. Aarhus: Aarhus University.

TCRA. (2018). Electronic and postal communications (online content). https://ww w.tcra.go.tz/images/documents/regulations/SUPP_GN_NO_133_16_03_2018_EP OCA_ONLINE_CONTENT_REGULATIONS_2018.pdf

Toesland, F. (2017, February 2). Africa's new media influencers. https://africanbusin essmagazine.com/sectors/technology/africas-new-media-influencers

UNCTAD. (2018). UNCTAD B2C E-commerce index 2018 focus on Africa. https:// unctad.org/en/PublicationsLibrary/tn_unctad_ict4d12_en.pdf

Wangari, N. (2017, February 27). African millennials; mobile usage and media con-sumption. https://www.geopoll.com/blog/african-millennials-mobile-usage-and-media-consumption

Chapter 6

It's a Whole New World

The Impact of Social Media Influencers on Type 1 Diabetics' Attitudes About, and Behaviors Regarding, Insulin Pump Therapy

Corey Jay Liberman

Social influence is an interesting process. Just recently, during a Thanksgiving dinner discussion, a family member and I began dialoguing about television shows in which we had been indulging as of late. He knew very few of mine, and I knew very few of his. When he began discussing one, however, I took particular interest and began watching the next day. As the closing credits of the first episode overtook the screen, I turned to my wife to see the extent to which she enjoyed it. She did. This created even more cognitive confusion for me because I was uncertain. Did I like it? Was I entertained? Was I enthused? Part of me wanted to answer these queries with a resounding "no." However, my family member, the social influencer, and my wife, an even more salient social influencer, both forced me to question my reactions. Perhaps I did like the show. Perhaps I enjoyed the characters and the character development. Perhaps I appreciated the dark sense of humor on behalf of the show's writers. I found myself in a cognitive conundrum: one within which social actors oftentimes find themselves. But why was I faced with this? Why do we so routinely encounter this dialectical tension between thought and knowledge (between thinking and knowing)? The answer lies in the power of social influence. We come to view so much of social life through the lenses of others that it is difficult for us to have the agency to decide, under our own volition, whether and to what extent something is deemed good or bad or funny or sad or just or unjust. We are primed to understand the world from the vantage point of other social actors in our myriad of social webs.

This chapter will not focus on the role of social influence in the world of television. Rather, it focuses on how Social Media Influencers (SMIs), a term originally adopted by, and employed for, those working in the world of digital marketing and public relations (see, for example, Freberg et al., 2011), have been effective persuasive agents regarding Type 1 diabetics' decision to begin insulin pump therapy. The chapter will first introduce, albeit briefly, the role of social influence in the process of persuasion, closing with a discussion about how social media has altered the process, not the product, of so doing. Next will be a discussion about insulin pump therapy and the particular variables necessary for influence from a communication perspective. The chapter will conclude with a discussion about the results from an empirical study dealing with how social influence seems to manifest itself online, in mediated platforms, examining why certain sources and messages are able to affect attitudinal and behavioral change.

WHAT IS SOCIAL INFLUENCE AND WHY DOES IT WORK?

The process of social influence is not new. It has likely existed, in some shape or form, since the beginning of recorded time. Yet, even as we swiftly enter the third decade of the twenty-first century, there has yet to surface a solid, unanimously agreed-upon definition for this phrase. One of the reasons for this lack of consensus is the seemingly fundamental question regarding the extent to which persuasion and social influence are, in fact, two distinct processes. That is, although social influence is oftentimes considered under the broad rubric of persuasion (Cialdini & Goldstein, 2004; Neuwirth & Frederick, 2004; Wood, 2000), do these two social phenomena refer to the same underlying processes or is there evidence (empirical and/or theoretical) to suggest that distinguishing one from the other would be profitable? After a review of the extant literature, one can make the claim that, while persuasion and social influence do share certain independent variables in common (e.g., source characteristics, the evocation of emotion), it is necessary to create a practical distinction between the two. In an attempt to provide a definition of social influence, it seems prudent to combine the ideas of several scholars, all of whom have spent their academic careers better understanding how social influence seems to work. As such, here seems to be an acceptable way of defining *social influence*:

> The process whereby people directly or indirectly influence the thoughts, feelings, and actions of others (Turner, 1991, p. 1) by [changing] one person's attitudes, cognitions, or behaviors (Cialdini, 1995, p. 257), ultimately leading to compliance (Cialdini & Goldstein, 2004, p. 592) or conformity. (Turner, 1991, p. 144)

In short, the study of social influence is an attempt to understand (and under-score) the importance of social relationships when the process of decision-making manifests itself. Returning to the chapter's opening example, it is quite likely that the variables producing my desire to watch the show endorsed by my relative were influenced, to a large extent, by my relationship with him. Perhaps I did not even wish to begin a new show. However, due to his role in my life, and his position in my familial social web, I felt the need to comply with this recommendation or conform to his behavioral choice. To state this differently, social influence is oftentimes the result of a fear of non-conformity: social actors want to engage in behaviors that are endorsed by those with which we have strong relationships and seek affinity. Why and how, however, does social influence seem to work?

Although the definition of *social influence* remains somewhat ambiguous, there is little doubt that the theoretical and empirical investigation of this social process has its roots in the oft-cited research experiment conducted by renowned social psychologist Solomon Asch in 1951. Among the major conclusions of his study was that social actors have a strong need and desire to make decisions that prove congruous with the opinions and attitudes of the majority. More specifically, results of his study indicated that, even though subjects had the intuitive knowledge that answers given by a majority were incorrect, "[when] confronted with opinions contrary to their own, many subjects apparently shifted their judgements in the direction of the majori-ties or experts" (Asch, 1966, p. 319). That is, even though the majority of experimental subjects knew that the confederates were offering erroneous answers, as became evident in the post-experimental exit interviews (see Asch, 1956, pp. 24–53), approximately 33 percent of all individuals fell prey to the pressures of a group majority. Since this pivotal experiment, scholars have devoted their academic careers to better understand why individuals were so willing to "yield" to the majority, rather than remain "independent," despite their knowledge that the answers provided by others were incorrect. While a detailed explanation of the experiment is well beyond the nature and scope of this chapter, Asch (1951) concluded that, when confronted with a situation where an individual is either in the minority (real or perceived) or has decision-based ambiguity or uncertainty, there is an established social pressure to conform to the majority for five major reasons: to avoid major-ity disapproval (p. 31); to avoid the fear and loneliness that accompanies a separation from others (p. 31); after making the a priori assumption that the majority must be correct (p. 43); to avoid exposure of a personal/intellectual deficiency (p. 43); and/or to not appear as a social outsider or misfit (p. 45).

Richard Crutchfield, another social psychologist interested in social influ-ence and social conformity, termed the foregoing tendency "deliberate con-forming," or the process whereby individuals "[choose] to express outward agreement with the group consensus even when believing the group to be wrong" (Crutchfield, 1955, p. 197). Among the first attempts to explain why this deliberate conforming is so likely to happen in certain social situations but not others was that undertaken by Morton Deutsch and Harold Gerald, both social psychologists, when they developed two terms that have become instrumental for understanding both the process and outcome of social influence: normative influence and informational influence. According to these scholars, *normative influence* is defined as an "influence to conform with the positive expectations of another," and informational influence is defined as an "influence to accept information obtained from another as evidence about reality" (Deutsch & Gerald, 1955, p. 629). Put more succinctly, normative influence is one's desire to yield to others due to a desire for social approval, whereas *informational influence* is one's desire to yield to others due to a desire to engage in correct behavior.

In the end, social influence is perhaps best summarized by Cialdini and Trost (1998), when they claim that "[since] approval by others is one of the underlying goals of socially responsible behavior, the source of influence should have a marked effect on our felt obligation to follow the norm of social responsibility" (p. 158). In other words, it is the process whereby social actors are influenced by a certain need to align their thoughts, attitudes, and behaviors with some salient in-group (or member of some salient in-group), ultimately adopting the shared standards produced within it. Why is such social influence so likely to be effective regarding insulin pump therapy? As Deutsch and Gerard (1955) claim, "the more uncertain an individual is about the correctness of his judgement, the more likely he is to be susceptible to social influences in making his judgment" (p. 634). Insulin pump therapy is still a medical technology rife with hesitations and questions.

While the phrase Social Media Influencer was not yet established when the previously mentioned academics published their groundbreaking studies (since social media was not yet available for use), the same underlying processes are at work. For example, if one were to look at a post on Facebook, Instagram, Twitter, Yelp, or Pinterest, do the same effects about which Asch (1951), Crutchfield (1955), and Deutsch and Gerard (1955) speak surface? Might one likely desire a new article of clothing because his friend posted a photo on Facebook? Might one likely create, change, or solidify her political identification as a result of reading a tweet? Might one decide to visit (or not visit) an eating establishment as a result of having seen a bad review on Yelp? It is likely that anyone reading this chapter can answer all of these three queries with a reverberating "yes." The remainder of this chapter will provide a detailed account of how SMIs, collectively connected to a not-for-profit organization, came to affect the decision-making processes of Type 1 diabetics pertaining to insulin pump therapy.

WHAT IS INSULIN PUMP THERAPY?

Type 1 diabetics are those who do not have a functional pancreas, creating the inability of the human body to produce insulin: a hormone necessary for the breakdown of sugar and carbohydrates into a usable form. While the discovery of insulin occurred nearly a century ago (1922 to be exact), there has since been developed multiple strategies for Type 1 diabetics to control their condition, including insulin pump therapy. As Lenhard and Reeves (2001) mention, there was a time, prior to the late 1970s, when Type 1 diabetics had but one option for disease control: MDIs (Multiple Daily Injections). In short, each and every time that one wanted to ingest something (liquid or solid) containing carbohydrates, he/she would need to administer an injection of insulin (the amount determined by an endocrinologist, likely in combination with a nutritionist, based on a carbohydrate-to-insulin algorithm). This type of injection is known as a bolus. This same individual would need one or more injections, throughout the day, to manage his/her blood sugar levels during non-ingestion times. This type of injection is known as a basal. Over the last forty years, however, technological advancements have provided the ability for Type 1 diabetics to engage in insulin pump therapy, known to the medical field as Continuous Subcutaneous Insulin Infusion (CSII) (see, for example, Dimeglio et al., 2004). In short, insulin pump therapy allows one to control his/her blood sugar levels, both throughout the day and night (basal), as well as at moments of ingestion (bolus), using a small, battery-operated, programmable machine.

In order to properly and effectively use an insulin pump, there are four necessary requirements: the pump, a reservoir, an infusion set, and tubing. The pump, itself, is programmable, meaning that the user, under the strict guidance of an endocrinologist, can determine and program such things as basal rates (the amount of insulin that an individual's body requires each hour of every day in order for his/her blood sugar to remain within a normal range), bolus rates (how many units of insulin one needs for every carbohydrate that he/she ingests), and even a correction bolus (how many units of insulin one needs if his/her blood sugar is elevated above the normal range). Clearly, this makes life with diabetes much more efficient for the user, and has been linked to many health benefits (see, for example, Nulli & Shashaj, 2006). The reservoir is a small, plastic, tubular device that stores the insulin needed for continuous injection into the body of a Type 1 diabetic. The reservoir oftentimes holds enough insulin for up to three days, after which it must be changed. The infusion set is what is administered, through injection, into the fatty tissue (oftentimes in the abdomen, upper leg, or buttocks), enabling insulin to flow from the pump's reservoir into the human body, via a thin, plastic tubing: the final necessary requisite for insulin pump therapy. The infusion set, along with the plastic tubing, is often changed every three days: similar to the reservoir (as per the recommendation of most manufacturers of insulin pumps). As a brief overview, insulin flows from the pump's disposable reservoir to the human body, by way of disposable tubing, through a disposable infusion set.

Approved twenty years ago (1999 to be exact), Type 1 diabetics now also have the opportunity to pair their insulin pumps with a Continuous Glucose Monitoring System (CGMS). Similar to insulin pump therapy, there are two necessary requisites for using this form of technology. First is the sensor: a small, canula-infused device that enters the body of the Type 1 diabetic through injection. The sensor is usually inserted into one's abdomen (or another fatty tissue found on the human body) and perpetually reads the body's blood sugar level. This is then communicated to the insulin pump (or another form of receiver) through a transmitter: a technological device that connects (either directly or remotely) to, and links with, the sensor, enabling the insulin pump to receive the user's blood sugar levels, ultimately making the management of diabetes astronomically less difficult.

In the end, the health goal of individuals with Type 1 diabetes is to control their blood sugar levels through the use of artificial insulin. Insulin pump therapy, coupled with continuous glucose monitoring, has revolutionized one's ability to manage diabetes: a disease that has been linked with serious health outcomes (damage to blood vessels, high blood pressure, heart disease, nerve damage, kidney disease, glaucoma etc.). So, the question, at this point, might be why certain individuals who are able to afford such therapeutic options decline to do so? While the answer(s) to this query would require an additional chapter, what follows is a detailed discussion about how Social Media Influencers, as part of a non-profit organization, were able to effectively persuade potential users to become eventual users.

SOCIAL INFLUENCE STRATEGIES WITHIN THE "NORTHEAST DIABETES CONNECTION" NETWORK

For purposes of anonymity and confidentiality, the name Northeast Diabetes Connection network (sometimes, and henceforth, referred as NDC) will be used to refer to the organization in question. The NDC's major mission is to raise money in an effort to support ongoing research efforts to provide a cure for Type 1 diabetes. Collectively, among the Executive Board of Directors, the Board of Trustees, volunteers, and members, the organization has, over the past two decades, had membership numbers exceeding 1,000. The organization has multiple media platforms, including a Facebook page, an Instagram page, and a Twitter account, in an effort to communicate with all affiliated constituents and provide social connectivity. Those connected to these three media outlets range in affiliation to Type 1 diabetes, from doctors to nurses to nutritionists to diabetics to family members and friends of diabetics. As such, there exist a myriad of different attitudinal reactions to, and impetuses for, communicative posts. From a content analytic perspective, I became quite interested in understanding how different posts about the use of insulin pump therapy and continuous glucose monitoring affected the decisions of those contemplating a switch from MDIs. Also, employing interview research, how did SMIs seem to condition, prime, and impact the decision-making practices of those who ultimately adopted this new form of diabetes management? Before moving forward, it is important to note that not all of those interviewed had, prior to social media engagement, a negatively valenced, or ambivalent, attitude toward insulin pump therapy. As such, some of the SMIs solidified the positive attitudes already held by subjects. This is well-aligned with Miller's (2002) argument that persuasion entails not only attitude formation, but also attitude reinforcement and attitude medication.

Health Care Professionals as SMIs

Based on both content analysis of social media posts, as well as interviews with active social media users, three broad populations of SMIs became influential in the decision-making processes of Type 1 diabetics within the Northeast Diabetes Connection network. First were health care professionals, including endocrinologists, nurse practitioners, and nutritionists. All told, there were a total of eighty-seven posts to Facebook, Twitter, and Instagram regarding the benefits linked to the use of insulin pump therapy, coupled with continuous glucose monitoring, by these health care professionals. An example of this was a Facebook post by Dr. X, who, along with three photos of her patient, Justin, also had the following to say to those connected via social media:

> Look at the smiles. Look at the difference. Nobody wants to live with this disease. But the *Tandem + Dexcom* system has worked wonders for so many and I would endorse this 100%. It is effective and it is easy to use and navigate. If you have any questions, whatsoever, about pump therapy, or CGMS in general, please reach out. My email address is xxxxx@xxxxx.xxx and my telephone number is xxx-xxx-xxxx.

Another example of an SMI is Dr. Y, who took to Twitter three days following the organization's annual fundraiser event, promoting the use of both insulin pump therapy and continuous glucose monitoring systems:

> It was great to see so many people at the event a few nights ago. We raised tons of money and hopefully a cure is in the foreseeable future. In the short

meantime, I know that we had some representatives from *Minimed* speaking about the new closed loop system. This has revolutionized the world of diabetes management. We have had hundreds of patients at our practice begin this and it has been life-altering. Their A1C levels, in just 18 months, dropped an average of nearly two points. Amazing!!! I would recommend this without reservation.

A nurse practitioner, Mr. Z, a longtime member of the NDC network, took to Instagram and posted a photo of the Omnipod (among the many insulin pump management systems available on the market today) with the phrase "It has made life with Type-1 diabetes so much easier!!!" This one, eleven-word phrase received 1,624 "likes."

As these three social media examples illustrate, there are ways to communicate about the benefits of insulin pump therapy and continuous glucose monitoring systems. However, why, in the end, were Dr. X, Dr. Y, and Mr. Z considered to be SMIs? How were they able to influence the attitudes and behaviors of Type 1 diabetics, just like Solomon Asch had demonstrated nearly seventy years prior? Data from interview research indicate that it was not the messages that were predictive of social influence, but rather the sources. For example, Daniel, a twenty-four-year-old sales associate, diagnosed with Type 1 diabetes two years ago, had the following to say about the post of Dr. X:

Of course I know about insulin pumps. My insurance will pay for much of it. That is not the issue. I am still learning a lot about this disease. Believe me . . . [this network] has helped tons. But when you hear a reputable doctor speaking about how great something like the *Tandem* system is . . . and how easy it is to use . . . especially for those of us not so good with technology . . . it makes you realize that it is time to invest. It sounds crazy to say . . . but she got me to call the company the next day and I ordered. Crazy stuff.

Miranda, the mother of a recently diagnosed boy, Seth, was equally influenced by the tweet from nutritionist Mr. Z:

The worst news of my life was four months ago when I found out that my little son, just three years old, was diagnosed with diabetes. This was going to be life changing for me, my husband, my daughter, and Seth. For all of us. To think about having to give a three-year-old shots every day . . . it crushes you. Absolutely crushes you. But when you hear a medical professional mention how easy something like the *Omnipod* is . . . it starts to put things into perspective. What we need is effective and easy. Painless would be nice, too. But easy is what we are looking for . . . and he provided that with his *Twitter* sentence.

And it was not coming from just anyone. It was coming from someone in the health field.

David, a sixty-eight-year-old man, a juvenile-onset Type 1 diabetic since the age of eight, admits that he had, for several reasons, never truly considered the switch over from daily multiple injections to insulin pump therapy, but, as a result of becoming connected to the NDC network, has since had an attitudinal change:

> Truth be told . . . I have spent the last 60 years of my life taking shots. If I did the math . . . I have probably used somewhere in the neighborhood of 100,000 needles. Crazy to think about. I have also stuck my fingers to check my blood sugar millions of times. Why have I never made the change over to a new form of health therapy? Not sure I can answer that. But when you see doctors post messages about how great these new technologies are, it makes you realize that it is absolutely the right thing to do. My kids say that 70 is the new 50 . . . so I am going to listen to these doctors and health care professionals and make the change.

What Daniel, Miranda, and David share in common is that they were targets of social influence because the sources of information were within the world of health care. This underscores the salience of normative and informational influence mentioned earlier and forces one to highlight the claim made by French and Raven (1959) sixty years ago: that sources of power, even the power to persuade or influence, are both interesting and perplexing. In this case, doctors, nurse practitioners, and nutritionists are able to influence the attitudes and behaviors of others due to a [likely] combination of expert power (the ability to influence due to what one knows) and referent power (the ability to influence due to one's level of admiration) (French & Raven, 1959, pp. 156–164). Again, citing a seminal publication from the field of social psychology, the reason for this goes back to Hovland and Weiss's (1951) finding that perceived credibility, in this case a combination of both expert and referent power, is inextricably linked to trustworthiness. Daniel, Miranda, and David, based on their interview reports, trusted these health care professionals, which provided the very context necessary for the creation and manifestation of social influence. In fact, one could argue that, in line with Petty and Cacioppo's (1986) contention, they engaged in mindless, not mindful, information processing: they were influenced merely because of the message source (source attractiveness, source liking). Daniel, Miranda, and David became cognitive misers and Dr. X, Dr. Y, and Mr. Z became SMIs (because of their health-related titles). Does this come to question the argument that, as per the Elaboration Likelihood Model, if motivation, ability to process a message, and need for cognition are all high, then the target of influence is more likely to centrally process the claims? Perhaps. After all, it is quite likely that this was the case for the aforementioned patients. What this *does* illustrate is Levine and Boster's (2001) idea of a moderating effect: if a target of social influence considers the source's message to exemplify justified power (the rewards of insulin pump therapy communicated by a health care professional), then the impact will be more effective than if unjustified power (the same rewards communicated by a non-expert) were to be employed.

Friends and Family Members as SMIs

The second major population of Social Media Influencers included friends and family members of those living with Type 1 diabetes. Based on an informal conversation with the president of the Northeast Diabetes Connection, friends and family comprise the great majority of the patronage and membership. Many of the individuals interviewed made particular mention of the import that the social media posts of friends and family played in affecting the attitudes and behaviors of those making the move to insulin pump therapy. One such interviewee was Jasmine, who revered a Twitter post made by Alexander (the brother of a Type 1 diabetic currently using an insulin pump and continuous glucose monitoring device):

> To hear Alexander speak about his sister's decision to switch from MDI to an insulin pump was that final push that I needed. He explained how much easier life became and how much happier she was as a result. It was transformative for her and for him. To hear the story told through the lens of her brother was amazing. I tweeted him back and thanked him for what he did and for what he provided our community. You used the term Social Media Influencer and that is exactly what this gentleman became in my life.

Another interviewee, Alicia, was, using her own verbiage, "brought to tears" by the visual and verbal story told by Denise on Facebook about her daughter, Sylvia: a thirty-three-year-old juvenile-onset Type 1 diabetic who switched to insulin pump therapy after nearly two decades of poor blood sugar control:

> Denise used photos and the power of stories to highlight the trials and tribulations linked to her daughter's difficulties with managing her diabetes. Her A1C levels were often high. Her depression level was high. Her motivation for work was low. Her overall energy levels were low. It was time for her to figure out a new plan of action. It was as though Denise used the before-and-after commercials that we are all too familiar with. Here is your life before insulin pump

therapy and here is your life after insulin pump therapy. And to hear the story told through the point of view of a mother is . . . well . . . let us just say that it is priceless. Priceless enough that it got me to call *Dexcom* the very next week and begin the ordering process. Thank you, Denise!!!

As a researcher, I was, at this point, interested more in the extent to which it was the messages posted by Alexander and Denise that sparked such attitudinal adjustment or whether it was merely a function of Alexander's and Denise's ability to become SMIs within a mediated web of social actors. Or perhaps both. After looking more deeply at the posts by family members and friends, it became clearer that there was nothing of substantive value in the postings, in terms of information, that came to affect attitude and drive behavior. Were emotions tapped? Absolutely. And, as Nabi (2002) argues, emotions are among the key driving forces behind persuasion. However, in this case, it was less about the strategic message design and more about the sources of the said messages, questioning the extent to which those exposed to media posts were engaging in the "careful thought" about which Wood (2000) speaks, or some other heuristic (Wood, 2000, p. 545). According to several interviewees, it was some other heuristic. For example, Eugene mentioned that it was the fact that the source was such a close friend of the insulin pump user:

> Honestly, there was nothing about the Instagram post that was so great. It was just that I knew that he was connected so closely to the family. There was some sort of emotional connection. I got hooked. I got persuaded. I got influenced. It had nothing to do with the post. It had everything to do with the fact that Jessica was a family friend. So emotional.

Timothy agreed, insofar as he saw a link between the ability for a social media post to influence one's attitude and the role of the source posting it:

> It is one thing for someone to post something about a product being so great from the company selling it. Even from someone who has been using the product. But when it comes from someone connected to our tight-knit community, it has so much more power. I don't really know why. It just does. I was 100% influenced because it was Alexandra who posted this about her sister. Had I not known Alexandra, I bet the impact would have been different.

The aforementioned examples, again, corroborate the argument that social influence is an interesting process. One would think that strong messages and salient information would be necessary in order to prime one's attitude and affect one's behavior. This is not the case. At least this was not the case given the data from the present study. What is needed for SMIs is to be embedded within a social network of those who are, for lack of a better word, influence-able. This highlights two of the major reasons that Turner (1991) argues that, as per Self Categorization Theory, social influence seems to work as a persuasive variable: the presence and cognizance of reference group membership (one is likely to be more influenced when the source is part of one's in-group) and social comparison (one is likely to be more influenced when comparing his/her attitude against that of a prototypical other). In the cases of Jasmine, Alicia, Eugene, and Timothy, we see reference group membership and social comparison producing positive attitudes about insulin pump therapy as a result of the communication by SMIs.

Type 1 Diabetic Patients as SMIs

The third, and final, major population of SMIs included those living with Type 1 diabetes and who were already using insulin pump therapy. Similar to Waldron's (2019) thesis that, within the public relations realm, the attitudes of followers are conditioned most by social influencers who are already consumers of products and services (p. 40); those considering insulin pump therapy and continuous glucose monitoring were, according to interview data, most affected by diabetic patients already using the said technology. Gillian, a Type 1 diabetic for the past six years, confirmed this finding:

> It is one thing for a doctor to say how great a new form of diabetes management is. But to then hear, and see, the same from a person already using it. This is a whole new ballgame altogether. [Daniel's] Instagram account is, quite literally, all that I needed to make that change. He showed me how easy this new *Dexcom* device really is. He showed me, through both visual and textual examples, the life-altering effects that the *Dexcom* and *Tandem* had on his health . . . and, truth be told, the well-being of others connected to him. Yes . . . it was Daniel who became my most important Social Media Influencer. So thank you, Daniel!!!

Similar sentiments were expressed during my interview with Stephanie: diagnosed with Type 1 diabetes not more than four months ago:

> As soon as I got into the hospital, with a blood sugar in the range of 850, I knew my life was about to change. But I also knew that, in 2019, there were technological ways to deal with this disease. In my first week of education, I got hundreds of bits of information. I was overwhelmed. But I also spoke with a small group of individuals as part of a support group. They were all part of the [Northeast Diabetes Connection network] that I have come to know and love. I went on to their Facebook page while still in the hospital and saw so many

success stories from so many people at such various times in their lives. Some were older. Some were younger. Some were working. Some had families. Some played sports. Regardless . . . it was the posts of those living with the disease, not so much the doctors or the nurses or the educators, who affected me. The Social Media Influencers? These were, without a doubt, the diabetics who I have become friendly with.

But just what were these Social Media Influencers posting that became such attitudinal and behavioral determinants? Based on a content analysis of Facebook, Instagram, and Twitter posts on behalf of those already using the diabetes management systems mentioned earlier in this chapter, 84 percent of all posts made mention of three independent variables in particular. First was the ease of use of the pump, the reservoir, the infusion set, the tubing, the sensor, and the transmitter. This aligns itself quite well with Ajzen's (1985) Theory of Planned Behavior, which argues that, along with having an interest in the said behavior, and knowing that others approve of the said behavior, individuals are more likely to engage in a behavior to the extent that they have the perceived behavioral control of so doing. A textbook example of perceived behavioral control is ability and a textbook example of ability is ease. Cecilia, in a tweet dated October 22, 2019, had the following to say about her recent site change:

> It was incredible. I changed my entire site, the reservoir, the infusion set, and the tubing, during the commercial of *Chicago Fire*. I was paying more attention to the advertisement for an insurance company and *Sonos* speakers than I was to changing my site. That is how easy this is.

Joan, a seventy-four-year-old Type 1 diabetic, posted, on Instagram, a ninety-second video of her changing her sensor, and adding her transmitter, likening the process to a public service announcement that aired in the 1980s:

> This is how easy it is to change, and add, your CGMS device. It is like the commercial, back in the day, warning about the dangers of drugs and drug addiction. Here is your life with constant finger sticks. Here is your life with a continuous glucose monitoring system. Any questions???

The second independent variable linked to attitudinal and behavioral changes is the extent to which the SMIs framed the experience of using an insulin pump and/or continuous glucose monitoring system as fun: an adjective rarely linked to this chronic disease. An example of this, mentioned in several post-study interviews, was the Facebook page of Elizabeth, a forty-year-old Type 1 diabetic who had been using an *Omnipod* insulin pump for the past seven months. Based on content analysis, the majority of her posts were of her smiling, laughing, and/or telling stories about the joys of technology for handling such a ruthless disease. Mentioning her posts, specifically, was Nathaniel, who, in his own words, was a soon-to-be insulin pump user:

> To see Elizabeth (although she goes by Lizzy) so overtaken by happiness and joy is something that I want to experience. She should be the marketing spokesperson for the *Omnipod* brand. She can sell anything. She has sold me. I guess it is the power of emotion, in this case positive emotion, that can really guide your behavioral decisions.

Tara, a close friend of Nathaniel, concurred that:

> Liz makes every day living with this disease seem not only manageable . . . but almost enjoyable. You know those people who feel the desire to post every fuc*ing thing about every moment of their lives, when, in actuality, nobody cares? Picture the exact opposite of that. Everyone cares. If not, then they have just not seen Liz's posts. She is amazing. A true and real Social Media Influencer and social media trailblazer.

While Nabi (2002) spends much time discussing the attitudinal and behavioral effects of negatively valenced emotions, such as fear, guilt, and anger, it is clear that, at least for purposes of this study, we can see the impact of more positively valenced emotions, such as envy, joy, pride, relief, and hope.

The third variable linked to attitudinal and behavioral changes is the overall effects that insulin pump therapy has had on Type 1 diabetics' increased ease of disease management. As the literature argues, among the most difficult (if not the *most* difficult) aspects of managing Type 1 diabetes is both knowing one's physiological reaction to blood sugar increase and knowing about his/her insulin-to-carbohydrate ratio (see, for example, Brazeau et al., 2013). Based on both empirical and testimonial evidence, insulin pump therapy, coupled with continuous glucose monitoring, helps alleviate many of the stressors associated with such things as carbohydrate counting, insulin recommendations, and overall ingestion options (see, for example, Bode et al., 2002). As such, members of the Northeast Diabetes Connection mentioned the sheer number of SMIs who posted mention not only about how easy it is to use an insulin pump, but rather how much easier life has become as a result of adopting this health behavior. For example, Tessa, a fifteen-year-old Type 1 diabetic, who admits to having difficulty managing her daily blood sugars, was marveled by the Twitter posts of fellow Type 1 diabetic, Albert:

His tweets, pre-pizza and post-pizza, were amazing. This is the food that I have most trouble with. He said "two hours ago my sugar was 181 . . . I ate three slices of pizza . . . and later my sugar was 166 . . . thank you, *Minimed 670.*" I then reached out to him so that we could discuss his ability to eat pizza, fruit, and wheat thins . . . my favorites. It was after my conversation with this Social Media Influencer that I decided to call my insurance company to begin the ordering process.

Similarly, Jacob, a forty-one-year-old Type 1 diabetic, currently using multiple daily injections, responded to the Instagram feed of Alessandra, a twenty-nine-year-old insulin pump user since 2012:

> The worst part of this entire disease is figuring out, before every meal, how much medicine I need to take. What if I take too little? What if I take too much? Alessandra seems to have it down pat. Her Instagram posts have her eating ice cream and skittles and cotton candy and popcorn and pizza. These would drive my blood sugar levels up the roof. But she also posts her three-month blood results and her A1C levels seem to keep going down . . . from 7.8 to 7.4 to 7.3. It is almost as though she is living the life of a non-diabetic. Well . . . close to that.

CONCLUSION

SMIs are everywhere. As mentioned at the start of this chapter, the process of social influence is not new. Rather, the social media enabling the mass communication and dissemination of messages are new. SMIs, according to Arora et al. (2019), "have highly established credibility for a specific industry . . . [and] have connections with a large audience . . . [leading to] support and trust . . . due to their admirable authenticity and position" (pp. 86–87). Whether it is Huda Kattan (a beauty expert who has upward of twenty-nine million Instagram followers), Kayla Itsines (a fitness guru with over ten million Instagram followers), or Zach King (an amateur filmmaker with more than twenty-one million Instagram followers), one thing is difficult to refute: such SMIs are having a noticeable impact on the decision-making practices of society at large. The Northeast Diabetes Connection network is no anomaly. It, too, has its fair share of SMIs, ranging from doctors to nurse practitioners to parents to friends to patients. As this chapter illustrates, each of the foregoing stakeholders has important implications for engagement with insulin pump therapy and continuous glucose monitoring systems. While Shelton and Skalski (2014) certainly explicate the darker side of social media use, the results from this chapter's study do highlight the beneficial, prosocial effects of Facebook, Instagram, and Twitter. In a world overtaken by mediated content, it is important to remember

Househ et al.'s (2013) conclusion that, from a health communication perspective, "although there are several challenges [associated with social media use] to be aware of for the patient, [there are] many more benefits for patients than harm" (p. 57). It is due time to begin capitalizing on the said benefits and it is clear that the communication between and among social agents within the Northeast Diabetes Connection network is one giant step toward this goal.

REFERENCES

Ajzen, I. (1985). From intentions to actions: A theory of planned behavior. In J. Kuhl & J. Beckmann (Eds.), *Action control: From cognition to behavior* (pp. 11–39). Heidelberg, Germany: Springer-Verlag.

Arora, A., Bansal, S., Kandpal, C., Aswani, R., & Dwivedi, Y. (2019). Measuring social media influencer index-insights from Facebook, Twitter, and Instagram. *Journal of Retailing and Consumer Services, 49*, 86–101.

Asch, S. E. (1951). Effects of group pressure upon the modification and distortion of judgment. In H. Guetzkow (Ed.), *Groups, leadership and men* (pp. 177–190). New York, NY: Carnegie Press.

Asch, S. E. (1956). Studies of independence and conformity: A minority of one against a unanimous majority. *Psychological Monographs, 70*, Whole Number 416.

Asch, S. E. (1966). Opinions and social pressure. In A.P. Hare, E.F. Borgatta, and R.F. Bales (Eds.), *Small groups: Studies in social interaction* (pp. 318–324). New York, NY: Alfred A. Knopf.

Bode, B. W., Tamborlane, W. V., & Davidson, P. C. (2002). Insulin pump therapy in the 21st century: Strategies for successful use in adults, adolescents, and children with diabetes. *Postgraduate Medicine, 111*, 69–77.

Brazeua, A. S., Mircescu, H., Desjardin, K., Leroux, C., Strychar, I., Ekoe, J. M., & Rabasa-Lhoret, R. (2013). Carbohydrate counting accuracy and blood glucose variability in adults with type 1 diabetes. *Diabetes Research and Clinical Practice, 99*, 19–23.

Cialdini, R. B. (1995). Principles and techniques of social influence. In A. Tesser (Ed.), *Advanced social psychology* (pp. 257–275). New York, NY: McGraw Hill.

Cialdini, R. B., & Goldstein, N. J. (2004). Social influence: Compliance and conformity. *Annual Review of Psychology, 55*, 591–621.

Cialdini, R. B., & Trost, M. R. (1998). Social influence: Social norms, conformity, and compliance. In D. T. Gilbert, S. T. Fiske, & G. Lindzey (Eds.), *The handbook of social psychology* (2nd Ed) (pp. 151–192). New York, NY: McGraw Hill.

Cruchfield, R. S. (1955). Conformity and character. *American Psychologist, 10*, 191–198.

Deutsch, M., & Gerard, H. B. (1955). A study of normative and informational social influences upon individual judgment. *Journal of Abnormal and Social Psychology, 51*, 629–636.

Dimeglio, L. A., Pottorff, T. M., Boyd, S. R., France, L., Fineberg, N., & Eugster, E. A. (2004). A randomized, controlled study of insulin pump therapy in diabetic preschoolers. *The Journal of Pediatrics, 145*, 380–384.

Freberg, K., Graham, K., McGaughey, K., & Freberg, L. (2011). Who are the social media influencers: A study of public perceptions of personality. *Public Relations Review, 37*, 90–92.

French, J. R., & Raven, B. H. (1959). The bases of social power. In D. Cartwright (Ed.), *Studies in social power* (pp. 150–167). Ann Arbor, MI: Institute for Social Research.

Househ, M., Borycki, E., & Kushniruk, A. (2014). Empowering patients through social media: The benefits and challenges. *Health Informatics Journal, 20*, 50–58.

Hovland, C. I., & Weiss, W. (1951). The influence of source credibility on communication effectiveness. *Public Opinion Quarterly, 15*, 635–650.

Lenhard, J., & Reeves, G. (2001). Continuous subcutaneous insulin infusion: A comprehensive review of insulin pump therapy. *Archives of Internal Medicine, 161*, 2293–2300.

Levine, T. R., & Boster, F. J. (2001). The effects of power and message variables on compliance. *Communication Monographs, 68*, 28–48.

Miller, G. R. (2002). On being persuaded: Some basic distinctions. In J. P. Dillard, & M. Pfau (Eds.), *The persuasion handbook: Developments in theory and practice* (pp. 3–16). Thousand Oaks, CA: Sage.

Nabi, R. L. (2002). Discrete emotions and persuasion. In J. P. Dillard, & M. Pfau (Eds.) *The persuasion handbook: Developments in theory and practice* (pp. 289–308). Thousand Oaks, CA: Sage.

Neuwirth, K., & Frederick, E. (2004). Peer and social influence on opinion expression: Combining theories of planned behavior and the spiral of silence. *Communication Research, 31*, 669–703.

Petty, R. E., & Cacioppo, J. T. (1986). The elaboration likelihood model of persuasion. *Advances in Experimental Social Psychology, 19*, 123–205.

Shelton, A., & Skalski, P. (2014). Blinded by the light: Illuminating the dark side of social network use through content analysis. *Computer in Human Behavior, 33*, 339–348.

Sulli, N., & Shashaj, B. (2006). Long-term benefits of continuous subcutaneous insulin infusion in children with Type 1 diabetes: A 4-year follow-up. *Diabetic Medicine, 23*, 900–906.

Turner, J. C. (1991). *Social influence*. Boston, MA: Brooks/Cole.

Waldron, S. (2019). *The PR knowledge book*. New York, NY: Business Expert Press.

Wood, W. (2000). Attitude change: Persuasion and social influence. *Annual Review of Psychology, 51*, 539–571.

Chapter 7

You "Can't Put Concealer on This One"

Crisis Management in an Influencer Context

Chelsea Woods[1]

Organizations have long used public figures to promote their brands. The new wave of social media influencers was initially considered a cheaper substitute for high-paid celebrities, but influencers quickly commandeered the landscape (Brown, 2018). By generating content and engaging in conversation with followers, social media influencers (SMIs) create the perception that they are "real, accessible and credible" (Dhananai, 2017, para. 7), enabling them to cultivate relationships with followers and increase consumer trust in brands they promote (Deloitte, 2015; Edelman, 2019).

Working with SMIs can introduce new opportunities for brands or generate reputational risks if the influencer commits a transgression, which may produce a crisis, defined as "the perception of an unpredictable event that threatens important expectancies of stakeholders and can seriously impact an organization's performance and generate negative outcomes" (Coombs, 2012, p. 2). Such events can portray both the influencer and the affiliated brand in a negative light. Thus, crises have implications for the brand–influencer relationship, influencer–follower relationship, and brand–consumer relationship.

Public relations research is ripe with studies on how organizations and individuals can employ strategies to protect and rebuild their reputations and relationships, yet literature on crisis management within the SMI context is lacking. Using relationship management theory and image repair theory, this chapter analyzes Laura Lee's 2018 tweet controversy and Olivia Jade's association with the college admissions scandal through analysis of news articles and social media user comments. Specifically, this study focuses on the response strategies of Laura Lee, Olivia Jade, and several of their sponsors (Amazon, Boxycharm, Sephora, and Ulta), in addition to evaluating public reaction. The findings of this chapter contribute to crisis management research and practice by offering implications for how influencers and affiliated brands can respond to influencer transgressions.

LITERATURE REVIEW

Relationship Management Theory

Dhanesh and Duthler (2019) defined a *SMI* as "a person who, through personal branding, builds and maintains relationships with multiple followers on social media" (p. 3). The relational dynamic between the influencers' personal brand and their followers is a key component in SMI success as it can lead to increased positive word-of-mouth and purchase intentions (Edelman, 2019; Jin et al., 2019), leading many brands to partner with SMIs to assist with their public relations endeavors.

According to Ledingham and Bruning (1998), advanced public relations should balance organizational and public interests to produce mutual benefits for both parties, and proposed communication should be used as a tool to establish, cultivate, and sustain relationships. Hon and Grunig (1999) identified outcomes of successful relationships, including control mutuality, trust, satisfaction, and commitment. Control mutuality is the extent to which the parties agree on who has the power to influence one another. Hon and Grunig (1999) suggested that the most stable relationships are those in which the organization and its publics have some degree of control over each other. Trust reflects the extent to which each party has confidence in and is willing to be open to the other party, including integrity (the organization is fair and just), dependability (the organization can be relied on to keep its word), and competence (the organization is capable of doing what it says it will do). Satisfaction occurs when one party feels positively about the other because their expectations are met. Finally, commitment reflects the extent to which one party values the relationship enough to exert energy to maintain it. Dhanesh and Duthler (2019) recently applied relationship management theory to examine the relational dynamics between influencers and their followers, proposing that the dimensions of control mutuality, trust, satisfaction, and commitment apply within this context. They advanced that "Perhaps the most defining characteristic of influencers' success is the relationships they build and foster between their personal brand and their followers" (p. 3) and highlighted the crucial roles of credibility and relatability in these relationships.

Organization–public and influencer–follower relationships are dynamic and can be altered by defining events (Ledingham, 2003). Each party brings its own set of expectations to the relationship, and if those expectations are violated, the relationship will be altered. The misbehaviors of individuals—such as athletes, celebrities, and influencers—can be perceived as an infraction of the rules underlying a relationship between two parties (Finsterwalder et al., 2017). When SMIs commit a transgression, the effects of their wrongdoing may impact followers' behavioral intentions toward the influencer and their affiliated brands. Following a crisis, SMIs and brands alike must act to protect or restore relationships and reputations, and scholars have identified strategies intended to mitigate negative outcomes.

Image Repair Theory

Research on celebrity and athlete transgressions frequently invokes Benoit's (1995, 1997) image repair theory (IRT), which offers a typology of options for the accused to adopt in order to salvage public perception following a crisis. IRT is based on the premise that the accused agent (an individual or organization) is held responsible for the perceived offensive act and advances that communication can be used to protect or rebuild the agent's image. Benoit (1995, 1997) proposed fourteen image repair strategies within five categories: denial, evading responsibility, reducing offensiveness, corrective action, and mortification.

The first strategy is denial of the offensive act (Benoit, 1995, 1997). When using this approach, the accused can *simply deny* the event occurred, or can attempt to reduce their perceived responsibility for the act, the offensiveness of the act, or the damage of the act. The accused may also attempt to *shift the blame* by asserting that another individual or organization is responsible for the event.

The second strategy, evading responsibility, includes four response options. An agent may use *provocation*, arguing that its behavior was a reasonable response to another's offensive act. A second option is *defeasibility*, when the accused maintains it had a lack of information or control over the inciting factors. The accused may also choose to portray the event as an *accident*, minimizing its responsibility. Lastly, the accused may admit that the act was performed but qualify that it was done with *good intentions*.

The third typology of responses is reducing offensiveness, which involves reducing the perceived severity of the act. The first approach is to adopt *bolstering*, or discussing the positive qualities of the accused, in an effort to increase positive perceptions of the accused and to combat negative feelings. A second response is *minimization*, which argues the act is not as egregious as it may seem. Alternately, the accused may choose to embrace *differentiation* by attempting to distinguish the act from similar but more offensive actions, making the act seem less serious. A fourth approach is *transcendence*, which seeks to justify the act by linking it to more important values. The fifth response is to *attack the accuser* by challenging those making assertions about the accused to undermine the accuser's credibility. Finally, the accused may use *compensation* by reimbursing the victim.

The fourth strategy is corrective action. When adopting this strategy, the organization or individual pledges to correct the problem(s) that led to the crisis. Benoit (1997) explains that this step may include restoring the state of affairs to pre-crisis status or promising to prevent a recurrence of the act or a similar offensive act. The fifth and final strategy is mortification, which requires the organization or individual to confess and beg forgiveness.

IRT strategies can be used alone or in combination, and the effectiveness of selecting a strategy depends on variables such as the audience and enactment of strategies (Benoit, 1995, 1997, 2013). When using a combination of strategies, individuals should ensure that the strategies do not contradict one another, such as simple denial and mortification (Benoit, 2013). Because of its adaptability to organizations and individuals, scholars regularly invoke IRT to examine crisis responses from organizations (Blaney et al., 2002), athletes (Brown et al., 2016; Meng & Pan, 2013), and entertainers (Moody, 2011). Although previous studies have explored the strategies used by public figures and brands, no known research has extended this application into the social media influencer arena. Thus, this study seeks to answer:

RQ1: What image repair strategies did Olivia Jade use, and how did the public react?

RQ2: What image repair strategies did Amazon and Sephora use, and how did the public react?

RQ3: What image repair strategies did Laura Lee use, and how did the public react?

RQ4: What image repair strategies did Boxycharm and Ulta use, and how did the public react?

Crises can also invoke negative repercussions for athletes' sponsoring brands (Brown et al., 2016; Lee & Kwak, 2016; Um, 2013) and can cause consumers to transfer their negative reactions from the celebrity to the brand (White et al., 2009). To extend this research, this study asks:

RQ5: To what extent are individuals' perceptions of the influencer related to their perceptions of the partnering brands?

METHOD

Data Collection

Seventy-seven online news articles and 1,839 social media comments were collected to analyze public reactions to the crisis responses for both the SMIs and affiliated brands.

News Articles

News articles were culled via Google News using the search terms "[influencer name]" and "Sponsors." For Olivia Jade, articles were collected beginning the day the news story (March 12, 2019) broke and the following week. Because of the magnitude of the college admissions scandal involving Jade, only the first fifty news articles were collected. For Laura Lee, news article collection corresponded with the week following the release of her first (August 13, 2018), second (August 19, 2018), and third (September 25, 2018) apologies. The Lee case drew less mainstream media attention, producing twenty-seven articles in total.

Social Media Comments

Facebook comments and tweets ($n = 1,839$) were used to gauge social media users' reactions. At the time of data analysis, Olivia Jade had not issued a response.[2] Thus, analysis relied on social media comments with reactions to Sephora, which publicly cut ties with Olivia Jade, and Amazon, which kept silent. Sephora tweeted twice about pulling out Olivia Jade's sponsorship, and both tweets were responses to Twitter users. Publicly available user replies to these tweets ($n = 220$) were saved. Second, because Amazon never issued a public response, 195 tweets from users to Amazon featuring "Olivia Jade" were collected using the Twitter advanced search function. Twitter and Facebook user comments ($n = 250$) on news articles posted by media organizations containing the terms "Olivia Jade" and "Amazon" in the headline were culled to evaluate public reaction. Estée Lauder Companies and TRESemmé also ended their relationship with Olivia Jade via a media statement but did not issue a response via social media; thus, the analysis compares reactions to Sephora and Amazon. Approximately 665 comments were collected for analysis in the Olivia Jade case.

Because Laura Lee issued multiple apologies, user responses were collected in stages. First, publicly accessible responses ($n = 330$) to Laura Lee's Twitter apology were saved. Second, Lee also posted two apology videos to YouTube. Because she changed the privacy settings on her first videos, public reactions ($n = 327$) were collected via the Twitter advanced search feature using the search terms "Laura Lee" and "video" between August 19 (the day she posted the video) and August 25. Lee posted her second video on September 25 but disabled comments. Public reactions (n = 181) were collected on Twitter using the search terms "Laura Lee" and "video" with dates ranging from September 25 to October 1. Boxycharm and Ulta were selected for analysis in this case. To evaluate individuals' reactions to Boxycharm CEO's apology on Facebook, 293 user comments on its post were collected for analysis. Ulta tweeted three replies to users about pulling out Lee's products, and user comments on these tweets (n = 11) were saved. An additional thirty-two tweets were gathered using the search terms "Laura Lee" and "Ulta" within the one-week time frame. Approximately 1,174 relevant comments were analyzed.

Data Analysis

News articles were analyzed using inductive thematic analysis to identify the larger themes present within the data. The articles were read through to gain an understanding of the content (Hsieh & Shannon, 2005). Then, the articles were re-read to identify several categories, which were combined based on their relationships: 1) background information, 2) the influencers' responses, 3) brand responses (including media statements), and 4) general public reaction to the scandals. SMI and sponsor responses were then thematically analyzed using a deductive approach grounded in IRT response strategies (Benoit, 1995, 1997).

Content analysis was used to derive meaning from all user-generated social media comments, with each comment serving as the unit of analysis. Emojis and images (e.g., GIFs and memes) were captured and included as part of the message, and direct quotes taken from comments are written as originally posted, including grammatical errors. A codebook was constructed using research that analyzed public comments in response to an organizational crisis (Coombs & Holladay, 2012; Kim et al., 2016) and an exploratory coding of 100 randomly selected comments. First, the coders indicated which influencer (Olivia Jade = 1 and Laura Lee = 2) and brand (Sephora = 1, Amazon = 2, Boxycharm = 3, and Ulta = 4) were discussed. User perceptions of the influencers were coded using four categories: perception of the influencer as responsible for the crisis (Yes = 1 and No = 0); defense of the influencer (Yes = 1 and No = 0); claims that the influencer's response was insincere (Yes = 1 and No = 0); and attitude toward the influencer (Negative = 1, Neutral = 2, and Positive = 3). User reactions to the brand were coded using five categories: calls for the brand to take action (Yes =1 and No = 0); support or disapproval of the brand's response (Yes =1 and No = 0); mention of purchase intention (Yes =1 and No = 0); stated purchase intention (1 = Negative, 2 = Dependent, and 3 = Positive); and attitude toward the brand (1 = Negative, 2 = Neutral, and 3 = Positive).

All social media posts were coded manually. Following a training session, four coders coded a random sample of 10 percent of the posts to establish intercoder reliability (ICR). Intercoder reliability was assessed using Krippendorff's alpha (Hayes & Krippendorff, 2007). Before coding the full sample, the coders discussed their experiences with coding the data and made changes to the codebook. Once ICR was established for all categories ($\alpha >$ .70), the four coders equally divided and coded all 1,839 comments.

THE CASE OF OLIVIA JADE

With 1.9 million YouTube subscribers and 1.3 million Instagram followers, SMI Olivia Jade Giannulli (known as Olivia Jade) attracted partnerships with brands including Amazon, Dolce & Gabbana, Estée Lauder Companies, Marc Jacobs Beauty, Sephora, and TRESemmé (Ross, 2019). In August 2018, she enrolled at the University of Southern California (USC) but drew criticism when she shared in a YouTube video "I do want the experience of game days, partying. I don't really care about school, as you guys all know" (Spangler, 2019). On March 12, 2019, Giannulli was swept up in the 2019 college admissions scandal, in which fifty individuals were accused of using bribes to influence admissions decisions at universities (see table 7.1 for a timeline). Her parents, actress Lori Loughlin and fashion designer Mossimo Giannulli, were accused of paying $500,000 to have Olivia Jade and her sister admitted to USC as members of the university's crew team, though neither participated in the sport (Ross, 2019).

RQ1: Olivia Jade's Response and Public Reaction

Olivia Jade Giannulli kept silent on the scandal and reduced her social media visibility. She posted to Instagram on July 29, 2019, to wish Loughlin a happy birthday. On August 12, she shared a since-deleted photo where she placed

Table 7.1 Olivia Jade Crisis Timeline

Date	Action
March 12, 2019	Federal prosecutors charged fifty individuals connected to the scheme; HP pulls out advertisement featuring Giannulli and Loughlin
March 14, 2019	Sephora ends partnership with Giannulli
March 15, 2019	Estée Lauder Companies and TRESemmé end partnerships with Giannulli
July 29, 2019	Giannulli returns to Instagram
August 12, 2019	Giannulli issues second Instagram post

both her middle fingers in the air with the caption "@dailymail @starmagazine @people @perezhilton @everyothermediaoutlet #close #source #says."

In total, 535 comments discussed Giannulli and leaned negative in tone (*M* = 1.38, *SD* = .53). Though she has not been formally implicated for playing any role in the scandal, 67.9 percent of user comments (*n* = 363) perceived she was complicit in or aware of the illicit activities (see table 7.2). One individual reasoned, "Let me know how she didn't know she was participating in the scandal? she literally posed as a rower to get in the school for sports." Many expressed outrage over the privilege and sense of entitlement of those implicated in the scandal, including a Twitter user who lamented:

> My kid works his ass off for good grades and to be even considered to a college let alone an elite one. This is a slap in the face to all the kids who work hard to succeed in academics. Olivia Jade and her mother should learn humility. Sick.

Around 13.6 percent (*n* = 73) of comments defended Giannulli, often arguing she was a casualty of her parents' actions: "Her parents did this! Not her. Unless you know some facts that everyone else doesn't know of her involvement in this? She's a teenager. I doubt she knew what her parents did." Other users wanted more information. For instance, one individual reasoned, "To be fair though, she's just a kid. This don't sit right with me. What happened to innocent till proved guilty? Who knows what she knew?"

RQ2: Amazon's and Sephora's Responses and Public Reaction

Brand Responses

Amazon never issued a response but received attention for a Prime Student–sponsored Instagram post in which Giannulli posed in her dorm room, captioned: "I got everything I needed from Amazon with @primestudent and had

Table 7.2 Frequencies of Public Reactions to Olivia Jade and Laura Lee

	Olivia Jade	Laura Lee's Twitter Apology	Laura Lee's First Video Apology	Laura Lee's Second Video Apology	Laura Lee (All Comments)
Influencer as Responsible	363, 67.9%	275, 83.3%	194, 59.3%	34, 18.8%	648, 60.1%
Defending the Influencer	73, 13.6%	31, 9.4%	14, 4.3%	4, 2.2%	69, 6.4%
Influencer's Insincere Response	2, < 1%	216, 65.5%	220, 67.3%	67, 37%	571, 53%
Total	535	330	327	181	1,078

it all shipped to me in just two-days. #ad #primestudent #allonamazon." The partnership was also touted in a *Teen Vogue* article (Howard, 2018). Amid the scandal, individuals flooded the since-deleted post with critical comments, and Amazon quietly replaced Giannulli in June (Costley, 2019).

Giannulli's partnership with Amazon was dormant at the time of the scandal, but her partnership with Sephora was active, including a collaboration on an "Olivia Jade collection" powder (Ross, 2019). The scandal provoked a wave of #boycottsephora tweets and one-star reviews on the collaboration, prompting the brand to remove the products and sever the partnership. Sephora issued a brief media statement using *provocation*: "After careful review of recent developments, we have made the decision to end the Sephora Collection partnership with Olivia Jade, effective immediately" (Spangler, 2019), which it repeated in two Twitter replies.

Public Reaction

In total, 176 comments collected for the Olivia Jade case captured user reactions to Sephora while 194 comments included perceptions of Amazon. An independent samples t-test showed there was a significant difference in public attitude toward Amazon and Sephora, $t(307.58) = 12.557$, $p < .001$. Public attitude toward Sephora was significantly more positive ($M = 2.48$, $SD = .645$) than Amazon ($M = 1.73$, $SD = .469$).

Sephora. Approximately 119 individuals (67.6%) supported Sephora's decision to cut ties with Giannulli (table 7.3). Many extolled the brand's perceived expression of virtues, such as integrity ("Thank you! I'm glad to see that Sephora has integrity") and justice ("Excellent news! [Thumbs up emoji] Olivia Jade is learning that there are consequences to cheating. So is her Mom"). A small number of individuals ($n = 27$, 15.3%) disavowed the brand following its announcement, defending Giannulli:

upsetting that y'all are doing this just to remain a "clean" brand. olivia did nothing but do good things for Sephora and y'all are just going to cut her off. y'all

Table 7.3 Frequencies of Public Reactions to Amazon, Sephora, Boxycharm, and Ulta

	Amazon	*Sephora*	*Boxycharm*	*Ulta*
Calls for Action	102, 52.6%	12, 6.8%	20, 13%	3, 7.1%
Support for Brand Response	2, 1%	119, 67.6%	83, 53.9%	10, 23.8%
Disapproval of Brand Response	70, 36.1%	27, 15.3%	2, 1.3%	3, 7.1%
Positive Purchase Intention	0, 0%	20, 11.4%	18, 11.7%	0, 0%
Dependent Purchase Intention	12, 6.2%	2, 1.1%	5, 3.2%	1, 2.4%
Negative Purchase Intention	7, 3.6%	7, 4%	2, 1.3%	1, 2.4%
Total	*195*	*176*	*154*	*42*

should know what kind of a person she is considering she was an ambassador for years.

Twenty-nine individuals (16.5%) mentioned their purchase intent. These comments were largely positive ($n = 20$, 11.4%), as users claimed they would purchase products from Sephora ("brb I gotta go shopping at Sephora"). However, 4 percent ($n = 7$) of comments were negative as individuals indicated they would no longer support the brand ("Her parents commit a crime and you penalize the daughter. I'll be shopping at Ulta from now on. #ultabeauty").

Amazon. Approximately 53 percent of individuals ($n = 102$) who commented about Amazon called for the brand to take action, with around 36 percent of individuals ($n = 70$) disapproving the brand's failure to respond (see table 7.3). Many argued that Amazon lacked values by not distancing itself: "@amazon Drop any affiliation you have with Olivia Jade. The lack of doing so speaks volumes about the ethical integrity of your company. Drop her." Nineteen individuals (9.8%) discussed their purchase intentions. Twelve individuals (6.2%) claimed their buying decisions were dependent on Amazon's response to the situation with comments such as "@amazon cancel @oliviajadee or cancel my prime membership." In comparison, seven individuals (3.6%) shared negative purchase intentions, indicating they would already stop supporting the retailer ("I buy from you all the time but now that she represents you not anymore"). No comments indicated positive purchase intentions.

THE CASE OF LAURA LEE

In 2018, Laura Lee was a successful SMI who managed a beauty YouTube channel with approximately five million subscribers (Ohlheiser, 2018), acquiring brand partnerships with Boxycharm, ColourPop Cosmetics, Diff Eyewear, Morphe Brushes, and Ulta. In August, Laura Lee and three others ignited a feud with beauty influencer Jeffree Star, posting a photo with their middle fingers up and the caption "Bitch is bitter because without him, we're better" (Trainham, 2018). Many perceived the tweet to be directed at Star, who made racist and sexist comments for which he apologized in 2017. Star's fanbase unearthed racist and body-shaming tweets posted by Lee in 2012, including "Tip for all black people if you pull ur pants up you can run from the police faster.. #yourwelcome" (Williams, 2018). Lee was dropped from all of her business arrangements and lost half a million YouTube subscribers within the first two weeks (Abad-Santos, 2018), leading her to issue three apologies (see table 7.4).

Table 7.4   Laura Lee Crisis Timeline

Date	Action
2012	Lee posts and retweets several racist and body-shaming tweets
August 13, 2018	Lee posts a written apology on Twitter
August 19, 2018	Lee posts her first video apology on YouTube
August 20, 2018	Boxycharm's CEO posts a video response via Facebook; DiffEyewear removes Lee's products; Ulta discontinues Lee's upcoming makeup collection and releases statement
August 22, 2018	Morphe Brushes removes Lee from its website, deletes her favorites collection, and labels her items as sold out
September 25, 2018	Lee posts her second video apology on YouTube

RQ3: Laura Lee's Responses and Public Reaction

Twitter Apology

Following the discovery of the tweet, Lee temporarily deactivated her Twitter account and deleted the offensive tweets before returning to post a lengthy apology on August 13, 2018 (Sung, 2018). Written in the notes app on a smartphone, Lee incorporated appropriate IRT strategies. First, she invoked *mortification* as she apologized "from the bottom of her heart" for her "insensitive" and "inexcusable" comments and to those whom she had "hurt and offended." Second, she embraced *corrective action*, explaining she still had "room to learn and grow" and offered she would be "getting involved with foundations that focus on educating the importance of equality and social justice." Lee's response also included strands of *defeasibility*, weakening her use of mortification as she attempted to blame her upbringing for the tweets, claiming, "That girl who tweeted that isn't who I am today. . . . As a small town girl from Alabama I wish I had the cultural education six years ago that I have now."

First Video Apology

One week following her Twitter apology, Lee posted a four-minute video to YouTube. Similar to her tweet, she embraced *mortification*, claiming, "I'm so sorry to you guys. It hurts me so bad to disappoint you all who have supported me for many years" (Haney, 2018). At the end of the video, she apologizes to Star for "the pain we may have caused you in this." Although Lee notes she has "no excuses" for her behavior, she attempts to evade responsibility through *minimization*, claiming that the initial video where she and three other influencers held up their middle fingers was simply an attempt to mimic a photograph from Kylie Jenner's birthday party. She further deflected blame when apologizing to Star by using *defeasibility*, rationalizing, "I didn't know the picture was going to be taken out of context and that anything was going to be said to you." Lee also attempted to portray herself as a victim to gain sympathy by alleging that people were threatening her mother and niece. The most damaging hit to her arguments came as she ineffectively used *differentiation* by incorrectly claiming she retweeted the offensive tweets when she actually wrote them. The video remained public for approximately one month before Lee changed its settings to private.

Second Video Apology

Lee released a follow-up apology on YouTube in late September, in which she attempted to make amends for its predecessor. In the second video, Lee justified removing her first apology video because "it does not represent me well." She noted that the video attempted to present her as a victim before declaring, "I am not a victim in any way, form, or fashion in this situation." She again adopted *mortification* by taking responsibility for her tweets before invoking *denial* by clarifying which tweets were hers and which were falsely attributed to her. The bulk of her video focused on *corrective action* as she attested to her self-growth since writing the offensive tweets and experiencing the public backlash. She then shared her plans to help "turn [the beauty community] around and put it in a beautiful place where it's a positive place where we can grow together and feel good again."

Public Reaction

In total, 1,078 comments discussed Laura Lee and leaned negative ($M = 1.33$, $SD = .526$). A majority of comments ($n = 648$, 60.1%) discussed Lee's responsibility for the incident (table 7.2), attributing responsibility for her insensitive comments solely to her ("Living in a small town is no excuse for being racist! Racism is a choice you make, you were old enough in 2012 to know that what you said was hurtful and wrong!"). Around 6.4 percent ($n = 69$) of comments defended Lee ("Like yeah @Laura88Lee messed up but people need to stop trying to make the situation worse. Everyone messes up and makes mistakes.").

A one-way ANOVA was used to examine differences in how social media users responded to her three apologies and demonstrated significant differences in public perception of Lee based on her apologies, $F(2, 819) = 36.292$, $p < .001$. Post hoc comparisons using the Tukey HSD test indicated that the mean score for public perceptions following her Twitter apology ($M = 1.23$, $SD = .57$) was significantly different than public perceptions after the second video apology ($M = 1.61$, $SD = .489$). Additionally, the mean score for public perception following the first video apology ($M = 1.25$, $SD = .451$) was significantly different than public perception after second video apology ($M =$

1.61, *SD* = .489). In both instances, social media users had a more neutral than negative perception of Lee following the second apology video. Responses did not significantly differ between the Twitter apology and first video apology.

A chi-square test of independence found a significant association between Lee's three apologies and perceptions of insincerity, $\chi^2(2) = 49.97, p < .001$. Specifically, Lee's Twitter ($n = 216, 65.5\%, z = 2.14, p = .101$) and the first video apology ($n = 220, 67.3\%, z = 3.73, p = .09$) exhibited greater insincerity than her second video apology ($n = 67, 37\%, z = -7.01, p < .001$). Following her Twitter apology, many criticized Lee for her defensive approach, deleting her previous tweets, and blocking users. One individual commented:

> Be real with yourself. You deactivated your Twitter because you didn't want to read or see people's reactions, just like you disabled comments on your insta-gram. If you're going to type up a lengthy apology like this be 100% real with yourself and your fans.

After her first video, individuals chastised Lee for downplaying her respon-sibility, disabling comments, and appearing insincere. Many mocked Lee's crying, perceiving her tears to be an inauthentic emotional display ("My favorite part was the jump cuts to put the fake tears on"). Although reactions to the second video leaned more neutral, many individuals expressed that the attempt was too little, too late ("Late attempt at damage control"), and an attempt to salvage her career ("I guess losing thousands of subscribers doesn't pay her bills very well").

RQ4: Boxycharm's and Ulta's Responses and Public Reaction

Brand Responses

Yosef Martin, CEO of the beauty box subscription service Boxycharm, posted a Facebook video. He acknowledged the "hurtful" and "disturbing" nature of Lee's tweets before transitioning into *denial*, emphasizing "we are against anything like that." Martin also invoked *defeasibility*, noting the brand works with "a lot of partners" and "can't watch everything out there that was said . . . something one day in the past, a tweet that was made and so on" despite trying to do its "due diligence." He inoculated against future inci-dents by claiming that, "if we ever work with a person, company, or someone that has said something like this . . . I am just telling you now that we do not support that." Martin embraced a *bolstering* position, emphasizing the brand's "positive" persona, which includes "education about makeup, funny memes, funny statements." Yet, Martin was careful not to scapegoat Lee by discussing the salacious details of the situation. He commented, "We don't sip on tea," a slang expression for gossiping before turning the conversation to a lesson about posting insensitive comments online, noting the Lee case presented "a valuable lesson for all of us."

Ulta issued a two-sentence media statement that distanced its brand from Lee, explaining it would not launch her product line (Williams, 2018), reflecting *corrective action*. The company also underscored its principles through *bolstering*, eschewing that it "values equality and inclusivity in all that we do." The chain simultaneously removed all Lee-related products from its stores and website.

Public Reaction

In total, 154 comments collected for the Laura Lee case captured user reactions to Boxycharm while 42 comments reflected user perceptions of Ulta. An independent samples t-test showed there was a significant difference in public attitude toward Boxycharm and Ulta, $t(76.74) = 3.43$, $p = .001$. Public attitude toward Boxycharm was significantly more positive ($M = 2.5$, $SD = .69$) than Ulta ($M = 2.15$, $SD = .53$).

Boxycharm. Facebook users responded positively to Martin's video response ($M = 2.5$, $SD = .69$). Individuals praised Martin for his sincerity, commenting, "Thank you for staying genuine and loving. The world needs more of that Yosef!" and "I love Joe so much and all his wisdom it so right it doesn't cost you anything to be nice it just makes me respect him so much more." Several users commended his use of the slang expression "sip the tea" ("Omg, joe is so amazing! 'We are not trying to sip on the tea' [laughing smiley face with tears emoji] . . . ."). A majority of comments ($n = 83$, 53.9%) supported the brand's decision to end its ties with Lee (table 7.3). One Facebook user shared, "I'm happy to hear you are no longer supporting her. Doesn't matter if it was years ago or yesterday . . . Love Boxycharm [heart emoji] And thank you for addressing the issue with us." Thirteen percent of comments ($n = 20$) called for Boxycharm to take further action, such as offering refunds or exchanges for Lee's makeup palette. Sixteen percent ($n = 25$) of comments discussed purchase intent. Most of these comments ($n = 18$) indicated a positive purchase intent compared to two comments that claimed they would no longer use Boxycharm ("I don't tolerate racism and hatred and have canceled my subscription . . . ."). Five Facebook users claimed that their purchase intentions were dependent ("Hopefully they're going to make September amazing, to make up for it, or I'm done").

Ulta. Twitter users were largely neutral in their attitudes toward Ulta ($M = 2.15$, $SD = .53$). Ten comments (23.8%) exhibited support for the brand's decision ("Laura Lee was dropped by Ulta, Morphe, and Boxy Charm? Yikes. I love those moments when it doesn't pay to be a racist"), compared to three comments (7.1%) that were disapproving. Three other comments

(7.1%) called for the brand to take action. Only two comments discussed purchase intention and were split between negative ($n = 1$, 2.4%) and dependent ($n = 1$, 2.4%).

RQ5: Relationship between Influencer Perception and Brand Perception

A total of 175 social media posts incorporated both perceptions of Olivia Jade and Amazon. Perceptions of Giannulli and Amazon were found to be weakly correlated, $r(173) = .2$, $p = .008$. In comparison, sixty-nine social media posts included perceptions of Giannulli and Sephora. Perceptions of Giannulli and Sephora had a strong, negative correlation $r(67) = -.54$, $p < .001$, indicating that as the attitude toward the influencer decreased, perception of the brand increased.

For Laura Lee, eighty-one social media posts incorporated both perceptions of the influencer and perceptions of Boxycharm. Perceptions of Lee and Boxycharm were not significantly correlated, $r(79) = -.02$, $p = .858$. Thirty-five social media posts included perceptions of Lee and Ulta that had a strong, negative correlation, $r(33) = -.55$, $p < .001$, indicating that as the attitude toward the influencer decreased, perception of the brand increased.

DISCUSSION

Drawing from IRT and relationship management theory, this chapter offers implications for crisis management following SMI transgressions. The following section analyzes Giannulli's and Lee's responses before focusing on the brands' reactions.

SMI Responses

Giannulli's perceived entitlement and Lee's indefensible tweets sparked outrage among social media users, who perceived both SMIs as responsible for their respective crises. Publicly available tweets incriminated Lee, leading one individual to proclaim that you "can't put concealer on this one." Giannulli has yet to be formally implicated for playing any role in the scandal, yet many charged her as guilty. Failing to issue an appropriate crisis response further fueled public backlash for both influencers. More defensive strategies (denial, evading responsibility) are generally appropriate when crisis responsibility is low while accommodative strategies (mortification, corrective action) should be used when responsibility is high (Benoit, 2013; Blaney et al., 2002; Meng & Pan, 2013). Giannulli's only strategy was to remain silent. Scholars advise against silence during a crisis (Coombs, 2012) as it cultivates the perception of guilt and causes the accused to lose control of the narrative. Giannulli's case was also complicated because of legal implications, including an FBI investigation, which likely led her to take a reputational hit rather than risking legal repercussions.

In comparison, Lee issued multiple responses but still struggled with mitigating the damage. Although she invoked mortification and corrective action, she was slow to respond and ineffectively paired strategies such as mortification with evading responsibility. Further, her Twitter apology came *after* a sustained period of time in which she deactivated her account to remove the offending content instead of quickly addressing the situation. When she did respond, she blundered by attempting to deflect the blame to her upbringing. Then, during her first YouTube apology, she again tried to downplay her responsibility. Messages in her final apology aligned with IRT as she took responsibility and embraced corrective action, but the delay in issuing this response dampened its effectiveness.

Lee's other blunders also offer important lessons for SMIs. First, she never addressed the removal of her offensive tweets, leading social media users to share screenshots of the content and admonish her for trying to "cover up." SMIs should be transparent about what content they remove from their platforms, openly acknowledging the erasures. Second, multiple users complained that Lee's video appeared to be several videos spliced together and identified a cut before she cries, claiming her tears were fake. Sincerity is central to the influencer–follower relationship, and when posting apology videos, SMIs should be aware of the effects of tone and editing on the perceived authenticity of the video. Finally, individuals rebuked Lee and Giannulli for disabling the comment sections on their online platforms. Having the ability to respond to SMIs via these platforms is a crucial component of the influencer–follower relationship (Marwick, 2016), and removing this perceived access to the influencer may impact control mutuality (Hon & Grunig, 1999) by portraying SMIs as inattentive, thereby leading followers to believe that their feedback is insignificant (Dhanesh & Duthler, 2019).

SMI transgressions and crisis responses led all four brands analyzed in this case to terminate their relationships with Giannulli and Lee, and jeopardized the influencers' relationships with followers. Trust between the SMIs and both their brands and followers was damaged as individuals questioned the SMI's integrity (Hon & Grunig, 1999). The crises also undermined the dependability and competency of the SMIs as a brand representative, and the influencers' failure to address followers and issue sincere apologies, along with deactivating comments, raised questions about their authenticity. Many individuals indicated a lack of satisfaction as Giannulli's and Lee's actions and responses failed to meet their expectations. Yet despite this displeasure, both still maintain millions of followers, and some users even defended the two SMIs, implying a commitment to the relationship. Because followers may develop parasocial relationships with influencers (Finsterwalder et al., 2017), strong associations could mitigate the negative effects of a crisis, warranting further investigation.

Brand Responses

Although the brands were not connected to the origins of either crisis, associations with Giannulli and Lee posed reputational risk. When public outrage is high, brands must address the situation. Giannulli's case attracted media attention, and individuals asked all four brands to disband partnerships, demonstrate integrity, and deliver justice. Lee's case attracted less media attention but sent shockwaves through the influencer community (Abad-Santos, 2018).

Boxycharm's, Sephora's, and Ulta's responses suggest that brands can effectively use defensive and accommodative strategies following an SMI's transgression. Brands may use defensive strategies to exhibit a lack of responsibility for the influencer's activities and distancing themselves, while accommodating strategies can be employed to show the brand's attentiveness to consumer concerns. However, public reaction to Amazon shows that silence is ineffective. Amazon had not actively worked with Giannulli in the six months prior to the scandal, but mainstream media outlets highlighted its Prime Student partnership with Giannulli, which touted her enrollment at USC. Along with individuals exhibiting displeasure at Amazon's refusal to publicly distance itself from Giannulli, ties between the content in Giannulli's sponsored Instagram post and the scandal intensified scrutiny and produced outrage.

While traditional statements using appropriate crisis management strategies are effective, Boxycharm's response demonstrates that replying through a video and using a conversational approach can further heighten public approval. Customers were particularly taken with CEO Yosef Martin's conversational manner, praising its authenticity and lauding his reference to the slang expression "sip the tea." Brands should adapt their communication efforts for a social media environment, which requires "a greater openness and a more human voice" (González-Herrero & Smith, 2008, p. 146) to facilitate connections with publics. Reactions to Boxycharm's video also suggest that brands should include a positive perspective in their crisis responses when possible. Although an innocent brand can use a hard denial strategy to distance itself, followers praised Martin for choosing not to demean Lee as part of his response and for encouraging them to consider the lessons they could glean from the crisis.

Next, the findings demonstrate the need for brands to engage in issues management by investigating all SMIs. Several comments on Boxycharm's video underscored that consumers expect brands to do their research. Most of these individuals acknowledged Boxycharm was not responsible for Lee's remarks but questioned why the brand was unaware of the posts when it could have surveyed her prior tweets. The Internet opens up brands to increased scrutiny from publics, and relationships with social media influencers are no exception. Although Boxycharm claimed that it "can't watch everything out there that was said" by Lee, such justifications will not be accepted by consumers for long.

Finally, the relationship between perceptions of the SMI and perceptions of the brand requires further attention. This study found no relationship between attitudes toward Lee and Boxycharm. Attitudes toward Giannulli and Sephora, and Lee and Ulta were negatively correlated, and attitudes toward Amazon and Giannulli were weakly correlated. Because Sephora and Ulta removed their affiliations with Giannulli, the inverse relationship suggests that as individuals' opinions of the SMIs diminished, their approval of the brands increased. Amazon never publicly addressed its relationship with Giannulli, which many social media users interpreted as supporting Giannulli. Given her high levels of unpopularity, the correlation suggests that negative attitudes may have spilled over onto the brands perceived support for her. These findings cautiously suggest that perceptions of the influencer and the brand are linked, and organizations should consider how consumers feel about the influencer before making decisions about preserving or extinguishing relationships. Future research should test the role of other factors, such as identification with the influencer or the brand, in shaping these relationships.

CONCLUSION

This study contains limitations. The findings rely on the perceptions of individuals who were motivated to post on social media, reflecting the views of the general public but not necessarily the attitudes of the SMI's followers or the brands' primary publics. Additionally, because this study relied on real social media comments, the strength of individuals' attitudes toward influencers and brands was not available. Similarly, many codes were dichotomous, and some categories (e.g., purchase intent) were not discussed by all social media users, limiting data analysis capabilities.

The success of an SMI is largely dependent on their ability to be authentic and connect with followers. Following a transgression, SMIs must openly communicate with followers and exhibit sincerity for their remorse or risk diminishing key relational pillars such as trust, satisfaction, and commitment (Hon & Grunig, 1999). As SMIs become a prominent part of social media strategy, brands should recognize not only the benefits but also the potential risks of these partnerships and thoroughly investigate influencers prior to affiliation. Perceptions of the influencer may also transfer to their partnering brands, which must be prepared to respond to these incidents, even if innocent.

NOTES

1. The author would like to thank Emma Baumgardner, Sarah Derrick, Jocelyn Hotter, and Andrew Knight for their assistance.

2. Jade later issued a statement via her YouTube channel on December 1, 2019.

REFERENCES

Abad-Santos, A. (2018, August 31). Laura Lee, Jeffree Star, and the racism scandal upending the YouTube beauty community, explained. *Vox.* https://www.vox.com

Benoit, W. (1995). *Accounts, excuses, apologies: A theory of image restoration strategies.* Albany, NY: State University of New York Press.

Benoit, W. (1997). Image repair discourse and crisis communication. *Public Relations Review, 23*(2), 177–186. doi:10.1016/S0363-8111(97)90023-0

Benoit, W. (2013). Image repair theory and corporate reputation. In C. E. Carroll (Ed.), *Handbook of communication and corporate reputation* (pp. 214–221). Hoboken, NJ: Wiley-Blackwell.

Blaney, J. R., Benoit, W. L., & Brazeal, L. M. (2002). Blowout!: Firestone's image restoration campaign. *Public Relations Review, 28*(4), 379–392. doi:10.1016/S0363-8111(02)00163-7

Brown, S. G. (2018, December 21). How Instagram influencers replaced the modern day celebrity. *HuffPost.* http://www.huffingtonpost.co.uk

Brown, K. A., Anderson, M. L., & Dickhaus, J. (2016). The impact of the image repair process on athlete-endorsement effectiveness. *Journal of Sports Media, 11*(1), 25–48. doi:10.1353/jsm.2016.0004

Coombs, W. T. (2012). *Ongoing crisis communication* (3rd ed.). Thousand Oaks, CA: Sage.

Coombs, W. T., & Holladay, S. J. (2012). Amazon.com's Orwellian nightmare: Exploring apology in an online environment. *Journal of Communication Management, 16*(3), 280–295. doi: 10.1108/13632541211245758

Costley, D. (2019, June 23). Amazon replaces Olivia Jade with Reese Witherspoon's daughter Ava post cheating scandal. *SFGate.* http://wwww.sfgate.com

Deloitte. (2015). Navigating the new digital divide: Capitalizing on digital influence in retail. https://www2.deloitte.com

Dhanani, Z. (2017, October 31). Why social influencers outsell celebrities. *Forbes.* https://www.forbes.com/

Dhanesh, G. S., & Duthler, G. (2019). Relationship management through social media influencers: Effects of followers' awareness of paid endorsement. *Public Relations Review, 45*(3), 1–13. doi: 10.1016/j.pubrev.2019.03.002

Edelman. (2019). 2019 Edelman trust barometer special report: In brands we trust? https://www.edelman.com

Finsterwalder, J., Yee, T., & Tombs, A. (2017). Would you forgive Kristen Stewart or Tiger Woods or maybe Lance Armstrong? Exploring consumers' forgiveness of celebrities' transgressions. *Journal of Marketing Management, 33*(13–14), 1204–1229. doi:10.1080/0267257X.2017.1382553

González-Herrero, A., & Smith, S. (2008). Crisis communications management on the web: How Internet-based technologies are changing the way public relations professionals handle business crises. *Journal of Contingencies and Crisis Management, 16*(3), 143–153. doi 10.1111/j.1468-5973.2008.00543.x

Haney, S. (2018, August 24). YouTube makeup guru apologizes in emotional video as she is dropped by sponsors over racist and fat-shaming tweets she posted six years ago. *Daily Mail.* https://www.dailymail.co.uk

Hayes, A. F., & Krippendorff, K. (2007). Answering the call for a standard reliability measure for coding data. *Communication Methods and Measures, 1,* 77–89. doi:10.1080/19312450709336664

Howard, H. (2018, September 13). Olivia Jade shares her USC dorm décor. *Teen Vogue.* http://www.teenvogue.com

Hsieh, H. F., & Shannon, S. E. (2005). Three approaches to qualitative content analysis. *Qualitative Health Research, 15*(9), 1277–1288. doi: 10.1177/1049732305276687

Jin, S. V., Muqaddam, A., & Ryu, E. (2019). Instafamous and social media influencer marketing. *Marketing Intelligence & Planning, 37*(5), 57–579. doi:10.1108/MIP-09-2018-0375

Ledingham, J. A. (2003). Explicating relationship management as a general theory of public relations. *Journal of Public Relations Research, 15*(2), 181–198. doi:10.1207/S1532754XJPRR1502_4

Ledingham, J. A., & Bruning, S. D. (1998). Relationship management and public relations: Dimensions of an organization-public relationship. *Public Relations Review, 24*(1), 55–65. doi: 10.1016/S0363-8111(98)80020-9

Lee, J. S., & Kwak, D. H. (2016). Consumers' responses to public figures' transgression: Moral reasoning strategies and implications for endorsed brands. *Journal of Business Ethics, 137*(1), 101–113. doi:10.1007/s10551-015-2544-1

Marwick, A. E. (2016). You may know me from YouTube: (Micro-) celebrity in social media. In P. D. Marshall & S. Redmond (Eds.), *A companion to celebrity* (pp. 333–360). Malden, MA: John Wiley & Sons.

Meng, J., & Pan, P.-L. (2013). Revisiting image-restoration strategies: An integrated case study of three athlete sex scandals in sports news. *International Journal of Sport Communication, 6,* 87–100. doi:10.1123/ijsc.6.1.87

Moody, J. (2011). Jon and Kate Plus 8: A case study of social media and image repair tactics. *Public Relations Review, 37*(4), 405–414. doi:10.1016/j.pubrev.2011.06.004

Ohlheiser, A. (2018, August 23). A guide to the racism scandal that's tearing Beauty YouTube apart. *The Washington Post.* https://www.washingtonpost.com

Ross, M. (2019, March 13). Will Lori Loughlin's Instagram-famous daughters get kicked out of USC, face other fallout because of parents? *Mercury News.* http://www.mercurynews.com

Spangler, T. (2019, March 13). Olivia Jade, Lori Loughlin's daughter, stands to lose brand deals over college-admissions scandal. *Variety.* http://www.variety.com

Sung, M. (2018, August 23). The art of the YouTube apology video. *Mashable.* https://www.mashable.com

Trainham, E. (2018, August 23). Laura Lee: Beauty guru loses sponsorships over racist tweets. *The Hollywood Gossip.* https://www.thehollywoodgossip.com

Um, N.-H. (2013). Celebrity scandal fallout: How attribution style can protect the sponsor. *Psychology & Marketing, 30,* 529–541. doi: 10.1002/mar.20625

White, D. W., Goddard, L., & Wilbur, N. (2009). The effects of negative information transference in the celebrity endorsement relationship. *International Journal of Retail & Distribution Management, 37*(4), 322–335. doi: 10.1108/09590550910948556

Williams, J. (2018, August 23). YouTube beauty blogger Laura Lee's racist tweet leads makeup brands to drop sponsorships. *Newsweek.* https://www.newsweek.com/

Chapter 8

Ethical Responsibilities for Social Media Influencers

Jenn Burleson Mackay

Social media influencers (SMIs) demonstrate their passion for everything from new technology to fashion. Thousands of dollars flood the industry every year. For example, some video game influencers make up to $50,000 an hour to play games live online (Needleman, 2019). Meanwhile, one cosmetic influencer reported making $18 million in a single year (Kelly, 2019). Followers develop a parasocial relationship with specific SMIs and are willing to buy products affiliated with these Instagram and YouTube celebrities (Sokolova & Kefi, 2019). Yet, it can be difficult for followers to distinguish between editorial content and native advertising, which may look like unbiased reviews rather than sponsored commentary, which in turn creates an environment that can be deceptive to consumers who may not recognize that their favorite online stars are being paid to promote products. While the Federal Trade Commission (FTC) regulates advertising, it is difficult for the government to regulate the vast influencer industry (Campbell & Grimm, 2019).

While other media agencies, such as the Public Relations Society of America or the Society of Professional Journalists, have well-established codes of ethics to guide their professions, SMIs operate in new territory. The Influencer Marketing Association, which purports to be the trade organization for the profession, formed in 2018, and has since pledged to develop ethical guidelines for the profession, but as of the writing of this chapter, the organization had not posted an ethics code to its website (Influencer Marketing Association, n.d.). The end result is that SMIs have no ethical codebook to help them determine what they should or should not do in their industry. Similarly, people in more traditional professions such as journalism or advertising often get college degrees in their fields, where they may be exposed to the ethical expectations of their field. SMIs, on the other hand, operate in a billion-dollar industry that lies in the Wild West of the Internet.

This chapter argues that SMIs have an occupation that falls somewhere between advertiser and journalist. They may receive free items for review or are paid to endorse specific products. At the same time, however, their content is presented in a format similar to a product review composed by a journalist. This unique position can lead SMIs into an ethical minefield, where followers can be confused or even deceived by influencer content. This chapter suggests that SMIs should be treated as quasi-journalists who hold themselves accountable for making sound ethical choices that support the community.

This chapter will consider ethical issues within the influencer profession, such as transparency, truth, and body image. By relying on normative ethical theory communitarianism, it will argue that SMIs should make ethical choices that are for the good of society. Communitarianism purposes that individuals have responsibilities to their communities. The chapter will argue that SMIs have a right to make money by discussing products that they have received directly from advertisers. Nonetheless, they have a duty to be transparent about how they received the product and should describe their legitimate experiences with the product. As quasi-journalists, SMIs should supply factual information to their followers and pay attention to the effect that their commentary may have on society, which will improve the influencer's credibility and support societal values. SMIs are well-positioned to make contributions that not only support the community but also pad their savings accounts.

WHY SMIS SHOULD CARE ABOUT ETHICS

SMIs as Quasi-Journalists

SMIs occupy a unique position in society. They work with brands and receive free products or are paid to endorse particular items. They operate like advertisers by sharing information about those products. At the same time, they publish information in the style of a journalist sharing content for the opinion or commentary page of a news site. In some ways, the relationship between advertising and journalism places SMIs in a category similar to that of a music reviewer for a news site, who might receive music files in exchange for reviewing content. Yet, journalists have professional codes of ethics and editors to ensure that published content is fair and accurate. SMIs, on the other hand, act as individual contractors. They don't have a formally established ethics code to guide their decisions. Likewise, some SMIs operate independently and do not have anyone double-checking that they have handled a review appropriately.

One might think of SMIs as quasi-journalists—people who share product news, but who have may a direct, personal stake in brands that supply the merchandise they review. Research has shown that SMIs have the power to influence consumer purchase decisions (Lim et al., 2017). This means that SMIs have the ability to directly affect the community. With that in mind, SMIs as quasi-journalists should consider the responsibilities they have to society.

The social responsibilities of the press were widely popularized after a group of scholars led by University of Chicago president Robert M. Hutchins formed the Commission on Freedom of the Press. The group, which is often referred to as the Hutchins Commission, published a report which argued that a press can only be free if it is responsible. A critical aspect of that responsibility is for the press to uphold the needs of the society it serves (Commission on Freedom of the Press, 1947). The Commission's report outlines the way for news organizations to be responsible. It argues that the press must be truthful, it should serve as a platform for the exchange of ideas, it should give people the information that they need to know in order to vote, it should help people to understand the values of society, and it should provide the public with intellectual information (Commission on Freedom of the Press, 1947). Siebert et al. (1956) later developed the idea into social responsibility theory. The revised theory argues that news organizations have a social responsibility to provide society with information to ensure that the political system can function and that people can self-govern. It added some additional concepts, however, including the argument that the press has a responsibility to bring together buyers and sellers, provide entertainment, and make a profit (1956).

Certainly, individual SMIs should not be expected to provide society with the information related to government elections, as quasi-journalists, the three additional responsibilities added by Siebert et al. (1956) fit the role of the influencer. If they want to maintain followers, the influencers must provide some degree of entertainment. Similarly, in order to continue their endeavors, they need to be able to make a profit. Likewise, they provide an avenue for bringing together buyers and sellers. At the same time, some of the responsibilities outlined by the Commission on Freedom of the Press (1947) also fit with the role of the quasi-journalist. As they can influence purchase intention, they need to be truthful about their experiences with products and should recognize and help the public understand the values of society. By doing these things, SMIs can make a profit and still benefit the community. Upholding social responsibilities can help SMIs build a relationship with their followers.

Influencer Credibility

Trust and ethics are intertwined, and lie at the heart of successful business entrepreneurship (Gensler, 2015, July 15). Research has suggested that the credibility of a source (in this case, a social media influencer) helps determine whether audience members will rely on user-generated content to make purchases (Demba et al., 2019). Brands, who hope to increase product profitability by relying on SMIs, need to know that followers view specific SMIs as credible information sources. Therefore, it is advantageous for SMIs to make ethical decisions that will help followers view them as trustworthy.

As a whole, ethics is important to the advertising industry. Advertising Professor Wally Snyder explains it the following way:

> My answer, and proposition, to my advertising colleague, and to you, is that being ethical does not make one less competitive. To the contrary, if you are doing the right thing, you will connect with your clients and customers in a powerful and positive sense. (Snyder, 2017, p. 3)

To make wise decisions about investing in SMIs, brands need to know that they can trust the ethics of these social media spokespeople. For example, if SMIs inflate their follower numbers by purchasing fake followers, they will be unable to provide brands with the return on investment they expect. The likely end result of that broken trust is that SMIs will no longer be a valuable resource to brands (Barker, 2019, September 24). Therefore, SMIs who hope to maintain long-term success should value their own credibility.

Ethical behavior is one way that journalists seek to separate themselves from non-professionals, such as citizen journalists (Craft, 2017). If SMIs want to be recognized as legitimate information providers and as purveyors of a respectable profession, the key may be adopting a set of ethical guidelines that assures the public that they intend for their information to be reliable and trustworthy. Thus, by emphasizing ethical behavior, SMIs can help strengthen their own field.

ETHICAL QUESTIONS RAISED BY SMIS

The FTC requires SMIs to reveal their relationships with brands and explain financial, personal, employment, or family connections they have with the brands. The FTC also provides guidance on how the relationship should be presented (Federal Trade Commission, 2019). The goal is to protect the public from misleading advertisements (Zialcita, 2019). Essentially, SMIs are required to be transparent about their relationship with the product or brand they are reviewing. Plaisance (2007) describes transparency as truth and argues that transparency is important to what, why, and how we share information. From a journalist's perspective, transparency helps the public to understand how news is gathered and presented, and journalists reveal to the public the process they use to report the news. The process helps hold journalists accountable and increases their validity to their audience (Allen, 2008).

Issues of Disclosure

SMIs might find it tempting to hide their relationship with sponsors when they post or to bury indications of the post as an advertisement in hashtags. It is difficult for the FTC to police every influencer post across every platform. Reports indicate that some SMIs publish content without identifying their sponsorship, such as Jemma Lucy, who posted a photo of herself with a weight-loss coffee while she was pregnant. The post did not acknowledge sponsorship and included content that was written by the advertiser (BBC News, 2019, July 31). One marketing study found that a third of advertisers admit that they do not disclose their SMIs. They argue that revealing the partnership will make their company seem less trustworthy (Tesseras, 2018, November 14).

One might compare the influencer's acknowledgment of sponsorships to the mainstream journalist's concerns for conflicts of interest. If a journalist has a potential conflict of interest, such as the publication that employs him or her also owns the company that produces the product that is being reviewed, the commentary should make that relationship clear. For example, if a journalist for *Time* magazine wrote an article about a film produced by their parent company, Time Warner, the article should make that affiliation clear to the audience; withholding that information would be potentially damaging to the community (i.e., the readership of *Time*). It could also damage the credibility of the publication as people question whether the journalists might be hiding other important information. Likewise, journalists are expected to label native advertisements, which without a label may appear to be editorial content (see Bachmann et al., 2019; Iversen & Knudsen, 2019). Research has shown that unlabeled native advertisements can deceive readers into believing that the advertisements are legitimate news content (Wojdynski, 2016). As explained by Sirrah in the *Columbia Journalism Review*, these advertisements "borrow the credibility and authority of their respective news publishers" (Sirrah, 2019, Key Findings, para. 1). When SMIs post sponsored content, the advertiser borrows the credibility from the influencer. As a result, it is important for the influencer to maintain credibility in the eyes of their followers.

Issues of Truth

Truth can be a murky area for SMIs. There are allegations that some SMIs accept or request money to post negative comments about a company's competitor. Brand consultant Kevin James Bennett posted on Instagram that he was contacted by a marketing team for an influencer who requested $75,000 to $85,000 for a negative review (Wischhover, 2018, August 31). Similarly, some less established SMIs have posted content that made it appear as though they had been paid by large brands when they, in fact, did not have a relationship or agreement with the brand. While not explicitly lying about these relationships, the influencers might post content that implies a sponsorship that doesn't exist. For example, influencer Taylor Evans paid for her own trip to Miami, but posted content such as "Thanks so much XYZ restaurant for the hospitality" (Lorenz, 2018, December 18). The content did not specifically state that the influencer was paid by the restaurant for the post, but it gave that impression. While this kind of content might potentially help a less established influencer catch the eye of larger brands, it also raises questions for followers. If an influencer is willing to imply a relationship that doesn't legitimately exist with a brand, how else might he or she mislead their followers?

Misleading posts might take other forms, as well, such as through computer-generated images (CGIs) of SMIs who do not exist in the real world. Marketers argue that CGI influencers can persuade consumers to make purchases. For example, Miquela Sousa is a CGI creation on Instagram. Her photos often look realistic. The avatar secured sponsorships with major brands such as Samsung. *Time* magazine ranked her as one of the most influential people online in 2018, along with the likes of Rihanna and President Trump (Trepany, 2019). She has helped promote fashion brands such as Prada (Time Staff, 2018, June 30). The CGI influencer phenomenon raises several important questions related to trust. Sousa's Instagram profile does identify her as a robot, but might there be those people who stumble across her photos without seeing that single line on her profile? What might this mean to the unsuspecting consumer who doesn't realize that the opinion he or she is trusting is completely fabricated? Furthermore, what's the potential damage to consumers who want to have the Sousa look, but find that their real-life physique is not as perfect as a CGI persona?

Unrealistic social media imagery is a potential ethical concern for SMIs who frequently depict themselves living extraordinary lives with flawless faces and perfect physiques. Legacy media, such as television and magazines (Grabe et al., 2008), as well as social media, such as Instagram and Facebook (Fardouly & Rapee, 2019; Cohen et al., 2017), have been criticized for presenting unrealistically beautiful images that make people feel unhappy with their own appearance. Fardouly and Rapee (2019) found that images of women not wearing makeup did not have a negative effect on the audience, while images of women in makeup tended to make people feel less satisfied with their own appearance. The concern about appearance can start very young, as suggested by Tiggerman and Slater (2013), who found that preteen girls who spent more time on Facebook and Myspace, were more concerned about their own weight and dieting. Men who use more social media also tend to show a tendency to self-objectify (Fox, 2015). As SMIs continue presenting idealized versions of themselves in order to make money, they may actually do some emotional damage to the fans who regularly view their posts.

COMMUNITARIANISM

Communitarianism is a philosophical theory that argues that one should make decisions that will benefit the community as a whole. The term *community* might be interpreted in different ways, such as neighborhoods or counties, but a community isn't necessarily defined by geographic boundaries. Borden (2014) suggests that a *community* refers to a group of people who share values. Likewise, one can be a member of multiple communities at once (Coleman, 2000). When applied to journalism, the theory shares some commonality with social responsibility theory, which suggests that journalists have responsibilities to society, such as ensuring that the public is well-informed. The same concept might be applied to quasi-journalists. While they don't carry all of the same burdens as traditional journalists, they do have certain responsibilities to the community they serve.

Individualism encourages an emphasis on having rights such as freedom of speech or the right to vote. The communitarian, on the other hand, says that responsibilities should accompany those rights. Therefore, if one is unwilling to fulfill his or her responsibilities, that individual should lose their rights. One might think of rights as being focused on the individual, whereas responsibilities are those obligations that an individual has to society. In order to deserve one's individual rights, one should uphold the responsibilities that are required to support the community. For example, Americans have duties to be informed, vote, and pay taxes. Similarly, while Americans embrace freedom of speech, they also should recognize that the right to speak does not mean that they should say anything they want. The responsibilities that we have to our community should be embedded in our speech. While we can state our opinions, we should not use our speech in a way that might take away or damage the rights of other people in our community. We should use our speech to help other people to be well-informed, for example. As Etzioni (1993) explains, "There is a gap between rights and rightness that cannot be closed without a richer moral vocabulary—one that invokes principles of decency, duty, responsibility, and the common good, among others" (p.263). Furthermore, a community should have a set of moral responsibilities that are non-discriminatory, easy to comprehend, founded on a common understanding of justice, and represent a variety of values (Etzioni, 1993).

Communitarians suggest that the problem with American society is the emphasis on individualism (Bellah et al., 1985). Individualism emphasizes autonomy and suggests that institutions hinder individual freedoms. Communitarianism, on the other hand, suggests that individuals are part of institutions. As Bellah et al. (1991) explains, "better institutions are essential if we are to lead better lives" (p. 5).

Communitarianism has been applied to journalism (Mackay, 2017), and scholars have suggested that the news media should serve as a platform for public discussion rather than an outlet for entertainment (Anderson et al., 1994). Christians et al. (1993) say, "Universal solidarity is the normative core of the social and moral order" (p. 178). A commitment to the community and the ability to imagine how others might perceive situations are important to communitarian journalism (Christians et al., 1993). This framework suggests that journalists need to work together to support institutions in a fashion similar to the civic journalism movement, which encourages journalists to be directly involved with discussing problems and potentially offer solutions to social ills (Craig, 1996). People should feel like they are equals as they discuss problems and issues (Borden, 2014). Furthermore, the theory suggests that the news media should strive to inform and empower the public (Christians et al., 1993).

Communitarianism and the Responsibilities of the Influencer

A capitalistic society driven by individual profits fits the traditional lifestyle of the social media influencer nicely. They act as advertisers who promote products in exchange for pay. However, if one thinks of SMIs as quasi-journalists, people who provide information as a service and entertainment to followers, their platforms take on a different meaning. They become a group of people who have social responsibilities. They have an obligation to support institutions and important social values and should use their online platforms as a place to foster honest discussions.

Responsibilities to Community

SMIs may be members of multiple communities. They are members of their hometown community, their university, social organizations, religious groups, and so on. While those communities are important to the overall identity of the influencer, for the purposes of this chapter, they are less relevant to the influencer's role as a quasi-journalist than communities that are more directly related to their profession. If one looks beyond the geographic communities, SMIs also could be considered members of the social media influencer community. In terms of communitarianism, this means that the moral choices they make should serve the overall community of SMIs.

More specifically, SMIs tend to do reviews for a specific type of product such as fashion, makeup, video games, technology, and so on. In other words, SMIs tend to have topical communities. One influencer may be a member of a fashion community, whereas another is a member of the technology community. These topics-based communities would include followers who consume reviews because they relate to a specific area of interest.

This topical community structure parallels the beat system in the world of journalism where a journalist might cover a specific topic such as government, entertainment, fashion, technology, sports, and so on. In the case of most beats, such as crime or government, journalists are expected to leave personal feelings out of their stories. When other topics are covered, however, such as music, restaurant, or technology reviews, the expectations are different. In these cases, journalists are expected to incorporate their personal experiences into their stories. Their commentary, like that of the influencer, is expected to be honest and opinionated.

If SMIs are treated as quasi-journalists, it stands to reason that they also should label their sponsored content so that the public understands the boundaries of the influencer's product review. If they have been paid to endorse a particular product, they need to share that information with the public. If they have been provided a product for free in exchange for sharing their opinion, they should explain that to viewers as well. This way, SMIs maintain their right to make money via sponsorships, but are also transparent about their relationship with specific brands and adhere to FTC guidelines, thus fulfilling their legal and ethical responsibilities.

Responsibilities to Truth

If one considers the responsibilities that the quasi-journalists have to the community, truth takes on even more importance. SMIs need to discuss their actual experiences with products rather than fabricating information to please a sponsor. They should only agree to represent those brands that generally align with their own preferences and values. This will make it easier for them to be honest. SMIs certainly have the right to freedom of speech, but this does not imply that they *should* lie. The right to freedom of speech comes with a reasonable responsibility for telling the truth. The word *reasonable* is key because SMIs should not be expected to provide every tiny detail relevant to their experience with a product. For example, they shouldn't be required to say how much money they made for testing a product any more than a journalist should be expected to publish his or her salary. Likewise, they should not be expected to describe every infinitesimal aspect of using a product. The same can be said of mainstream journalists who must pick and choose which details they include in a news story. Not every detail can be included. Some information must be left out. The information that is left out of the review/ story should not be detrimental to the truth of the story, however.

Responsibilities to Followers

It is inappropriate for SMIs as quasi-journalists to buy fake followers. Fake followers create an unrealistic community and mislead followers as well as potential advertisers. The deception weakens the credibility of the influencer and creates a false sense of community. It makes it difficult for advertisers to know the extent of the actual community that can be reached by an endorsement. The influencer should build a legitimate community that is both profitable for the influencer and informative for the public. This will be valuable to both brands as well as engaged followers.

SMIs should not take money in exchange for saying something negative about a sponsor's competitor. If they have had a negative experience with a product, there is nothing wrong with discussing that; however, it is important that SMIs are truthful with their followers. Honesty can help foster a discussion in the influencer's community and allow the influencer to engage with their followers, which can help strengthen the credibility of the individual influencer as well as the overall profession of SMIs. Honest reviews also contribute to the information flow throughout the community, ensuring that people are capable of making wise purchase decisions. This can strengthen the economic institutions. Taking money in exchange for publishing negative commentary sacrifices the credibility of the influencer and serves no value within the community. Its sole purpose is greed, which can be destructive to a well-informed public. Expressing honest opinions helps reinforce truth, an important social value.

Fabricated or highly edited images that make the influencer appear more physically perfect than he or she is should be avoided. These images can damage the mental health of young women and men, who may not recognize how extensively an image has been altered. This can cause emotional damage and lead to eating disorders, and eventually lead to long-term damage to the health of the community. By being more honest with their imagery, and possibly even discussing their own insecurities with the followers, SMIs can help strengthen their community and help followers to feel comfortable discussing their own insecurities. This can improve public health as people develop a more realistic expectation for their own physical appearance and the appearance of others.

SMIs have a platform that is ripe with the ability to foster discussions. Their social media sites should serve as avenues for information and debate. While conversations might begin by discussing a particular makeup or technological creation, they may evolve to higher-level discussions where people can discuss healthy living choices, the environment, or other issues important to society. This allows the influencer to provide entertaining information, while also supporting higher-level discussions that can support the welfare of society. More specifically, SMIs should use their platforms to promote programs that serve the community, such as sustainable and ethically created products. This can help SMIs to serve as a partner for business initiatives that are profitable but also beneficial for society, such as products that are recyclable, support a cleaner environment, have not been tested on animals, and so on. By publicizing sustainable companies and ethical business practices, SMIs can help drive sales toward programs and products that are beneficial to society, which can have long-term implications that strengthen the health of the community.

Using communitarianism as a lens to view the ethical responsibilities of SMIs can help SMIs find a balance between making a profit and supporting community standards. It can help SMIs as quasi-journalists support their followers and to help strengthen social institutions such as health and the economy. Likewise, a communitarian approach can help SMIs strengthen their own credibility. Trust is an important aspect of the influencer–follower relationship. Efforts to support community goals and strengthen social standards can help SMIs to build and maintain that trust.

GUIDELINES FOR ETHICAL SOCIAL MEDIA INFLUENCERS

While there is no official ethics code for the influencer profession, there are some guidelines that can help SMIs to publish ethical content.

- SMIs should uphold FTC recommendations about identifying sponsored content. In other words, products that were provided to the influencer for free should be identified. If the influencer was paid to discuss the product, a photo or review should clearly be identified as an advertisement. The sponsorship information should be easy to see to ensure that followers don't overlook it.
- Social media content should express influencer's legitimate opinions and experiences with a product. The influencer should actually use or test the product that is reviewed.
- Just as sponsorships should be indicated, SMIs should not publish content that implies that a sponsorship exists when it doesn't. Posts should be honest.
- SMIs should not accept payment in exchange for publishing negative content about a sponsor's competitor.
- Photo editing should be limited. There are numerous filters and editing tools that allow individuals to easily alter images of themselves or products.

These edits, however, can misrepresent an individual or product. This is an area where SMIs can take a lesson from mainstream journalists who avoid editing photos in order to assure that history is accurately reflected.

- SMIs should foster conversations on their social media sites and allow their community members the opportunity to talk with one another about their personal experiences. This can help strengthen the community.
- SMIs as quasi-journalist should strive to support social values. Use their social media platform as a means to re-enforce the values that are important to society such as honesty, justice, and fairness.
- SMIs should create legitimate online communities populated by actual social media users, and should not purchase fake followers in order to create an unrealistic online presence.

CONCLUSION

SMIs walk a thin line between advertising and journalism. Followers develop parasocial relationships with the online personalities, which causes viewers to feel as though they have a personal relationship with the SMIs (Sokolova & Kefi, 2019). This fake relationship provides SMIs with an advertising prowess. Yet, they present commentary in the style of a journalist writing a review. This quasi-journalist status puts SMIs in a unique ethical position where they should balance their responsibilities to their sponsors with their social responsibilities as journalists.

An application of the normative theory communitarianism suggests that SMIs have rights, but they need to balance those rights with the responsibilities that they have to the community. While they have the right to post content online, they owe it to the community to be honest. Certainly, SMIs have the right to accept sponsorships and make money for publishing advertisements on their social media sites; yet, they are expected to uphold FTC recommendations by acknowledging sponsorships clearly for viewers (Zialcita, 2019). This helps ensure that followers can separate endorsements from other content. Just as transparency helps journalists strengthen their accountability with audiences (Allen, 2008), it can help SMIs to increase their perceived credibility.

SMIs have a powerful platform at their disposal. They can use it to help reinforce the core values of the community, such as treating one another with respect and doing the right thing (Etzioni, 1993). By being truthful about their work and their experiences and engaging their followers in productive conversations, SMIs can strengthen the community while also maintaining profitable businesses. They can maintain a balance between the worlds of advertising and journalism.

REFERENCES

Allen, D. S. (2008). The trouble with transparency. *Journalism Studies, 9*, 323–340.

Anderson, R., Dardenne, R., & Killenberg, G. (1994). *The conversation of journalism: Communication, community, and news.* Westport, CT: Praeger.

Bachmann, P., Hunizker, S., & Ruedy, T. (2019). Selling their Souls to the Advertisers? How native advertising degrades the quality of prestige media outlets. *Journal of Media Business Studies, 16*, 95–109.

Barker, S. (2019, September 24). How to maintain trust and transparency in influencer marketing. *Forbes.* https://www.forbes.com/sites/forbescoachescouncil/2019/09/24/how-to-maintain-trust-and-transparency-in-influencer-marketing/#514804724224

BBC News. (2019, July 31). Pregnant Jemma Lucy's 'irresponsible' Instagram post banned. https://www.bbc.com/news/technology-49163138

Bellah, R., Madsen, R. L., Sullivan, W., Swidler, A., & Tipton, S. (1985). *Habits of the heart. Individualism and commitment in American life.* Los Angeles, CA: University of California Press.

Borden, S. L. (2014). Communitarian journalism and the common good: Lessons from the Catholic worker. *Journalism, 15*(3), 273–288.

Campbell, C., & Grimm, P. E. (2019). The challenges native advertising poses: Exploring potential federal trade commission responses and identifying research needs. *Journal of Public Policy & Marketing, 38*, 110–123.

Christians, C. G., Ferre, J. P., & Fackler, P. M. (1993). *Good news: Social ethics and the press.* New York, NY: Oxford University Press.

Cohen, R., Newton-John, T., & Slater, A. (2017). The Relationship between *Facebook* and *Instagram* Appearance-focused Activities and Body Image Concerns in Young Women. *Body Image, 23*, 183–187.

Coleman, R. (2000). The ethical context for public journalism: As an ethical foundation for public journalism, communitarian philosophy provides principles for practitioners to apply to real-world problems. *Journal of Communication Inquiry, 24*, 41–66.

Commission on Freedom of the Press. (1947). *A free and responsible press.* Chicago, IL: University of Chicago Press.

Craft, S. (2017). Distinguishing features: Reconsidering the link between journalism's professional status and ethics. *Journalism & Communication Monographs, 191*, 260–301.

Craig, D. A. (1996). Communitarian Journalism(s): Clearing conceptual landscapes. *Journal of Mass Media Ethics, 11*, 107–118.

Crawford, A., & Etzioni, A. (1996). The spirit of community: Rights, responsibilities, and the communitarian agenda. *Journal of Law and Society, 23*(2), 247–262.

Demba, D., Chiliya, N., Chuchu, T., & Ndoro, T. (2019). How User-generated content advertising influences consumer attitudes, trust and purchas intention of products and services. *Communicare, 38*, 136–149.

Etzioni, A. (1993). *The spirit of community: Rights, responsibilities, and the communitarian agenda.* Crown Publishers.

Fardouly, J., & Rapee, R. M. (2019). The impact of no-makeup selfies on young women's body image. *Body Image, 28,* 128–134.

Federal Trade Commission. (2019). Disclosures 101 for social media influencers. https://www.ftc.gov/

Gensler, A. (2015, July 28). Trust is the most powerful currency in business. *Fortune.* https://fortune.com/2015/07/28/trust-business-leadership/

Grabe, S., Ward, L., & Hyde, J. S. (2008). The role of the media in body image concerns among women: A meta-analysis of experimental and correlational studies. *Psychological Bulletin, 134,* 460–476.

Influencer Marketing Association (n.d.). https://influencermarketingassociation.org/about/

Iversen, M. H., & Knudsen, K. (2019). When politicians go native: The consequences of political native advertising for citizens' trust in news. *Journalism, 20,* 961–978.

Kelly, C. (2019, February 12). Frye Festival to fashion week, how do influencers make so much money? *USA TODAY.* https://www.usatoday.com/story/news/investigations/2019/02/12/instagram-youtube-influencer-rates-fyre-festival-fashion-week-money-rich-branding-ads-girls/2787560002/

Lim, X. J., Mohd Radzol, A. R., Cheah, J., & Wong, M. W. (2017). The impact of social media influencers on purchase intention and the mediation effect of customer attitude. *Asian Journal of Business Research, 7*(2), 19–36.

Lorenz, T. (2018, December 18). Rising Instagram stars are posting fake sponsored content. *The Atlantic.* https://www.theatlantic.com/technology/archive/2018/12/influencers-are-faking-brand-deals/578401/

Mackay, J. B. (2017). What Does Society Owe Political Cartoonists? *Journalism Studies,* 28–44.

Needleman, S. E. (2019). Top 'live-streamers' get $50,000 an hour to play new videogames online. *The Wall Street Journal.* https://www.wsj.com/articles/top-live-streamers-get-50-000-an-hour-to-play-new-videogames-online-11558184421

Plaisance, P. L. (2007). Transparency: An assessment of the Kantian roots of a key element in media ethics practice. *Journal of Mass Media Ethics, 22,* 187–207.

Siebert, F., Peterson, T., & Schramm, W. (1956). *Four theories of the press.* Chicago, IL: University of Illinois Press.

Sirrah, A. (2019, September 6). Guide to native advertising. *Columbia Journalism Review.* https://www.cjr.org/tow_center_reports/native-ads.php

Snyder, W. (2017). *Ethics in advertising: Making the case for doing the right thing.* New York, NY: Routledge.

Sokolova, K., & Kefi, H. (2019). Instagram and YouTube bloggers promote it, why should I buy? How credibility and Parasocial interaction influence purchase intentions. *Journal of Retailing and Consumer Services.* Print edition in press. https://www-sciencedirect com.ezproxy.lib.vt.edu/science/article/pii/S0969698918307963

Tesseras, L. (2018, November 14). A third of brands admit to not disclosing influencer partnerships [Blog post]. https://www.marketingweek.com/influencer-mark eting-partnerships/

Tiggermann, M., & Slater, A. (2014). NetTweens: The internet and body image concerns in pre-teenage girls. *Journal of Early Adolescence, 34*, 606–620.

Time Staff. (2018, June 30). The 25 most influential people on the Internet. *Time.* https://time.com/5324130/most-influential-internet/

Wojdynski, B. W. (2016). The Deceptiveness of Sponsored News Articles. *American Behavioral Scientist, 60*, 1475–1491.

Wischhover, C. (2018, August 31). The shady world of beauty influencers and the brands that pay them, explained. *Vox.* https://www.vox.com/2018/8/31/17801182/ beauty-influencers-pay-negative-reviews

Zialcita, P. (2019, November 5). FTC issues rules for disclosure of ads by social media influencers. *NPR.* https://www.npr.org/

Chapter 9

The Case of Dina Tokio

Using Symbolic Theory to Understand the Backlash

JoAnna Boudreaux

This chapter will draw upon Ernest G. Bormann's 1972 Symbolic Convergence Theory (SCT) to examine the controversy surrounding Dina Tokio, a Muslim vlogger and social media influencer (SMI), considered one of the most visible and famous faces of the "modest fashion movement" (Osman, 2018). Tokio, a British Egyptian Muslim, began vlogging in 2011, at the age of twenty-one. Tokio connected with young Muslim women by posting YouTube videos offering beauty and style tips and tutorials. She also regularly expressed her musings and frustrations about living as a Muslim woman who wears a hijab. She was featured in *Elle* magazine as part of a new generation of Muslim women "reclaiming the narrative" of what being a Muslim woman means by asserting themselves as modern, fashion-forward, progressive, and glamorous (Rodulfo, 2017). She collaborated with brands such as Tom Ford, H&M, ASOS, and Revlon to promote their products across her social media pages. In November 2017, she premiered her documentary project "#YourAverageMuslim," as part of the *Creators for Change* series produced by YouTube. She was listed as one of *Vogue*'s "New Suffragette's" in January 2018 and published her autobiography *Modestly* (2018). And yet, while Tokio initially wore her hijab, or Islamic head covering, very traditionally, she evolved over time and began experimenting with more styles that showed off her hair and neck. Eventually, in November 2018, Tokio announced that she would only be wearing the hijab when "she wanted" and soon began posting pictures of herself without wearing the scarf at all (Prideaux, 2019). Tokio suffered a swift and immediate backlash from her millions-strong follower community. Her decision was publicly debated across social media platforms resulting in countless tweets, and entire YouTube videos and Instagram posts dedicated to the topic. Most notably, followers took to the comments section of her social media pages to deliver their rage. On January 1, 2019, Tokio posted a YouTube video in which she reads off over forty-five minutes of abusive misogynist, sexual, and threatening comments. Followers encouraged each other to unsubscribe and accused Tokio of leaving Islam and using the Muslim community for fame and attention (Dina Tokio, 2019).

I use Symbolic Convergence Theory (SCT) as a guide to examine the community that formed around Tokio and to better understand the fallout experienced when she ceased behaving as her community expected. SCT is a communication theory developed to account for how a shared rhetorical vision can converge among a group of people, developing into one collective group consciousness (Bormann, 1972, 1985). Collective group consciousness is formed when people exchange shared "fantasies." "Fantasy" takes on its technical definition as the "creative and imaginative interpretation of events that fulfills a psychological or rhetorical need" (Bormann, 1985, p. 5). These fantasies develop in response to issues that are happening to the members of a community—as experienced by them personally, as recorded in historical accounts, or as reported in the news media. This chapter posits that a cultural climate of anti-Islamic political rhetoric and negative media stereotypes create the psychological need for the cultivation of "fantasy," or rather, a need for some Muslim women to respond to questions of what a Muslim woman looks like, what a Muslim woman should look like, and who looks Muslim.

Social media is an easily accessible platform that facilitates a transnational way to answer these questions. One way that Muslim women have used social media to rearticulate their identity is through visual narratives that take the form of Instagram posts and YouTube vlogging. It is from this context that glamorous young Muslim women began to emerge as SMI, popularly referred to as "hijabi influencers." Aggregate members of the global Muslim community view, comment, exchange, reproduce, and emulate these social media posts, creating a virtual community. As per SCT, members cease thinking of themselves as "I" or "me," but as "us" and "we." Members of the community form a collective group consciousness, develop a shared vision, and cultivate a unified set of goals. As Tokio and other hijabi influencers gained popularity, they became the public faces of their community. When Tokio removed her hijab, she was seen as abandoning those goals and betraying a community that she helped create. This chapter will consider SCT's applicability to the hijabi influencer community that formed around Dina Tokio while considering each of the theory's five stages: (1) emergence or creation, (2) consciousness-raising, (3) consciousness-sustaining, (4) vision-declining, and (5) terminus.

STAGE 1: EMERGENCE OF A COMMUNITY

Bormann (1972, 1985) discusses how communities emerge from a dramatic social event or series of events that compel individuals to communicate with others in an effort to make sense of a fearful or unstable reality. I argue that the mainstream social and political climates surrounding visibly Muslim women over the past few decades provide these conditions. Scholars have long documented the tendency for Western media depictions of Islam and Muslims to be profoundly negative (Said, 1978; Arjana, 2019). While Muslim men are portrayed as violent, uncivilized, savage, and threatening, Muslim women are often not portrayed at all (Arjana, 2019). In the instances in which Muslim women are portrayed, they are presented as mute, silent, veiled, and foreign (Arjana, 2019). Furthermore, in recent years, the hijab and other Islamic coverings have become politized as European countries such as France, Germany, and Belgium publicly banned the niqab or face-covering worn by some Muslim women. France took an additional step by banning "burkinis," a full-covering swimsuit worn by Muslim women, from its beaches. Al-Saji (2010) argues that Muslim women are scripted as oppressed and subjugated; thus she stands antithetical to the Western woman who is scripted as free. Consequently, the Muslim woman's erasure and exclusion from the public sphere is demanded and enforced. As a result, in her day-to-day interactions, the Muslim woman possesses a hypervisibility in which she is seen as both a victim of gender oppression and a member of a deviant religion. I further posit that Muslim women choosing to wear a hijab are seen as actively rejecting democratic values of individual autonomy, freedom, and self-expression.

It is from within this context that social media becomes a vehicle from which Muslim women can control the rearticulation of their own identities. While SCT has traditionally focused on how group members share a rhetorical vision through ordinary talk and stories, the innovation of social media provides new platforms and methods for the development of new kinds of communicative rituals. Among these new rituals is the construction of visual narratives that take the form of Instagram posts and YouTube vlogs. Social media holds particular allure as it allows individuals to selectively control the information displayed to the public. Once an image or an exhibition is uploaded for public viewing it can be viewed repeatedly, and for a continuous stream of time, until someone removes it. One can specifically craft a certain kind of visual narrative by being selective about how an image or video is cropped, photoshopped, edited, and filtered, and deciding which images and videos to upload.

Erving Goffman (1959) offers a dramaturgical theory to explain the meaning and activity behind these visual narratives. Goffman (1959) refers to a "public presentation of self" and posits that individuals perform an idealized self rather than an authentic version. Goffman describes the performance as an "activity of an individual which occurs during a period marked by her continuous presence before a particular set of observers and which has some influence on those observers" (p. 22). A photo displayed on Instagram can be thought of more aptly as an exhibition rather than performance (Hogan, 2010). Whether in a public performance or a social media exhibition, individuals selectively control the information they allow to be known about them in a technique Goffman (1959) termed "impression management" (p. 49). Muslim women, specifically those who live in Western countries, are faced with the unique dilemma of reconciling the values and ideologies of their own internal religious communities with those of the larger secular world. The individual question of identity illuminates the collective question of identity. "Who am I, as a Muslim woman?" becomes "Who are Muslim women?" The question "What am I supposed to look like" becomes "What are we supposed to look like?" While much is said about how Muslim women choose to dress (or not to dress), different and competing perspectives remain challenging to reconcile. Western Muslim women are members of a secular society that extols multifarious ideologies of feminine identity and womanhood. These ideologies often contradict and compete with dominant Islamic ideals. Muslim women struggle with navigating the realms of femininity, feminism, and Islamic notions of modesty in piety. Thus, as young Muslim women navigate these ideologies and struggle to synthesize various facets of "self," social media sites, such as Instagram and YouTube, become a public platform for a quotidian exhibition of not only being—but of becoming.

Thus, social media becomes a space for Muslim women to create a narrative of self that showcases them as both members of their religious community and members of a democratic society. Additionally, social media also serves to fulfill the psychological need for acceptance and community. Essentially, a rhetorical vision is formed that allows the group to have a collective identity. Of course, it cannot be overlooked that follower communities also comprise a number of male followers who leave adoring remarks in the comment sections. I speculate that the fantasy presentation of the modest and fashionable Muslim woman most certainly holds a particular allure for men who also seek to reconcile ideas of traditional religiosity with contemporary progressiveness.

STAGE 2: CONSCIOUSNESS-RAISING: THE
RISE OF THE HIJABI INFLUENCER

Borman (1972, 1985) identifies the second stage of a growing rhetorical community as "consciousness-raising." During this stage, the fantasy chains grow and swell as members of the group contribute more and more to the shared rhetorical vision. Followers share, comment, tweet, blog, and reblog the Instagram posts and YouTube vlogs of certain SMIs as a way of saying, "This is us" or "This is who we are." To that end, hijabi influencers become the symbolic persona of a collective movement (Bormann, 1985). They are celebrated by a community that shares their images and vlogs as a way of articulating how they are different and unique from the rest of society. In other words, the follower communities of hijabi influencers become a space for young Muslims to challenge the marginalization they experience in other aspects of their lives.

Thus, hijabi influencers are propelled into public consciousness by a rhetorical need to identify and define the online social media community of their followers. In this stage of consciousness-raising, there is an increase in excitement, communion, and joy. Insiders to the community are celebrated as the rhetorical vision is grounded in high moral standards and opposition to evil (Cragan & Shields, 1981). Muslim women, historically marginalized and misrepresented in mainstream media, were successfully reclaiming the public narrative of their own identity. They had become agentic characters in their own storylines. Bormann (1972) refers to Burke's (1950) *Dramatism* to explain that rhetorical visions always reflect themes of character, settings, and actions. The plotlines of rhetorical visions often denote the themes of popular cultural narratives. I suggest that the rise of the hijabi influencer hearkens toward a "rags to riches" story. Hijabi influencers are scripted as Muslim women who are assumed to be submissive, backward, and foreign, but overcome social discrimination and prejudice to recreate themselves as progressive mainstream beauties. One blogger, Ruqaiya Haris (2018) wrote of hijabi influencers as:

> Wearing hijab and becoming a "practising" Muslim seemed more attainable through them. They broke certain stereotypes about religious women that I didn't even know I had. They made it look easy; they were outspoken and principled, they could laugh at themselves, and they were glamorous, but they weren't selling sex like many other women I had fangirled over growing up. It was different and it was refreshing. I was already enamoured by Islam, but these women really beautified the religion for me. (para. 9)

Of all hijabi influencers, Dina Tokio is noted as possibly the most famous and most followed. Tokio, originally referred to as Dina *Torkio,* still maintains 1.3 million Instagram followers and over 800,000 YouTube followers. Tokio's popularity has been attributed to her sense of style, enthusiasm for fashion, and an outspoken, witty personality. She launched her first YouTube channel in 2011, and her most popular videos include "THE MOST BEAUTIFUL

LIPSTICK IN THE WORLD," TURBAN TUTORIAL WITH LIBERTY LONDON| OOTD!" and "AIRPORT SECURITY DON'T BELIEVE I'M BRITISH." In 2015, she established her own website, "Days of Dolls," where she would eventually launch her own clothing line. The now-defunct site featured her modeling glamorous, trendy styles in an urban setting. She is credited with leading global fashion trends among Muslim women, notably inspiring the popular turban-style hijab (Kadri, 2018). Tokio was also featured in a 2015 BBC Three documentary film titled "Muslim Miss World." The film focuses on Tokio's entry into the World Muslimah pageant that is held annually in Indonesia and features participants from countries including Bangladesh, Singapore, and Iran.

In the wake of the precedent set by Dina Tokio, it is difficult to track the complete timeline of the hijabi influencers. Omar (2018) found that hijabi influencers had a combined following of over three million. One Muslim influencer, Amena Khan, has over 600,000 followers. Khan was noted for collaborating with L'Oreal for a haircare and skincare campaign in 2016. Maria Ali has over 400,000 followers on Instagram. Ali uses her Instagram to share photos of her international travels as a model for Muse Management NYC. Yasmeena Rasheed, who models for brands like H&M, has over 100,000 followers. Noor Tagouri, controversially noted for being the first hijab-wearing Muslim woman to be featured in *Playboy*, boasts over 300,000 Instagram followers.

Articles about hijabi influencers began appearing in mainstream beauty sites such as *About Her* (Stock, 2018) and *Elle* (Rudolfo, 2017). Eventually, the settings of the Muslim influencer transgressed over into the offline cultural mainstream. The impact of Dina Tokio and other hijabi influencers is evidenced by the rise of the modest fashion industry. The modest fashion industry is a growing commercial market that supports the dressing styles of Muslim women and those of other Abrahamic faiths (Gander, 2017; Sarkar, 2019). In a *Forbes* magazine article, fashion journalist Meghna Sarkar (2019) comments on the relationship between hijabi influencers and the modest fashion industry noting:

> Modest fashion influencers have proliferated mainstream media thanks to the relatability, authenticity and the sense of ownership in their content. The compelling Instagram stories, real-time live chat sessions and effectively marketed posts are directed towards building a lasting relationship with one's followers, where transparency is the most effective trump card. (para. 7)

Hijabi influencers and the community that surrounds them took their vision offline and transformed the image of modest fashion from "frumpy" and "dowdy" to "glamorous" and "trendy," by promoting, sharing, exchanging, and emulating a shared cultural narrative of what a Muslim woman looks like. The collective social media activities of Dina Tokio and other hijabi influencers told a story of the contemporary Muslim woman. It is a story of reclamation. Old foundations were shattered as they became forerunners of a new consciousness. No longer were Muslim women beholden to erasure and negative stereotyping of the mainstream media. Muslim women themselves had taken control over their own image.

STAGE 3: CONSCIOUSNESS-SUSTAINING

As the rhetorical vision formed by the online hijabi community expanded and transcended into the offline world, the next stage focuses on maintaining the enthusiasm and commitment of the vision. Bormann (1972, 1985) describes this stage as "consciousness-sustaining." As certain young women became defined as hijabi influencers, they subsequently became the central characters of a shared rhetorical vision. Hijabi influencers sponsored fashion brands and beauty products on their personal social media pages and successfully influenced the mainstream fashion industry. They provided interviews to mainstream beauty sites. Everyday Muslim women became a recognizable marketing demographic. For the first time in modern history, Muslim women saw themselves on the catwalk, in beauty ads, and in commercials.

Hijabi influencers were the central characters in a new narrative. As central characters, it implies they possess certain character traits. The Muslim woman could be beautiful, sexy, and modern without sacrificing the core tenant of Islamic modesty. She did not have to show her hair or skin. Thus, it is important to note that since hijabi influencers wore Western clothing, high-heels, and makeup, the only symbolic boundary that truly distinguished them as insiders to the community is the head covering. Therefore, the hijab became an elevated and naturalized as an essential component of the new Muslim woman. What made hijabi influencers identifiable as forerunners to their community is, well, their *hijab*. Hijabi influencers were literally essentialized to the scarf on their head. In other words, to remove the head covering would be considered a profound betrayal to the community. It meant abandoning the rhetorical vision.

Thus, in October 2018, when Dina Tokio began posting pictures of herself without wearing the hijab, she was met with immediate outrage. Her followers took to the comment section of her social media pages to express their anger and disappointment. Srouji (2018) quotes a letter Tokio posted on her social media accounts that stated:

There's been a lot of speculation and madness over the weekend regarding the
way I've been wearing or not wearing my headscarf . . . sometimes I feel more
comfortable covering my hair and other days I am more comfortable showing
it. That's just it. (para. 3)

Her followers responded by posting hateful comments suggesting that she
had used the Muslim community for fame and was never genuine nor authentic. Later in November 2018, Tokio posted a story referring to the "hijabi"
community as a "very toxic cult" (Srouji, 2018). In a later Twitter thread,
Srouji (2018) quotes Tokio as further explaining:

To address my "hijabi community starting to become like a toxic cult" comment. I'm referring to the onslaught of slander and insults I've received from a
community that I was very much a part of and helped build . . . all because of
my personal decision to basically wear it when I want to. (para. 6)

Critiques of Tokio continued in comments, tweets, blog posts, and even
YouTube videos. In December 2018, popular American Muslim YouTuber
Adam Saleh posted an entire video devoted to discussing Dina Tokio, aptly
titled "Why Dina Tokio Took Her Hijab Off." The video earned over 500,000
views and featured Saleh in the company of three friends. All four give their
opinions on why they think Tokio made the "wrong" choice. When asked for
his opinion, one man in the video remarks, "To overnight just change everything you ever believed in . . . to me, that's just crazy" (Adam Saleh Vlogs,
6:27). Saleh himself replies, "I mean if I was a girl and I had a hijab on and
I out of nowhere took it off . . . my mom would pretty much slap the shit out
of me" (Adam Saleh Vlogs, 6:44). Another man in the video states that "you
can't be on earth and stuff, opposing the religion . . . you can't disagree with
God's law" (Adam Saleh Vlogs, 9:23). While the comment section of the
video has since been deleted and disabled, Saleh ends by asking the audience
to leave comments and share their thoughts. This video was one of several
that debated Tokio's decision and can still be found on YouTube.

In order to maintain the momentum of the collective consciousness, any
evidence of backsliding by one individual is severely criticized by other
members of the community. Bormann (1985) explains that one strategy is to
"accuse the person of having a bad character (that is, one that departs from
the models of good personae in the basic shared fantasies). They also criticize
the person for enacting bad scenarios and failing to emulate good scripts"
(p. 15). As a backslider, Dina Tokio endured an incredible level of abuse. In
addition to being the subject of video discussions by fellow YouTubers, she
was lambasted with vitriolic comments left in the comments of her various
social media pages. In her January 1, 2019, YouTube video, Tokio wore an

oversized lime green hoodie with her blonde hair hanging loose and casual around her shoulders. A baby walker can be seen in the background. Without any introduction or explanation, she holds up her smartphone and begins reading while a screenshot of the text she is looking at appears at the bottom of the screen. For forty-seven minutes, Tokio reads a non-stop continuous stream of misogynist hatred, slurs, and threats from comments posted across her various social media pages. There are dozens and dozens of comments targeting Tokio's looks, her faith, and her family. The comments include "dog," "I hope u and ur family die painfully and slowly. Absolute disgrace," "Satan in disguise," "You look trashhh without your hijab," and "Used Islam to gain popularity, the absolute rat" (Dina Tokio, 2019, 1:07, 1:16, 8:07, 13:26, 21:39 [*sic*]). Tokio's video sparked divisions in the Muslim social media community, as members reacted in tweets, comments, and blog posts. Most notably, Tokio's decisions underscored the tremendous scrutiny Muslim women face from within their own communities. The controversy further raised questions about what it means to become the face of a movement. What do SMIs owe their communities? Are they expected to maintain continuity in their own personal lives? Do followers have a right to tell them what to do?

STAGE 4: VISION-DECLINING

I suggest that Dina Tokio's public removal of the hijab and the subsequent backlash signaled the stage that Bormann (1985) described as *vision-declining*. In this stage, the rhetorical community undergoes rapid changes and the vision is not capable of successfully adapting. This is referred to as the *principle of explanatory power*, meaning that the rhetorical vision can no longer explain its reason for being. While Tokio faced notorious backlash for publicly removing the hijab, she was not the first hijabi influencer to take it off. Kareem (2018) wrote a brief article about the trend two months before Tokio publicly announced that she would no longer be wearing the hijab regularly. In her article, "The Rise and Fall of the Hijab on Social Media," Kareem speculated that the decline of the hijab could be due to the tremendous expectations that are put upon hijabi influencers to perfectly represent Islamic womanhood. Hijabi influencers, even when wearing a headscarf, face numerous criticisms about their online self-presentation. Tokio, for example, began receiving criticisms about the styles in which she wore her hijab long before she completely took it off. For example, writing for the online Islamic magazine, *IlmFeed*, Mahuja Ahmed (2017) criticized the turban style stating, "Showing your hair and neck is not hijab and should never be promoted as hijab" (para. 8). As Instagram and YouTube are spaces to present an idealized version of the self, eventually living up to an ideal becomes exhausting.

Therefore, I suggest that for many, the online community ceases to fulfill the psychological need for belonging and community.

In returning to Goffman's (1959) theory of dramaturgy, he suggests that the performance, or rather, the "presentation of self," offered for public viewing is dictated by the audience, rather than the individual. Social media offers a universal audience composed of Muslims, non-Muslims, and everyone beyond and in-between. While the images Muslim women posted on social media were always meant to be the most idealized versions of the self, reconciling the religiously pious self with the secular, fashionable self certainly requires a degree of emotional and spiritual labor. In order to address unseen labor involved with constructing an idealized version of the self, Goffman (1959) dichotomized these two settings into notions of "front stage" and "backstage." The front stage is the space where the individual presents the idealized self while the backstage is the space where the individual labors to keep up the ideal. He explains, "When the individual presents himself before others, his performance will tend to incorporate and exemplify the officially accredited values of the society, more so, in fact, that does his behavior as a whole" (p. 23). According to Goffman, individuals are driven to play their roles as convincingly as possible in order to succeed in a particular setting. In Goffman's dramaturgical theory, the settings were bounded by time, place, and a specific audience. I suggest that the online environment complicates the audience. Muslim influencers simply grow tired of attempting an ideal version of the self for a community that they will never be able to satisfy. Muslim women occupy a complex space in which what they wear is always scrutinized by people both from within and outside their community. As evidenced by the case of Dina Tokio, the online world may not provide a respite for this.

Additionally, in considering the *principle of explanatory deficiency*, it is perhaps important to note that as the hijab entered the mainstream via *the principle of rapid implosion*, the need for an alternative community of inclusivity may become less and less needed as time goes on. The rhetorical vision created by the community surrounding hijabi influencers became too big to be contained in the realm of social media. Worth over $240 billion, modest fashion is one of the industry's fastest-growing sectors (Omar, 2018). As Muslim women have become increasingly recognized as a marketing demographic with tremendous spending power, they began to see themselves featured in mainstream fashion advertisements and marketing campaigns (Gander, 2017; Sarkar, 2019). Dolce & Gabbana, Nike, and H& M have all launched clothing lines featuring the hijab and marketed toward Muslim women. Halima Aden emerged as the first hijab-wearing Muslim woman to walk on the runway during a New York fashion week while Ikram Abdi Omar soon followed as the second (Haute Hijab, 2018). Additionally, Nura Afia was signed as the first

Covergirl ambassador to be featured in ads wearing the hijab (Paton, 2016). Even the toy manufacturer Mattel released the first hijab-wearing Barbie to recognize Olympic athlete Ibtihaj Muhammad (Sarkar, 2019).

Bormann (1985) also asserts that another reason for declining vision is the *principle of exploding free speech*. This principle refers to the problem of a barrage of counter-rhetoric. As central characters and public figures, hijabi influencers always faced criticism and constant policing on their dress and behavior from their own followers, from the orthodox Muslim community, and from misogynist men hiding behind keyboards. Tokio discussed criticism she faced from men in an interview in September 2018, a month before she publicly removed her hijab. In the interview, she explained that she no longer had any tolerance for men who choose to criticize her for the way she chooses to dress or wear her headscarf. She suggested that if they feel so conflicted about it then perhaps, they should not be looking at her at all (Fearon, 2018).

It is also important to note that not all Muslim women were ever on board with the hijab entering the realm of mainstream fashion. Hijabi influencers and the communities that supported them faced a backlash from the international orthodox Muslim community almost from the inception of the movement. In February 2017, the Al-Madina Institute, a non-profit American Muslim institution of higher education, published an article titled "More than a Headscarf: How Hijab has Lost its Soul" by a student of Islamic studies, Shazia Ahmad. Ahmad (2017) targeted beauty blogging hijabi influencers and argued that the hijab has become devoid of its foundational component of modesty. She stressed the importance of conformity to religious rulings of dress—these rulings include covering all of the body except for the face, hands, and feet, not wearing clothing that is too tight or revealing, and the avoidance of makeup, jewelry, and accessories. She stated that it is improper to "reduce" hijab to an indicator of identity or cultural heritage and that in doing so, one has neglected the "the important relationship between the body's disciplined conformity to sacred law and the heart's ascendance to the Divine" (para. 4). Similarly, author Shelina Janmohamed argues that "today's fashion industry is about consumerism and objectification," which she considers antithetical to core Islamic values (Sanghani, 2016, para. 10).

Conversations surrounding Tokio elucidated many of these criticisms. There were widespread accusations that Tokio only pretended to be Muslim to use the community for fame and profit (Pridaux, 2016). While completely unfounded, these accusations raise questions surrounding the meanings behind the public presentations of hijabi influencers. Do representations of Muslim women as beautiful and fashionably dressed challenge discriminatory stereotypes or encourage materialism? Are Muslim women agentic creators of their own cultural narratives or just passive consumers endorsing products? Are hijabi influencers creative entrepreneurs or profiting off a community?

STAGE 5: TERMINUS

Terminus is the last and final stage of a rhetorical vision. It is marked by the *principle of rapid implosion*. In this stage, the rhetorical vision implodes upon itself due to a barrage of problems explained in the previous section. The rhetorical community becomes overwhelmed by being unable to explain its reason for being, incapable of keeping up with rapidly changing external factors, and growing contradictory motives and visions. The vision fragments into so many moving parts and pieces that it eventually shatters. While Dina Tokio is still vlogging on YouTube, she would not be considered a hijabi influencer. While she still has a large following, it is difficult to determine the demographics of her audience, which community she represents, or whether she represents any single community at all. It is important to note that despite encouraging each other to unsubscribe from Tokio, it appears that no one really did. At the end of 2019, she still had roughly the same number of followers that she did when she was featured in *Elle* in 2017. It is possible that as Tokio has grown and evolved, so did her original fan base. Perhaps her most loyal followers recognize Tokio's humanity and believe in allowing her the space to be a human who is entitled to grow and change. It is also certainly worth mentioning that the forty-seven-minute video, "The Bad, the Worse, the Ugly," in which Tokio reads the mean-spirited comments, has over one million views. It is one of Tokio's most-watched videos and may have certainly gained her new followers for any that she lost.

There is also evidence that hijabi influencers are not completely terminated, but the narratives surrounding them have changed and shifted. In January 2019, Haute Hijab published a list titled "10 Hijabi Influencers to Look Out for in 2019." While the women listed were all fashion and lifestyle SMIs, they were also noted for being personally successful as entrepreneurs and educated professionals. The list includes an interior designer, a bridal stylist, a chemist, an ophthalmologist, and a radiologist (Mostafa, 2019). I also note that the women listed are diverse in race, ethnicity, and body type. In consideration of Bormann's (1985) theory, it may be that a new type of fantasy is being shared as more and more young Muslim women seek professional careers and financial independence. I suggest that based on the Haute Hijab list, meanings attached to modernity and progress are rapidly moving away from notions of consumeristic beauty and more toward the ideals of diversity, meritocracy, and individual success.

CONCLUSION

In summary, SCT offers a way of understanding how the hijabi influencer community rapidly emerged, became cohesive, and crafted a rhetorical vision. SCT illuminates the tendency for individuals to try and make sense of events and assume agency in unstable social or political conditions. SCT also elucidates how the hijabi influencer community cultivated a group consciousness through recurring visual narratives that took form in Instagram posts and YouTube vlogs. These visual narratives communicate a shared story of a progressive Muslim woman shattering traditional stereotypes. Personalities like Dina Tokio were upheld as the main characters in the story. SCT also illustrates how the consciousness of the group began to fail and the methods employed in an effort to sustain the rhetorical vision. While this chapter remains ambivalent about the current state of the hijabi influencer community, I conclude that the community is in a definite state of vision-declining. However, I also suggest that as culture rapidly shifts and a new generation of young Muslim women comes of age, a declining vision can also be interpreted as a vision that is simply changing and taking a new form.

REFERENCES

Ahmad, S. (2017, February 20). More than a headscarf. How hijab has lost its soul. *Al-Madina Institute.* https://almadinainstitute.org/blog/more-than-a-headscarf-how-hijab-has-lost-its-soul/

Ahmed, M. (2017, March 14). The problem with 'hijab fashion'. *Ilmfeed.com.* https://ilmfeed.com/the-problem-with-hijab-fashion/

Akhtar, A. (2018, August 27). Meet the first hijab-wearing runway model, who started making money at 10 and loves paying taxes. *Time.com.* http://time.com/money/5375079/halima-aden-money-work-ethic/

Al-Saji, A. (2010). The racialization of Muslim veils: A philosophical analysis. *Philosophy and Social Criticism, 36*(8), 875–902.

Arjana, S. R. (2019). *Veiled superheroes: Islam, feminism, and popular culture.* Lanham, MD: Lexington Books.

Bormann, E. G. (1972). Fantasy and rhetorical vision: The rhetorical criticism of social reality. *Quarterly Journal of Speech, 58*(4), 396–407.

Bormann, E. G. (1985). *The Force of Fantasy.* Carbondale; Edwardsville: Southern Illinois University.

Canela, M. (2018, March 15). Ikram Abdi Omar becomes the second hijabi model to be signed to a modeling agency. *Hautehijab.com.* https://www.hautehijab.com/blogs/hijab-fashion/ikram-abdi-omar-becomes-the-second-hijabi-model-to-be-signed-to-a-modeling-agency

Cooney, S. (2016, September 28). A Muslim woman made history for appearing in playboy. *Time.com.* http://time.com/4511338/noor-tagouri-hijab-playboy/

Cragan, J. F., & Shields, Donald. (1981). *Applied communication research on a dramatist approach.* Prospect Heights, IL: Waveland Press.

Fearon, F. (2018, September 20). 'I make a bully look silly': modest fashion star Dina Torkia on outsmarting the hijabi haters. *The National.* https://www.thenatio nal.ae/lifestyle/fashion/i-make-a-bully-look-silly-modest-fashion-star-dina-torkia -on-outsmarting-the-hijab-haters-1.772332

Gander, K. (2017, October 16). Modest fashion: how covering up became mainstream. *The Independent.* https://www.independent.co.uk/life-style/fashion/modest y-fashion-shopping-covering-up-hijab-abaya-muslim-jewish-orthodox-christian -a8003726.html

Goffman, E. (1959). *The presentation of self in everyday life.* Garden City, NY: Doubleday.

Haris, R. (2018, December 11). Exploring modest fashion blogger Dina Tokio's hijab controversy. *DazedDigital.Com.* https://www.dazeddigital.com/beauty/head /article/42189/1/exploring-modest-fashion-blogger-dina-tokios-hijab-controversy

Hogan, B. (2010). The presentation of self in the age of social media: Distinguishing performances and exhibitions online. *Bulletin of Science, Technology & Society, 30*(6), 377–386.

Islam, I. (2019). Redefining #YourAverageMuslim woman: Muslim female digital activism on social media. *Journal of Arab &Muslim Media Research, 12*(2), 213–233.

Kadri, M. (2018, April 7). The rise of Muslim influencers- and why this is something you can't ignore. https://www.wearemin.co/blog/the-rise-of-muslim-influencers-and-why-this-is-something-you-cant-ignore/

Kareem, H. (2018, September 19). The rise and fall of the hijab on social media. *Muslim Influencer Network.* https://www.wearemin.co/blog/the-rise-and-fall-of-the-hijab-on-social-media/

Khoja-Moolji, S. (2017, June 22). The "new" Muslim woman: A fashionista and a suspect. *Blarb.* https://blog.lareviewofbooks.org/essays/new-muslim-woman-fashi onista-suspect/

Mangla, I. S. (2015, November 10). Meet the hijabi fashionistas of Instagram: Chic muslim women share their modest style on social media. *International Business Times.* https://www.ibtimes.com/meet-hijabi-fashionistas-instagram-chic-muslim -women-share-their-modest-style-social-2178021

Mostafa, M. (2019, January 30). 10 Hijabi influencers to look out for in 2019. *Haute Hijab.* https://www.hautehijab.com/blogs/hijab-fashion/10-hijabi-influencers-to-look-out-for-in-2019

Now This Entertainment. (2018, October 3). *Yasmeena Rasheed is an influencer putting modest fashion on the map* [Video File]. https://www.facebook.com/NowTh isSeen/videos/703766489981511/

Olumide Olufowote, J. (2017). Symbolic Convergence Theory. In C. R. Scott, J. R. Barker, T. Kuhn, J. Keyton, P. K. Turner and L. K. Lewis (Eds.), *The International*

Encyclopedia of Organizational Communication. doi:10.1002/9781118955567. wbieoc202

Omar, S. (2018, October 8). 10 hijabi influencers you should already be following. *Elle.com.* https://www.elle.com/uk/beauty/make-up/g22696236/hijabi-beauty-influencers-to-follow-now/

Paton, E. (2016, November 9). Covergirl signs its first ambassador in hijab. *The New York Times.* https://www.nytimes.com/2016/11/09/fashion/covergirl-beauty-hijab.htmlaux

Prideaux, S. (2019, January 6). 'I hope you die': influencer Dina Torkia shares shocking amount of abuse she's received since taking hijab off. *The National.* https://www.thenational.ae/lifestyle/i-hope-you-die-influencer-dina-torkia-shares-shocking-amount-of-abuse-she-s-received-since-taking-hijab-off-1.809869

Rodulfo, K. (2017, April 19). Why over 150 million watch these hijabi beauty influencers. *Elle.com.* https://www.elle.com/beauty/a44241/hijabi-beauty-influencers/

Said, E. W. (1978). *Orientalism.* New York: Pantheon Books.

Saleh, A. [Adam Saleh Vlogs]. (2018, December 9). *Why dina tokio took her hijab off* [Video File].

Sanghani, R. (2016, February 18). How the hijab went high-fashion and divided muslim women. *The Telegraph.* https://www.telegraph.co.uk/women/life/how-the-hijab-went-high-fashion-and-divided-muslim-women/

Sarkar, M. (2019, April 4). It's time we stop ignoring modest fashion influencers. *Forbes.com.* https://www.forbes.com/sites/meghnasarkar/2019/04/04/its-time-we-stop-ignoring-modest-fashion-influencers/#c802b955da11

Srouji, M. (2018, October 30). A case of sexism and the responsibility of influencers: This is why Dina Tokio and her hijab are at the center of debate. *Mvslim.Com.* https://mvslim.com/a-case-of-sexism-and-the-responsibility-of-influencers-this-is-why-dina-tokio-and-her-hijab-are-at-the-center-of-debate/

Torkia, D. (2018). *Modestly.* London: Ebury Press.

Tokio, D. [Dina Tokio]. (2019, January 1). *The bad, the worse and the ugly* [Video File]. https://www.youtube.com/watch?v=i3kIJd-_yiY

Chapter 10

Connecting via Social Media for Weight Loss

An Exploration of Social Media Influencers in a Weight-Loss Community

Carrie S. Trimble and Nancy J. Curtin

Americans spend so much time, eleven or more hours daily, according to Hutchinson (2019a), engaged with digital media, it is a wonder that they can spend time doing anything else. Part of that engagement is an ever-increasing amount of time on social media. In 2019, Americans spent almost an hour or more daily on social media than they did in 2012 (Hutchinson, 2019b). That time likely includes exposure to social media influencers (SMIs), a segment of social media users worth more than $6.5 billion by the end of 2019 (Min, 2019).

With almost half of a day spent with media and over two hours spent on social media, digital and social media seem likely sources of health and medical information. In fact, when looking for information on health or medical issues, 80 percent of Americans will search the Internet in addition to asking a health professional or a family member or friend (Fox, 2014; Weaver, 2019). However, the use of social media for seeking health information is different. According to previous research, the general public claims that social media is not a typical source for their health and wellness information (Fox, 2014; Weaver, 2019). More specifically, while 44 percent of Americans search in particular for diet and nutrition information, they claim to not search for this information on typical social media platforms like Facebook or Instagram.

This leads to a number of questions, especially when thinking about weight loss as a health concern. Is the same true for those interested in weight loss? Does the general public not use social media for weight-loss information and/or their weight-loss journeys? More specifically, do the findings for the general public and general social media platforms hold true in weight-loss-specific social media platforms like WW (formerly Weight Watchers) Connect, which is limited to members of WW and can only be accessed through the WW app? Or do WW members turn to influencers on WW Connect while they avoid those on other social media platforms? In short, what is social media's role in people's weight-loss journeys?

Technology- and Internet-based weight-loss programs can provide social support that facilitates weight-loss efforts (Bradford et al., 2017; Hwang et al., 2010; Khaylis et al., 2010), which might suggest that these online programs are a good source to search for information. In fact, some participants prefer online or Internet-based programs over traditional, face-to-face programs because they provide anonymity, accessibility, and less judgmental comments (Ballantine & Stephenson, 2011; Bradford et al., 2017). General social media platforms like Facebook can be a vehicle for providing emotional and informational support for a weight-loss community through a program-specific Facebook page (Ballantine & Stephenson, 2011). Weight-loss-specific online communities like SparkPeople also provide emotional and informational support as well as a sense of shared experiences (Hwang et al., 2010).

With this dichotomy in mind—consumers say they don't use social media for health-related search, but weight-loss communities have successfully used social media as a means for sharing information — we designed a WW-specific study to identify the role social media apps (in this case WW Connect), play in users' weight-loss journeys. In exploring the role of WW Connect, this research focused on SMIs within the app. More specifically, this exploratory study investigated the following: (1) the function of WW Connect for WW members' social support; (2) the development of parasocial relationships with SMIs through the WW Connect app; and (3) characteristics of SMIs' credibility within the WW connect app. In short, this exploratory study analyzed the degree and efficacy that WW members on the WW Connect platform serve as social media influencers in people's weight-loss journeys.

LITERATURE REVIEW

Role of Social Support in Weight Loss

Social support improves weight-related health conditions, including weight loss and weight maintenance (Wing & Jeffery, 1999). Participants on a weight-loss journey who had social support in a face-to-face setting tended to lose more weight and keep that weight off longer than those who participated in a program alone (Wing & Jeffery, 1999). Specifically, participants who were recruited with friends tended to lose 6.5 more pounds than those recruited alone. A higher percentage of participants who were recruited with friends and encouraged to provide social support for each other (66%) maintained their weight loss compared to those who were recruited alone (24%) (Wing & Jeffery, 1999).

The concept of social support encompasses interpersonal exchanges that include elements of assistance such as emotion, information, or judgment (House, 1981). These exchanges can result in positive affective responses such as feelings of love, motivation, acceptance, esteem, value, care (Cobb, 1976; Wills, 1985) as well as improved health conditions (Barefoot et al., 2005; Rosengren et al., 2004; Vogt et al., 1992).

Successful technology-based weight-loss programs typically include the following: feedback and communication from counselors or experts, a structured program with potential for tailoring, self-monitoring, and social support (Khaylis et al., 2010). The sense of social support can be found by both observing online discussions and posting in online discussions. In online weight-loss networks and discussions, social support is characterized as emotional, informational, or judgmental (House, 1981). Emotional support is often felt through a sense of acceptance and caring by fellow members. It can also be manifested as encouraging or motivating comments (Hwang et al., 2010). Informational support in this setting includes helping participants understand what foods to eat and which activities to pursue. In addition to the emotional and informational support, shared experiences also characterize a theme in social support (Hwang et al., 2010).

Another critical element of social support is receiving the appropriate amount and type of support (Yan, 2017). Under-provision (less support than necessary) or over-provision (too much support) can impact program participants negatively. Additionally, some participants may feel more comfortable receiving support than offering support. Both receiving and providing social support offers benefits to recipients (Shumaker & Brownell, 1984; Yan, 2017). Social support providers may prefer sharing as a style of communication (Ballantine & Stephenson, 2011), may feel better about themselves for offering aid (Verhijden et al., 2005), may develop better coping strategies for themselves, and may develop relationships they can depend on in future situations when they may need assistance (Stewart, 1993). Providing support is also a means of publicly declaring a commitment to a program or weight-loss effort. Those that receive support often highlight the informational aspect of the support they need (Ballantine & Stephenson, 2011), including recipe and activity ideas as well as the emotional support of companionship, inspiration, and a means of publicly committing to a program.

As previously stated, it is important that the social support be the amount and type that participants need. SMIs may be considered active supporters—as defined by Ballantine and Stephenson (2011)—who typically report that their sharing provides both informational and emotional support. This would likely come through the engagement (comments and likes) with a post. Active supporters, like SMIs, may still feel the strain of continually helping others (Yan, 2017). The imbalance of providing more support than receiving, which could take place if posts have little engagement, can lead to feelings of exploitation and resentment (Newsom, 1999; Rook, 1987).

Additionally, passive recipients (Ballantine & Stephenson, 2011), who prefer to browse and read posts instead of initiating their own, also need to receive the correct amount of support. When passive recipients are exposed to over-provision, they can feel indebted (Greenberg, 1980) or the overabundance of support may make recipients doubt their own ability to manage a weight-loss program (Nahum-Shani et al., 2011). According to Ballantine and Stephenson (2001), passive recipients "received a high level of informational and emotional support" by being passive members of a social media weight-loss network (p. 334). In order to explore the role of social media apps (in this case WW Connect) specific to the weight-loss context, we pose the following research question:

RQ 1: How do WW members use WW Connect for social support?

Parasocial Interactions and Relationships

Different from participating with friends, online social support typically is provided by participants who have weak social ties with each other (Wright et al., 2010). The weak social ties work even for participants who prefer a more passive approach to communicating in an online or technology-based program. Both passive and active communicators report that the online groups provide informational support as well as emotional support (Ballantine & Stephenson, 2011). Because the effectiveness of online and technology-based weight-loss programs seems to work through weak social ties, it is worthwhile to consider the influence of parasocial interactions. Ballantine and Martin (2005) assert that passive support is similar to the idea of parasocial interaction and parasocial relationships.

Parasocial interaction was originally conceptualized by Horton and Wohl (1956). Rubin et al. (1985) evolved and operationalized the *parasocial interaction* definition as involvement between the media user and the media they consume that results in taking advice from a media personality, wishing to meet, or hoping to be friends with media performers. While *parasocial interaction* has been defined and tested through televised new programs and in the fictional world of television shows, the heart of the theory is that media viewers become emotionally attached to media personalities over time as exposure to a particular personality increases (Russell & Stern, 2006). The individual interactions that happen over long-term exposure lead to a parasocial relationship, and, consequently, the terms *parasocial interaction* and *parasocial relationship* are often used interchangeably (Dibble et al., 2016). For weight-loss programs, repeated interactions with anonymous users on weight-loss apps can be considered parasocial interactions, and subsequently as those relationships develop, they should have implications for online communities and SMIs (Ballantine & Martin, 2005). The idea is that long-term exposure can lead to feelings of intimacy with a media personality and vicarious participation in the lives of the personality (Maccoby & Wilson, 1957) that are not limited to fictitious characters and plots.

Parasocial Relationships and SMIs

While the concepts of parasocial interactions and parasocial relationship were developed in light of television viewers' emotional responses to media characters, the literature has started to address how the same type of relationships could develop on social networking sites and with SMIs. Twitter can make parasocial relationships seem more authentic (Stever & Lawson, 2013), and those parasocial relationships can satisfy a need to belong to a group (Iannone et al., 2018). While many SMIs today are famous based solely on their social media presence and following, celebrities who became famous before the advent of social media were some of the first SMIs (Leadem, 2017).

Celebrities' use of Twitter is of particular focus for research on parasocial relationship development through social media interaction because of the relative ease of following an account without ever having interpersonal interaction with a celebrity or SMI (Stever & Lawson, 2013); the same can be said for Instagram or YouTube. With Facebook, however, the necessity of getting approval to "friend" someone or, even possibly, join a fan group, means that Facebook connections are primarily those a person has had at least minimal interpersonal interactions with (Cohen, 2011). Therefore, researchers have often focused on Twitter, Instagram, and YouTube to study the possibility of parasocial relationships developing through the weak social ties of celebrity and SMI accounts. Celebrities and other SMIs find that social media brings them "closer to fans than we've ever really been before" (Hammer, 2009, p. 8).

Perhaps one of the most successful SMIs on multiple social networking sites, Lady Gaga (with follower counts as high as 57 million on Facebook, 37 million on Twitter, and 1.2 billion views on YouTube), used her influence to create her own social media platform for her fans, LittleMonsters.com (Click et al., 2013). The appeal of joining the invitation-only LittleMonsters.com speaks directly to fans' parasocial relationships with Lady Gaga where they refer to Gaga as the "Mother Monster," as a friend, and as a mentor. This relationship contains both emotional and behavioral elements such as collection, fantasizing, and mirroring Lady Gaga's pro-social opinions and values.

For SMIs in the health and weight-loss arena, research suggests that SMIs also act as opinion leaders (Stehr et al., 2015). SMIs as parasocial opinion leaders can direct and restrict discussion topics as well as influence the opinions of their followers by limiting the flow of information online. While this can be of concern if the SMIs post about topics in which they have no expertise, research has found that parasocial relationships with weight-loss vloggers can improve compliance with weight-loss programs (Sakir et al., 2019). Specifically, Sakir et al. found a direct and positive relationship between perceptions of SMI attractiveness and the development of a parasocial relationship with an SMI, as well as a direct and positive relationship between parasocial relationships and compliance with weight-loss advice.

The development of a parasocial relationship with members of an online community provides an explanation for how weak social ties online still feel like social support in weight-loss programs. Parasocial attachments or relationships are often indicated by media viewers who report feeling like they are a member of a group and that the emotions of the media personality affect the emotions of the viewer (Dibble et al., 2016). If the findings of Dibble et al. (2016) can be applied to an online environment and SMIs, it seems likely that participants in a weight-loss program who identify with an SMI will also report that the emotions and behaviors of SMIs in the weight-loss sphere will affect the emotions and behaviors of the participants.

One of the critical elements of social support for successful use of online weight-loss programs is a stated public commitment to a goal (Bradford et al., 2017). While SMIs, like food bloggers and celebrities with Instagram accounts, frequently post about diet (9% of posts) and exercise (8% of posts) (Muralidhara & Paul, 2018), as of yet there is no evidence that these posts constitute sufficient public commitment for weight-loss success, and some suggest that these posts that were meant as inspiration can actually have the opposite effect (Arnold, 2018). Therefore, it is unclear if members of a weight-loss program like WW can receive the social support and structure from SMIs that Khaylis et al. (2010) found was necessary for successful technology-based weight-loss programs. However, if WW members have developed a parasocial relationship with SMIs on WW Connect, the impact of influencer posts should be similar to face-to-face social support that members might receive. After all, media viewers feel like they know a media personality, so responses to posts are not the responses of strangers. As such, the following research question is posed:

RQ 2a: Do WW members develop parasocial relationships with SMIs?

The "actively vested" term derives from Russell and Stern (2006) where the authors point out that viewers might develop an attitude toward a fictional character after a single exposure but that any vicarious or emotional response to the characters develops over long-term viewing. Applying that logic to SMIs, the presumption is that followers might form an attitude toward an SMI after a single post, but that on social networking sites, long-term exposure would be necessary for followers to become emotionally involved with SMIs or for SMI behavior to influence the behavior of their followers. Therefore, the following research question is posed:

RQ 2b: Through those parasocial relationships, do WW members become "actively vested" in SMIs as evidenced by emotional involvement and behavioral response?

Additionally, other research has suggested that exposure to a high frequency of social media posts from SMIs can lead to feelings of "ambient intimacy" (Lin et al., 2016) or a sense of closeness with strangers. While high frequency of exposure can come from heavy consumption of a single social media. The high frequency of exposure it could also come from media migration when followers are exposed to SMIs on more than one social networking site or on a social site and a television program (Jahng, 2019). In general, SMIs have a high level of media representation (Stehr et al., 2015). The existence of media migration and the importance of long-term exposure for the development of parasocial attachment lead to the following research question:

RQ 2c: Does the development of parasocial relationships rely on cross-platform exposure?

Credibility

In an era of so many weight-loss programs and a plethora of weight-loss information, credibility is critical. According to Machackova and Smahel (2018), "The varying quality of information available on the internet has increased the need for the assessment of the trustworthiness of online information" (p. 1534).

Source credibility is an important factor in who becomes an SMI (Lou & Yuan, 2019). Over the years, many researchers have explored and analyzed what comprises source credibility (Hovland et al., 1953; McGuire, 1985; Ohanian, 1990). Based on previous research conclusions about source credibility, Ohanian (1990) constructed a scale to measure celebrity endorser's source credibility using three constructs: trustworthiness, expertise, and attractiveness. Later research added a fourth construct of source credibility, similarity (Munnukka et al., 2016).

As Lou and Yuan (2019) note, "In the context of social media, several studies have tested the impact of source credibility on consumers and demonstrated its persuasiveness across different scenarios (e.g., Djafarova & Rushworth, 2017; Lopez & Sicilia, 2014; McLaughlin, 2016)" (p. 61). Based on these studies, Lou and Yuan (2019) then explored the role of influencers' source credibility on followers' trust. They found, "Influencers' trustworthiness, attractiveness, and similarity all positively affected followers' trust in influencers' branded content" (Lou & Yuan, 2019, p. 65), whereas expertise did not play a role in followers' trust.

None of these studies looked at online weight-loss communities and social media influencers. This study addresses the role of SMIs' credibility in the context of a weight-loss community. More specifically, we pose the following research question:

RQ 3: What factors contribute to SMI credibility in the weight-loss community?

METHOD

Researchers gathered data via an online survey posted on SurveyMonkey for WW members to complete anonymously. Recruitment for participants occurred through researchers' posts on WW Connect, and the distribution of postcards, including the survey link at WW meetings. The authors' Institutional Review Board approved the survey. Before beginning the survey, participants read the informed consent page and then indicated if they voluntarily consented to completing the survey. All respondents had to indicate that they were eighteen years or older to participate. Survey completion took about five minutes.

Survey Development

Fourteen questions comprised the survey. All questions were closed-ended questions, and respondents were free to answer any or all questions. Respondents indicated the following: (1) demographic information (age, gender identity, and level of education); (2) type of WW membership (workshop only, online only, or both); (3) degree and type activity on WW Connect (frequency and function); (4) parasocial interaction with other WW members; and (5) feelings about favorite WW members' posts. The survey included statements with five-point Likert scales.

WW Connect Activity Measures

In terms of the degree and type of activity on WW Connect, respondents indicated (1) how often they use WW Connect: (a) more than once/day; (b) once/day; (c) once or twice/week; (d) once/month or less; and (e) never and (2) how they primarily use WW Connect: (a) to create content; (b) to find a group of similar people; (c) to get new ideas like recipes or activities; (d) to maintain honesty about progress; (e) commitment to the WW plan; and (f) to use WW Connect to check others' posts for motivation and/or to lurk on WW Connect. Respondents could indicate multiple answers.

To gather information about interaction with other WW members, respondents were asked if they used other social media platforms to follow WW Connect members as well as typical posting behavior to other WW members' posts; more specifically, respondents were asked whether they asked questions, gathered information, and/or posted encouraging comments.

Parasocial Interaction

To explore the nature of the parasocial interactions, a portion of the survey questions was derived from parasocial interaction and parasocial relationship scales. It must be noted that Dibble et al. (2016) argue that these two concepts are not interchangeable but rather distinct. Furthermore, Dibble et al. (2016) argue that previous scales used often (e.g., Rubin et al., 1985) lacked content validity with Horton and Wohl's (1956) original conceptual definition of *parasocial interaction*. Thus, Dibble et al. (2016) constructed and tested new scales, notably the Experience of Parasocial Interaction (Hartman & Goldhoorn, 2011), and some of the items for this survey were adapted from that scale. In general, survey statements focused on cognitive, affective, and behavioral responses to WW Connect posts.

Parasocial relationship survey items focused on respondents' feelings (affective) toward SMIs as well as possible behavioral responses to those WW members who they followed most closely on WW Connect. Survey statements also assessed if SMIs' behavior affected respondents cognitively, affectively, and/or behaviorally. More specifically, respondents were asked: (1) Feelings for SMIs who struggle and if/how that affects respondents' behaviors (If the WW members struggle to follow the WW plan, I see that as permission to make less healthy choices for myself) and (2) Feelings for SMIs who succeed and if/how that affects respondents' behaviors (If the WW members succeed in following the WW plan, I feel good for them). A complete list of items is found in table 10.2.

SMI Credibility

To assess SMI credibility, the survey included statements focused on three areas of SMI credibility: expertise, trustworthiness, and attractiveness. These three main areas, which comprise SMI credibility, were adapted from Newell and Goldsmith (2001) and Ohanian (1990). A complete list of items is available in table 10.3.

Sample Information

Thirty-four surveys were completed in their entirety. Some questions allowed for respondents to choose more than one answer. Respondents indicated the frequency in which they use WW Connect, and the majority (70.6%) indicated they use WW Connect at least once a day. Of the daily users, 55.9 percent use WW Connect more than once per day. Of the thirty-four responses, thirty-two (94%) respondents were female. Two respondents did not indicate their sex. The mean age of respondents was 52.3 years old and the age range was 27–71 years old. Thirty-two respondents indicated their education level and the majority of respondents were college graduates (43.8%). The next highest segment of education was graduate school with 31 percent of respondents having completed some amount of graduate school. High school came in third with 15.6 percent respondents. The smallest percentage of respondents, 9.4 percent indicated some college for their education level.

This sample is representative of the typical WW membership which is 85–90 percent female (Raphael, 2017; MRI-Simmons, 2018) and has a median age of thirty-eight (Raphael, 2017) while 43 percent of WW members are fifty-five or older (MRI-Simmons, 2018). The respondents' reported education is similar to that of WW membership as well (Numerator, 2020). Additionally, this sample seems to fit the trend in social media use for the demographic of a typical WW member. Social media platform usage varies by demographics, and that it can be inferred from trade reports that women over fifty who are WW members are more apt to use WW Connect than they are to use any other social media platform. For example, 54 percent of Facebook users are women and 22 percent are fifty-five years or older (Chen, 2020). On Instagram, 50 percent are women and only 5 percent are fifty-five years or older (Tran, 2020). Contrast those percentages with the fact that 85–90 percent of WW members are women (Raphael, 2017; MRI-Simmons, 2018) and 43 percent of WW members are fifty-five or older (MRI-Simmons, 2018). In this research, 100 percent of respondents were female, and the mean age was fifty-two. Furthermore as noted above, a majority of the survey respondents

(70.6%) use WW Connect at least once a day are active WW Connect users. So, while this sample is not generalizable to all social media users or even heavy social media users, it is appropriate for WW Connect users.

RESULTS

WW Connect Function

RQ1 asked how WW members use WW Connect for social support. Respondents could indicate more than one response (any or all answers that apply) and provide a comment if they chose the *other* category. Findings indicated the two most popular social support uses of WW Connect app are for motivation and new ideas for recipes and activities. Less than a quarter of respondents stated they used WW Connect as a means of publicly committing to the WW program. (See table 10.1 for a full list of reported social support uses.)

Forming Parasocial Attachments and Their Impact

To investigate the relationship between parasocial interactions and SMIs for weight-loss efforts, two related research questions were posed: (RQ2a) Do WW members develop parasocial relationships with SMIs? and (RQ2b) through those parasocial relationships, do WW members become "actively vested" in SMIs as evidenced by emotional involvement and behavioral response? To determine if parasocial attachment existed, the responses from the fifteen-item parasocial scale were measured, and a mean and standard deviation were calculated for individual items as well as the scale as a whole. table 10.2 lists all the parasocial items as well as participant responses; items related to emotional involvement, behavioral responses, and social support are also highlighted on table 10.2.

Overall, respondents reported a trend toward parasocial relationships ($M = 3.46$; $SD = 1.16$). Related to emotions, participants did report that their

Table 10.1 Functions of WW Connect Usage

WW Connect Functions	n	% of respondents
Motivation	22	64.7%
New recipes & activities	15	44.1%
Find people like me	11	32.4%
Keep commitment	8	23.5%
Lurk	7	20.6%
Create content & share	5	14.7%

Table 10.2   Responses to Parasocial Scale Items

Parasocial Scale Items	Mean	SD
Have sense of SMI personality	3.59	.86
SMIs are like me	3.82	.76
Closely follow SMIs posts	3.06	1.18
SMIs understand what I want to know	3.74	.86
Want to meet SMIs	2.88	.95
I miss SMIs when they don't post[EI]	2.97	1.40
SMIs posts motivate me[SS]	4.27	.57
SMIs posts help to follow WW[SS]	4.12	.78
SMIs posts valuable or helpful	4.09	.63
I feel bad when SMIs struggle. [EI]	3.91	.91
I feel good when SMIs succeed[EI]	4.47	.56
SMIs struggles gives me permission to be less healthy [BR]	1.76	.65
SMIs success motivates me to follow WW [BR]	3.82	.80
SMIs struggles increase my less healthy behavior [BR]	1.91	.79
SMIs success increase my healthy behavior[BR]	3.59	.95
Scale (all items)	3.46	1.16

SS = social support; BR = behavioral response; EI = emotional involvement

emotions were affected by the success and struggles of SMIs (success $M = 4.47$, $SD = .56$; struggle $M = 3.91$, $SD = .91$). However, they did not report emotional attachment as they indicated that they did not miss SMIs when they did not post to WW Connect ($M = 2.97$, $SD = 1.40$). As to social support, participants found SMIs motivational (motivate me $M = 4.27$, $SD = .57$) and helpful (help me follow WW $M = 4.12$, $SD = .78$).

Responses were mixed as to whether the success and struggles of SMIs had an impact on WW member behavior. Participants found that SMI success motivated them to follow WW ($M = 3.82$, $SD = .80$), and increased members' healthy behavior ($M = 3.59$, $SD = .96$). However, when SMIs reported struggling with the plan, it did not constitute permission to be less healthy ($M = 1.76$, $SD = .65$) or decrease members' healthy behavior ($M = 1.91$, $SD = .79$).

The parasocial relationships participants formed with SMIs were not dependent on cross-platform exposure (RQ2c). Half of the participants reported that they only interacted with SMIs on WW Connect while less than 30 percent said they interacted with WW SMIs on one additional social networking site like Facebook or Instagram in addition to WW Connect. Therefore, the trend toward parasocial relationships developed mostly in the absence of cross-platform exposure. Therefore, it seems likely that the necessary frequency or long-term exposure required for a parasocial relationship to form can be achieved on a single social networking site like WW Connect.

Credibility

To investigate the characteristics of SMI credibility (RQ3), respondents indicated the degree of SMI credibility according to nine statements using a five-point Likert scale. As stated earlier, statements centered on three areas of credibility: expertise, trustworthiness, and attractiveness. The mean and standard deviation were calculated for individual items as well as the scale as a whole are reported on table 10.3. All of the credibility statements' mean scores indicate that, in general, they neither agree nor disagree with the statements ($M = 3.28$; $SD = .79$).

One aspect of trustworthiness showed the strongest role in SMI credibility. For trustworthiness, statements gauged the level of agreement about SMIs' honesty, truthfulness, and trustworthiness dependability. Of all the credibility statements, SMIs' honesty scored the highest; respondents indicated a higher or stronger level of agreement in their belief that SMIs are honest ($M = 3.75$; $SD = .62$). Contrastingly and interestingly, respondents were more indifferent to the ideas that SMIs are truthful ($M = 3.24$; $SD = .78$) and trustworthy ($M = 3.38$; $SD = .95$).

Attractiveness played the smallest or weakest role for SMI credibility. More specifically, of all the credibility scale items, the reaction to the statement, "SMIs are attractive," respondents were indifferent ($M = 3.09$; $SD = .64$). One may even argue that because of the very low mean, respondents are trending toward disagreement about SMIs' attractiveness. Furthermore, respondents indicated a weaker degree of neutrality or indifference in their beliefs about SMIs' appealing appearance ($M = 3.13$; $SD = .66$) or appearing fit ($M = 3.13$; $SD = .61$).

For expertise, respondents indicated their level of agreement about SMIs having experience, skill, and knowledge expertise. Respondents indicated indifference in their beliefs about SMIs' expertise ($M = 3.24$; $SD = .83$), skill ($M = 3.23$; $SD = .89$), and experience ($M = 3.35$; $SD = .84$).

Table 10.3   Responses to Credibility Scale Items

Credibility Scale Items	Mean	S.D.
SMIs have great amount of experience	3.35	.836
SMIs are skilled	3.23	.890
SMIs have expertise	3.24	.830
I trust SMIs	3.38	.954
SMIs are truthful	3.24	.781
SMIs are honest	3.75	.622
SMIs are attractive	3.09	.641
SMIs have appealing appearance	3.13	.660
SMIs appear fit	3.13	.609
Scale (all items)	3.28	.789

DISCUSSION

Research consistently affirms the importance of public commitment in weight-loss programs (Bradford et al., 2017). Surprisingly, in this research less than 24 percent indicated that they use WW Connect to "keep . . . commitment to the WW plan." Thus, it seems that respondents do not perceive WW Connect's function to be about public commitment, but rather to serve other social support functions such as finding new recipes and new ideas for exercise. While past research has found that publicly declaring a commitment to a weight-loss program is important to successful weight-loss journeys (Hwang et al., 2010), this study did not differentiate between WW members who were succeeding and those that were merely beginning or possibly struggling. Therefore, it is difficult to deduce if the differences between past findings and this study related to publicly sharing the commitment were a function of the sample, cultural norms of the programs, or an effect of SMIs.

SMIs, Parasocial Interaction, and Weight-Loss Communities

Overall, participant responses to measures of parasocial relationships were moderate ($M = 3.46$, $SD = 1.16$), but there were some sharply mixed responses to these items. The concept of parasocial attachment or parasocial relationship was introduced as a means to explain how weak social ties could serve in online weight-loss programs just as primary, strong ties serve in face-to-face weight-loss efforts. The intent was to measure if any evidence of parasocial relationships could be found and, if found, to determine if parasocial relationships were seen as providing social support as well as the right amount of social support for an online weight-loss program to be effective.

Participants shared several indicators that parasocial relationships develop between WW members and SMIs and provide social support. They reported that their emotions were engaged, in a positive way, and that they were repeatedly motivated by posts from SMIs. WW members also seemed to find value in SMIs posts as they indicated those posts were most helpful and assisted them in following the program. These responses fit with the previous descriptions of social support, including both emotional and informational support. However, participants did not report that they viewed SMI behavior as permission to deviate from the program, nor was witnessing SMIs struggling with the program seen as an excuse for members to make less healthy choices themselves. Finally, WW members did not seem to confuse these parasocial relationships with primary social or face-to-face relationships as they do not report a need to meet SMIs. The willingness to use SMIs for motivation and information without a need for further interaction also suggests that SMIs can provide the correct amount and type of social support for an online weight-loss program to be effective.

Following SMIs on other social media in addition to WW Connect did not affect the degree of parasocial attachment. It seems that the value of WW Connect serves a unique, specific purpose in connecting WW members parasocially. Furthermore, this may imply that WW members are committed and happy with the functionality of WW Connect. This corresponds with consumer claims that they do not turn to general-purpose social media like Facebook or Instagram for advice on health and wellness and suggest that weight-loss-specific platforms such as WW Connect and SparkPeople serve a distinct purpose not replicated by other social media platforms.

Credibility

In short, for WW Connect users, SMI credibility did not play an influential or major role. In fact, WW Connect users are rather indifferent to influencers' credibility. Even though people are using the app for motivation, they do not seem to rely on influencers for that motivation, which is an interesting finding, especially when related to the previous discussion on social support. More specifically, of the three facets of credibility (expertise, trustworthiness, and attractiveness), this study affirmed the influential role of trustworthiness, specifically a stronger tendency of agreement about the role of honesty. However, the study indicated some conflicting information (i.e., more neutrality) about the role of truthfulness and trustworthiness. This inconsistency in ratings of SMIs trustworthiness definitely is puzzling. Perhaps, respondents trust SMIs for certain things, like recipes, but are distrusting of SMIs revealing the complete picture of their weight-loss journeys?

Attractiveness played the smallest role in SMI credibility in this weight-loss community. This finding is consistent with previous research (Breves et al., 2019), who examined the fit between influencers and brand and concluded that influencers' physical attractiveness did not matter as much as perceived trustworthiness and expertise when examining the fit between influencer and brand. However, our finding and Breves et al.'s finding contrast with Lou and Yuan (2019), who discovered that influencers' attractiveness did play a role in followers' trust in the influencers' branded content. It must be noted though that neither Breves et al. (2019) nor Lou and Yuan (2019) researched the weight-loss community specifically.

Finally, based on respondents' neutrality toward expertise, this aspect of credibility did not play a prominent role in how respondents regarded SMIs. This finding is consistent with Lou and Yuan (2019), who found that expertise did not play a role in followers' trust of SMIs. They speculate, "This may be because influencers, by default, have a status of expertise among their followers, yet such expertise does not necessarily promise followers' trust in their sponsored content" (Lou & Yuan, 2019, p. 68).

Limitations and Future Research

The biggest limitation to this research is the small sample size. Increasing the sample size would provide a more complete picture of the role WW Connect serves among various types of users, demographically (age, gender, education level) and categorically (influencer vs. passive recipient vs. lurker). More people completing surveys would depict a more comprehensive view of the function of social media posts as to how that may relate to parasocial interactions in the weight-loss environment.

Another limitation, and thus a suggestion for future research, was the small amount of choices for many of the questions. Granted, the authors did not want to have a long survey, and in some instances an "other" category was offered. However, more options could have been offered since the average completion time of the survey was only about 3.5 minutes. For example, follow-up questions when participant responses seem contradictory would be useful as in the case of the credibility scale items where respondents said SMIs were honest but not necessarily truthful. Similarly, it would be helpful to compare answers of respondents' opinions of SMIs in general to opinions of specific SMIs. This study only focused on general opinions of SMIs.

Suggestions for future research could include analyzing the role of SMI credibility in terms of expertise, trustworthiness, and attractiveness (Newell & Goldsmith, 2001; Ohanian, 1990) and how that relates to parasocial interactions and relationships. For example, future research could identify specific SMIs based on the number of followers to explore the nature of the influencer credibility.

Finally, future research could qualitatively explore what characterizes SMIs' credibility in the weight-loss context. More specifically, because of the contrasting findings in this study and previous research (Breves et al., 2019; Lou & Yuan, 2019), more research is needed focusing on the role of influencers' attractiveness in the weight-loss community. Additionally, the current study's findings indicated mixed results about the role of influencers' trustworthiness. Future research could explore this role in the weight-loss community.

Furthermore, research could investigate if and how SMI credibility contributes to parasocial relationships and the efficacy of those parasocial relationships in the weight-loss world. Another suggestion for future research would be to compare self-identified SMIs with WW ambassadors to discern the nature (characteristics) and efficacy of these influencers. If and how do self-identified influencers' posts vary with WW Ambassadors' posts? What characterizes the interactions? And, do these interactions lead to parasocial attachments?

CONCLUSION

This exploratory study examined the function of a specific social media app in a weight-loss community, WW Connect for WW members. In addition to identifying the function of WW Connect for WW members, the study also measured the role of credibility and parasocial relationships with SMIs. These findings may imply that WW members are committed and happy with the functionality of WW Connect. WW members reported evidence of parasocial relationships as they believed SMIs provided positive social support and motivation. Finally, negative behavior by an SMI did not negatively affect the follower. Thus, while parasocial relationships with SMIs can serve important, positive functions, it is reassuring that these relationships with SMIs are not negatively affecting their followers if the SMIs exhibit negative behavior. Simply put, WW members' commitment to their weight-loss journeys is only helped, not hindered, by SMIs on WW Connect. This study reaffirms the importance, to a degree, of connecting people via the WW Connect app.

Similar to Ballantine and Stephenson's (2011) assertions, this study also adds to the research that examines the reliance of online information for health information and weight-control programs as well as the role of social support in online communities. Some online content is more effective than others in the weight-loss and maintenance world. This study contributes to discovering what constitutes effective content and what respondents look for in the online community as they navigate their weight-loss/maintenance journeys.

REFERENCES

Arnold, A. (2018, November 26). Fitspiration on social media: Is it helping or hurting your health goals? *Forbes*. https://www.forbes.com/sites/andrewarnold/2018/11/26/fitspiration-on-social-media-is-it-helping-or-hurting-your-health-goals/#2fe6acb847f0

Ballantine, P. W., & Martin, B. A. S. (2005). Forming parasocial relationships in online communities. *Advances in Consumer Research, 32*, 197–202.

Ballantine, P. W., & Stephenson, R. J. (2011). Help me, I'm fat! Social support in online weight loss networks. *Journal of Consumer Behaviour, 10*, 332–337.

Bandura, A. (1971). *Social learning theory.* Stanford University, 1971. http://www
.esludwig.com/uploads/2/6/1/0/26105457/bandura_sociallearningtheory.pdf

Bradford, T. W., Grier, S. A., & Henderson, G. R. (2017). Weight loss through virtual support communities: A role for identity-based motivation in public commitment. *Journal of Interactive Marketing, 4,* 9–23.

Breves, P. L., Liebers, N., Abt, M., & Kunze, A. (2019). The perceived fit between Instagram influencers and the endorsed brand: How influencer-brand fit affects source credibility and persuasiveness effectiveness. *Journal of Advertising Research, 59*(4), 440–454.

Chen, J. (2020, January 14). Social media demographics to inform your brand's strategy in 2020. https://sproutsocial.com/insights/new-social-media-demograph ics/#Facebook

Click, M., Lee, H., Holladay, H. W. (2013). Making Monsters: Lady Gaga, Fan Identification, and Social Media. *Popular Music and Society, 36*(3), 360–379.

Cobb, S. (1976). Social support as a moderator of life stress. *Psychosomatic Medicine, 38,* 300–314.

Cohen, J. (2011, January 13). You don't know one-fifth of your Facebook friends. *Newsweek.*

Dibble, J. L., Hartmann, T., & Rosaen, S. F. (2016). Parasocial interaction and parasocial relationship: Conceptual clarification and a critical assessment of measures. *Human Communication Research, 42,* 21–44.

Djafarova, E., & Rushworth, C. (2017). Exploring the credibility of online celebrities' Instagram profiles in influencing the purchase decisions of young female users. *Computers in Human Behavior, 68,* 1–7.

Fox, S. (2014, January 15). The social life of health information. *Pew Research Center.* http://www.nbcnews.com/id/3077086/t/more-people-search-health-onl ine/#.Xci6LqjYrnE

Greenberg, M. (1980). A theory of indebtedness. In K. Gergen (Ed.), *Social Exchange: Advances in Theory and Research* (pp. 3–20). Boston, MA: Springer.

Hammer, M. C. (2009). It's Twitter time. *MediaWeek, 19*(28), 8.

House, J. S. (1981). *Work stress and social support.* Addison-Wesley.

Hovland, C. I., Janis, I. K., & Kelley, H. H. (1953). *Communication and persuasion.* New Haven, CT: Yale University Press.

Hutchinson, A. (2019a, January 16). How much time do people spend on social media in 2019? *Social Media Today.* https://www.socialmediatoday.com/news/how-muc h-time-do-people-spend-on-social-media-in-2019-infographic/560270/

Hutchinson, A. (2019b, July 25) How much time do people spend connected to media in 2019? *Social Media Today.* https://www.socialmediatoday.com/news/how-much -time-do-people-spend-connected-to-media-in-2019-infographic/559480/

Hwang, K. O., Ottenbacher, A. J., Green, A. P., Cannon-Diehl, M. R., Richardson, O., Bernstam, E. V., & Thomas, E. J. (2010). Social support in an Internet weight loss community. *International Journal of Medical Informatics, 79,* 5–13.

Iannone, N. E., McCarty, M. K., Branch, S. E., & Kelly, J. R. (2018). Connecting in the Twitterverse: Using Twitter to satisfy unmet belonging needs. *The Journal of Social Psychology, 158*(4), 491–495.

Jahng, M. R. (2019). Watching the rich and famous: the cultivation effect of reality television shows and the mediating role of parasocial experiences. *Media Practice and Education, 20*(4), 319–333.

Khaylis, A., Yiaslas, T., Bergstrom, J., & Gore-Felton, C. (2010). A review of efficacious technology-based weight-loss interventions: Five key components. *Telemedicine and E-health, 16*(9), 931–938.

Kozinets, R. V. (1999). E-tribalized marketing?: The strategic implications of virtual communities of consumption. *European Management Journal, 17*(3), 252–264.

Lauchlan, S. (2019, May 5). WW looks to digital transformation to add weight to its new operating model. https://diginomica.com/ww-looks-digital-transformation-add-weight-its-new-operating-model

Leadem, R. (2017, August 6). The evolution of influencers, From 1700s to today (Infographic). *Entrepreneur.*

Lin, E., Levordashka, A., & Utz, S. (2016). Ambient intimacy on Twitter. Cyberpsychology: *Journal of Psychosocial Research on CyberSpace, 10*(1), article 6.

López, M., & Sicilia, M. (2014). eWom as a source of influence: The impact of participation in eWOM and perceived source trustworthiness on decision making. *Journal of Interactive Advertising, 14*(2), 86–97.

Lou, C., & Yuan, S. (2019). Influencer marketing: How message value and credibility affect consumer trust of branded content on social media. *Journal of Interactive Advertising, 19*(1), 58–73.

Maccoby, E. E., & Wilson, W. C. (1957). Identification and observational learning from films. *Journal of Abnormal and Social Psychology, 55*(1), 76–87.

Machackova, H., & Smahel, D. (2018). The perceived importance of credibility cues for the assessment of trustworthiness of online information by visitors of health-related websites: The role of individual factors. *Telematics and Informatics, 35*(5), 1534–1541.

McGuire, W. J. (1985). Attitudes and attitude change. In G. Lindzey & E. Aronson (Eds.), *Handbook of social psychology* (vol. 2, pp. 233–346). New York: Random House.

McLaughlin, C. (2016). Source credibility and consumers' responses to marketer involvement in Facebook brand communities; What causes consumers to engage? *Journal of Interactive Advertising, 16*(2), 101–116.

Min, S. (2019, November 8). 86% of young Americans want to become a social media influencer. *CBS News.* https://www.cbsnews.com/news/social-media-inf luencers-86-of-young-americans-want-to-become-one/

MRISimmons. (2018). Weights watchers, wellness, and consumer targeting. Spring 2018 National Consumer Study. https://www.mrisimmons.com/2018/09/28/we ight-watchers-wellness-consumer-targeting/

Munnukka, J., Uusitalo, O., & Toivonen, H. (2016). Credibility of a peer endorser and advertising effectivness. *Journal of Consumer Marketing, 33*(3), 182–192.

Muralidhara, S., & Paul, M. J. (2018). #Healthy selfies: Exploration of health topics on Instagram. *JMIR Public Health and Surveillance, 4*(2), e10150. doi:10.2196/10150

Nahum-Shani, I., Bamberger, P., & Bacharach, B. (2011). Social support and employee well-being: The conditioning effect of perceived patterns of supportive exchange. *Journal of Health and Social Behavior, 52*(1), 123–139.

Newell, S. J., & Goldsmith, R. E. (2001). The development of a scale to measure perceived corporate credibility. *Journal of Business Research, 52*(3), 235–247.

Newsom, J. T. (1999). Another side to caregiving: Negative reactions to begging helped. *Current Directions in Psychological Science, 8*(6), 183–187.

Numerator. (2020). WW (formerly weight watchers) membership data. https://snap-shot.numerator.com/

Ohanian, R. (1990). Construction and validation of a scale to measure celebrity endorsers' perceived expertise, trustworthiness, and attractiveness. *Journal of Advertising, 19*(3), 39–52.

Raphel, R. (2017, December 4). How weight watchers transformed itself into a life-style brand. *Fast Company.* https://www.fastcompany.com/40500280/how-weight-watchers-transformed-itself-into-a-lifestyle-brand

Rook, K. S. (1987). Reciprocity of social-exchange and social satisfaction among older women. *Journal of Personality and Social Psychology, 52*(1), 145–154.

Rubin, A. M., Perse, E. M., & Powell, R. A. (1985). Loneliness, parasocial interaction, and local television news viewing. *Human Communication Research, 12*(2), 155–180.

Russell, C. A., & Stern, B. B. (2006), Consumers, characters and products: A balance model of sitcom product placement effects. *Journal of Advertising, 35*(1), 7–21.

Sakib, M. N., Zolfagharian, M., & Yazdanparast, A. (2019). Does parasocial interaction with weight loss vloggers affect compliance? The role of blogger characteristics, consumer readiness, and health consciousness. *Journal of Retailing and Consumer Services, 52*, 1–11.

Shumaker, S. A., & Brownell, A. (1984). Toward a theory of social support—Closing conceptual gaps. *Journal of Social Issues, 40*(4), 11–36.

Sternthal, B., Phillips, L. W., & Dholakia, R. (1978). The persuasive effect of source credibility: A situational analysis. *Public Opinion Quarterly, 42*(3), 285–314.

Stever, G., & Lawson, K. (2013). Twitter as a way for celebrities to communicate with fans: Implications for the study of parasocial interaction. *North American Journal of Psychology, 15*(2), 339–354.

Stewart, M. J. (1993). *Integrating social support in nursing.* Newberry Park, CA: SAGE Publications.

Tran, T. (2020, February 4). Instagram demographics that matter to social media marketers in 2020. https://blog.hootsuite.com/instagram-demographics/

Verheijden, M. W., Bakx, J. C., Van Weel, C., Koelen, M. A., U Van Staveren, W. A. (2005). Role of social support in lifestyle-focused weight management interventions. *European Journal of Clinical Nutrition, 59*, S179–S186.

Weaver, J. (2019, July 16). More people search for health online. *NBC News.* http://www.nbcnews.com/id/3077086/t/more-people-search-health-online/#.Xci6LqjYrnE

Willis, T. A. (1985). Supportive functions of interpersonal relationships. In S. Cohen & S. L. Syme (Eds.), *Social support and health* (pp. 61–82). Cambridge, MA: Academic Press.

Wing, R. R., & Jeffery, R. W. (1999). Benefits of recruiting participants with friends and increasing social support for weight loss and maintenance. *Journal of Consulting and Clinical Psychology, 67*(1), 132–138.

Wright, K. B., Rains, S., & Banas J. (2010). Weak-tie support network preference and perceived life stress among participants in health-related, computer mediated support groups. *Journal of Computer-Mediated Communication, 15*(4), 606–624.

Yan, L. (2018). Good intentions, bad outcomes: The effects of mismatches between social support and health outcomes in an online weight loss community. *Production and Operations Management, 27*(1), 9–27.

Chapter 11

Influenced by My Lifestyle Net Idols (#Contentcreators)

Exploring the Relationships between Thai Net Idols and Followers

Vimviriya Limkangvanmongkol

In Thailand, the vernacular term "net idol" refers to a group of people who have become famous online (Limkangvanmongkol & Abidin, 2018, p. 96). Shortened from "Internet idol," "net idol" denotes persons with extraordinary qualities worth admiring and adoring (Putnark, 2016). While there is no definitive meaning of net idol, it generally refers to two categories of people. The first group consists of exclusive people who are physically attractive and praised by their followers for their appearance, grooming, fashion, and aspiring lifestyle (Limkangvanmongkol & Abidin, 2018; Phahulo & Boonnak, 2015). The second group consists of those with talents or special abilities in the aspects of music, sports, and comedy (Limkangvanmongkol & Abidin, 2018; Phahulo & Boonnak, 2015). Although the term denotes positive meaning, much of the media and tabloid coverage pertaining to net idols has devoted the first page headlines for scandal, such as debts, drugs, and illegal gambling (Limkangvanmongkol & Abidin, 2018).

At the beginning, net idols were "ordinary" (Turner, 2010) consumers who used and reviewed products via online social space as a hobby. Once they acquired a certain number of followers, they became known as "opinion leaders" (Arndt, 1967; Kozinets et al., 2010), "microcelebrity" (Senft, 2008), "influencers" (Abidin, 2016), or "beauty bloggers" (Limkangvanmongkol, 2018) who have influential power to persuade other consumers to try consumer products, dine at restaurants, or stay at hotels.

Net idols are "skillful in using social media to create an online message using photography in conjunction with writing, design, presentation, and other sets of skills and abilities" (Meyer, 2015, p. 4) to brand their personas. Through collaborations with brands (Koeck & Marshall, 2015; Limkangvanmongkol, 2018; Limkangvanmongkol & Abidin, 2018) in multiple seeding campaigns (Kozinets et al., 2010; Koeck & Marshall, 2015), net idols post numerous advertorials (Abidin, 2016) to multiple popular platforms for Thai consumers, such as YouTube, Facebook, and Instagram. Their credibility is based on their ability to relate to the experiences of average consumers (Abidin, 2016).

This chapter aims to empirically highlight online word-of-mouth marketing (WOMM) within Thai social media platforms by examining the relationship between net idols in the lifestyle sector and their followers. This study draws on WOM theory in the network coproduction model (Kozinets et al., 2010) to examine net idols' relationship with followers by considering blogging/vlogging as a viable online marketing communications channel. In particular, the study takes net idols' blogging/vlogging as a subset of word-of-mouth marketing (WOMM) which is understood as "the intentional influencing of consumer-to-consumer communications by professional marketing techniques" (Kozinets et al., 2010, p. 71). The market messages and meanings are co-produced and exchanged among the members of the consumer network (p. 73).

The social media landscape in Thailand has allowed net idols to become key players in multiple WOMM campaigns. The current population of Thailand is 69.24 million people, and 57 million people use the Internet, of which 55 million people use mobile devices to access the Internet (Asean Up, 2019). In Thailand, there are around 51 million active social media users. The most popular social media platform in 2018 was Facebook (93%) (Asean Up, 2019), making Thailand the country with ninth-largest number of Facebook users (Thaitech, 2017). The second, third, fourth, and fifth most popular social media platforms are YouTube (91%), Line (84%), Facebook Messenger (72%), and Instagram (65%). The top five mobile apps are Line, Facebook, Facebook Messenger, Instagram, and Lazada (Asean Up, 2019). As Thai people are very active on social media, the consumer's journey inevitably involves digital platforms. In particular, influencer marketing has become an effective tool in influencing consumer purchase decisions (Mathew, 2018).

Previous research explored blogging as WOM focused on western blog content (McQuarrie et al., 2013; Zhao & Belk, 2007), the views and experiences of western tech-bloggers in online WOM (Koeck & Marshall, 2015), the rise of beauty bloggers in Thailand (Limkangvanmongkol, 2018), and the emergent microcelebrity genre in Thailand (Limkangvanmongkol & Abidin, 2018). However, this chapter focuses more on the experiences of Thai net idols' followers in online WOMM campaigns, and their views toward net idols' blogging/vlogging, and the relationship between the two parties. Following Kozinets et al. (2010), the core of WOMM is the ability to create perceived credibility among consumers when having WOMM activities. This chapter explores followers' perspective toward net idols whom they perceive as credible.

WORD-OF-MOUTH THEORY

The two-step flow of communication model introduced by Lazarsfeld originally explains the effects of media focusing on the flow of information disseminated through mainstream mass media. Katz and Lazarsfeld (1995) posit that mass media audiences are affected not only by news itself but also by opinion leaders' interpretation of the news. To illustrate, opinion leaders receive the news from mass media, and share it with other people via WOM. The information received from opinion leaders is modified, with opinion leaders' interpretation or ideas added. Some scholars (Robinson, 1976; Weimann, 1982; Burt, 1999) argue that the two-step flow of communication model has some limitations, and further propose the multi-step flow of communication model to explain information flow in different directions and iterations. In this model, opinion leaders not only receive information from mass media directly but also from the audience's reaction to the information. The opinion leaders could better relay the information received to their audience than mass media.

As marketing scholarship has evolved from centering on transactions to relationships among consumers and community building, WOM theory has been developed through the change of society (see figure 11.1). Initially, *the organic interconsumer model* explains the organic communications between one consumer and others without measurement by marketers. Consumers share their WOM as they intend to help other consumers about good or bad products (See Arndt, 1967; Rogers, 1962; Kozinets et al., 2010). As WOM practice advances, *the linear marketing influence model* focuses on influential persons known as "WOM-spreading consumers" (Kozinets et al., 2010, p. 72) in the WOM process. Marketers use traditional communications, such as advertising and promotions, to influence the opinion leaders who are perceived as trusted sources and expect them to further influence their friends (see Brooks, 1957; Engel et al., 1969; Kozinets et al., 2010).

In the newest WOM model afforded by the Internet (known as WOMM), *the network coproduction model,* the role of opinion leaders is very crucial (Kozinets et al., 2010). Serving as "active coproducers of value and meaning" (Kozinets et al., 2010, p. 72), consumers use WOMM communications that are coproduced in their networks. Two distinct characteristics explain the model as follows:

First is marketers' use of new tactics and metrics to deliberately and directly target and influence the consumer or opinion leader. Second is the

A: The Organic Interconsumer Influence Model

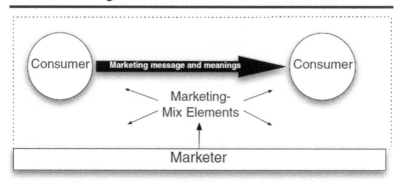

B: The Linear Marketer Influence Model

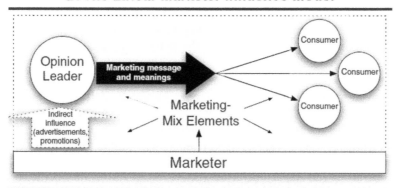

C: The Network Coproduction Model

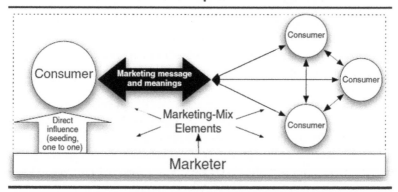

Figure 11.1   The Evolution of WOM Theory (Kozinets et al., 2010, p. 72).

acknowledgment that market messages and meanings do not flow unidirec-
tionally but rather are exchanged among members of the consumer network.
(Kozinets et al., 2010, p. 72–73)

Seeding campaigns emerge as opinion leaders (Arndt, 1967; Kozinet et al.,
2010) or influential consumers being selected as "seeds" communicate about
a product favorably to other consumers (Balter, 2005; Kozinets, 2010).
Marketers target one-to-one seedings in managing WOM activities. Seeds
take the role of not only sending out marketing messages and meanings to
other consumers who follow them but also exchange them with other consumers (Kozinets et al., 2010). Seeds create posts by gathering information
from various sources and diffuse the information via recommendations and
advice to their readers or followers (Weimann, 1994). Serving as influential
friends (Koeck & Marshall, 2015; McQuarrie et al., 2013) rather than sales-
persons representing the markets, seeds are able to engage with their audiences
through various presentational styles. Seeds take the dual role of consumer
and marketer to produce networked narratives, as seeds are the real consumers
who talk about products as part of brands' seeding campaigns. Not only are
seeds required to conform to communal blogger practice, but they also need to
strategize seeding contents that would lead to the campaign's objectives. The
market tactics filtered into posts that are expected to reflect sharing and caring
communal practice affect the perceived credibility of consumer-to-consumer
communication. The ability to balance "commercial and communal tensions"
(Kozinets et al., 2010, p. 83) largely affects bloggers' reputation.

Other scholars also shed light on online WOM ecosystems and factors that
influence successful WOMM campaigns. Henning-Thurau et al. (2004) suggest
four primary factors motivating online WOM behavior. First, consumers feel
fulfilled for social interaction with other like-minded consumers. Second, consumers are attracted by the economic incentives received as rewards for writing.
Third, consumers express their care for other consumers through warning about
a bad product or negative consumer experience. Fourth, consumers enhance
their self-worth, as their sharing about good judgment on product purchase
makes them a clever customer. Hinz et al. (2011) argue for the four factors
that have potentially introduced successful seeding campaigns. First, seeding
contents can be recommendations or updates. Second, seeding social networks
should be large enough to reach more potential targets. Third, seeds should be
willing to participate in the campaigns and agree on proposed incentives. Fourth,
seeding campaigns require the right initial sets of targeted consumers.

Knock and Marshall (2016) empirically explored seeding campaigns
focusing on relationships that bloggers form: "blogger–blogger relationship
and blogger–marketer relationship. For the former relationship, bloggers are

required to belong to the blogger community, which has shared practices to validate professionalization of bloggers and ensure transparency in terms of funding. However, those who fail to conform to the practices find themselves ostracized from other bloggers who align with the practice" (pp. 375–376). For the blogger–marketer relationship, bloggers develop new ways to interact with marketers, as it allows them access to information and new products that can be published on their blogs. Furthermore, collaborations apart from seeding campaigns may be possible. As time goes by, bloggers establish more permanent relationships with marketers. The roles taken by the marketers have changed, as they could potentially hold the positions of "influencer relations or blogger relations" (Knock & Marshall, 2016, p. 376). The new role allows them to be hired as external consultants or in the marketing or public relations department.

WOMM AND SOCIAL MEDIA INFLUENCERS

Leading media and communication agencies in Thailand propose the Pyramid of Influence which encompasses different types of social media influencers (SMIs), in terms of reach and relevance. The different types of SMIs are described as follows:

> *Mega-influencers* refer to actors, artists, athletes and social media stars who have 500k+ followers and could potentially drive 2% to 5% engagement per post. They have the highest reach on the influencer spectrum, with their influence driven by their celebrity. They have the lowest overall resonance when it comes to driving actions on behalf of a brand.

> *Macro-influencers* refer to professional bloggers and YouTubers who have 50,000 to 500,000 followers and could potentially drive 5% to 20% engagement per post. They have the highest topical relevance on the spectrum, with category-specific influence—such as lifestyle, fashion or business.

> *Micro-influencers* refer to everyday consumers who have 1,000 to 100,000 followers and could potentially drive 25%-50% engagement per post. Compared to other types of influencers, they have the highest brand relevance and resonance. They could exert influential power using personal experience with a brand and their strength of relationships with their networks.

> *Brand Advocates* refer to consumers who are passionate and willing to share, but have little influence. (StarNgage, n.d, para. 5)

While there are different types of social media influencers listed by agencies in Thailand, this chapter considers net idols as influential opinion leaders. They are "active coproducers of value and meaning" (Kozinets et al., 2010, p. 72) through online WOMM campaigns, which refer to their blogs/vlogs and social media content. In particular, this study focuses on the experiences of Thai net idols' followers in online WOMM campaigns and their views toward net idols' blogging/vlogging, and the relationship between the two parties. In particular, it sheds light on the roles of net idols as perceived by their followers. More specifically, as net idols' perceived credibility by followers depends largely on how net idols can relate to average consumers (Abidin, 2016), this chapter sheds light on how followers perceive net idols and what roles net idols take in their consumers' life. The perspective of followers, not opinion leaders', is the key focus.

METHODOLOGY

This chapter synthesizes two sets of data in which the author had face-to-face interviews with two groups of people who engaged with net idols. Each interview lasted forty minutes to two hours. All interviews were in Thai. A key strength of interviewing is its ability to probe individuals' thoughts and feelings in great detail, such that it has been described as a method by which "to explore meanings" (Arksey & Knight, 1999, p. 4) and to reach "people's subjective experiences and attitudes" (Denzin & Lincoln, 2011, p. 529). All the interviews were recorded and kept confidential. Each participant was assigned a pseudonym which was informed prior to recording the interview. The participants' identities were anonymous.

In the first data set, the author conducted in-depth interviews with twelve Thai social media followers who followed net idols for more than a year. Of the twelve followers, participants were twenty to twenty-five years old, identified themselves as undergraduate students or entry-level workers. Participants were asked how and why they began following Thai net idols, why they still followed the net idols, as well as the relationships between the net idols and themselves.

In the second data set, the author conducted in-depth interviews with two brand representatives who collaborated with net idols for more than a year. The representatives consistently worked with net idols by inviting them to attend workshops, product launches, and other commercial events hosted by their brands. Participants were asked about their collaborative experiences with net idols and to share their attitudes toward successful net idols. The second data set serves to strengthen arguments made by followers collected in the first set of data.

Data Analysis

To analyze data, the author used grounded theory as it seeks to construct a theory about issues of importance in peoples' lives (Glaser, 1978) through inductive data collection. This method allows for comparisons, initially between data with data, and progressing to between their interpretations carried out in forms of codes and categories (Mills et al., 2006).

First, the author used initial coding to sort large amounts of data with "a wide variance of possibilities" (Saldana, 2009, p. 85). For instance, posts were coded as "expanding my restaurant shortlists" and "giving rationale of product evaluation." In the second coding cycle, the author used focused coding, as it is suitable for studies employing grounded theory methodology. It aims to develop "the most salient categories" in the data corpus and "requires decision about which initial codes make the most analytic sense" (Charmaz, 2006, pp. 46, 57). For instance, "expanding my restaurant shortlists" and "giving rationale of product evaluation" were categorized as "information source for purchase decision process."

RESULTS

Thai net idols' followers discussed their positive experiences toward consuming net idols' seeding content for diverse campaigns relating to food, electronic gadgets, cosmetics, and fashion. To the followers, net idols cater content to their interests, and in some cases, solve their problems as well. They are aware of consumer-to-consumer communication through seeding campaigns and WOMM activities influenced by professional marketing techniques and usually evaluate how net idols negotiate between communal and commercial conflict of interest. However, seeding product or service information that is perceived as useful and/or entertaining has become crucial for net idols to be perceived as credible. Such contribution allows net idols to become more known for creating trustworthy content, authentic online communities, and having a cool image that followers admire.

NET IDOLS AS #CONTENTCREATORS

Thai net idols serve as content creators who "contribute to the online commons by creating or contributing to Web sites, posting photos, and sharing files. They are taking advantage of new Web applications like blogging and, in many cases, faster, bigger Internet connections to facilitate their contributions" (Lenhart et al., 2004, para. 2). Social media content circulates through online

WOMM, including content about beauty, food, travel, electronic devices, and others. From interviews with the two brand representatives who had collaborated with net idols, they discussed two important points. First, net idols' special ability was to tell engaging stories that make a good connection between marketed products and their readers or followers. As content creators, each net idol finds their own strengths and personal narratives that represent their own unique selling points. If content is controlled by brands rather than their own voice, they may lose credibility and trust perceived by their followers. Second, the content is of true fact. While storytelling is a required skill for a content creator to shine, fake information and fabricated stories tend to bring criticisms toward the content creator. Brands that partnered with net idols in such cases would also be negatively affected regarding brand reputation.

The co-created and coproduced social media content reflects two mixed characteristics: informative and entertainment. *Informative* refers to the characteristic of content which provides consumers with useful and resourceful information (Chen, 1999; Ducoffe, 1995). In the co-created and coproduced network, informative content makes net idols a crucial source of information for consumers to learn, follow (e.g., how-to, problem-solving content), and use as part of their decision-making process (e.g., reviews content). *Entertainment* refers to the characteristics of content that offer entertainment value, such as enjoyment and pleasure (Lee & Choi, 2005). Arguably, the presentability of entertainment content is a way to enhance and actualize consumers' hedonic needs (Fischer & Reuber, 2011). Net idols' ability to offer consumers' emotional release and diversion (Muntinga et al., 2011) through content that consumers experience and exchange among their networks (Kim et al., 2011) potentially encourages consumers to repeat the same media use (Dehghani et al., 2016). The entertainment characteristics were evidenced by net idols' pleasant or humorous appearance, creative communication, and trendiness.

FOLLOWER–NET IDOL RELATIONSHIPS

The following section presents three different types of relationships formed between net idols and followers in the co-created and coproduced platforms: how-to gurus, informational source for purchase decision process, and entertainers.

#Contentcreators: How-to Gurus

Thai followers are familiar with the how-to presentation style, as it is the core style net idols have adopted to use in their social media posts. As Limkangvanmongkol (2018) argued, the first-generation Thai beauty bloggers originally created how-to content for their blogging routine out of their passion for beauty-related issues. Net idols post how-to social media content and videos with detailed step-by-step instructions for different makeup looks, hairstyles, and manicures/pedicures. Followers consider how-to content as guiding instructions they could easily follow and adopt in their everyday life. For instance, one interviewee noted:

> I started following beauty bloggers when I was a freshman. At that time, cosmetics was a whole new world to me. A YouTube video by beauty blogger Achita came up in the recommended videos. I watched other beauty-related videos recommended by YouTube. I finally found Mayy R channel and have followed her since then. Our facial condition is similar, and her light make-up style is my favorite. I do not like to wear a full-coverage foundation, especially when I go to school. (Translated from Thai)

Recently, the how-to presentation style has become prevalent on social media, with more diverse content ranging from beauty, travel, electronic gadgets, and problem-solving tips. Followers found these videos very useful, easy-to-follow, and time-saving (see figure 11.2). For example, an interviewee said:

> I usually watch how-to videos for solving problems on laptops. The first time I searched for the videos was when my laptop ran very slow. I finally could fix the problem by following the video, "How to Fix a Slow Laptop" (Win7/8/10), by NotebookSPEC. To me, it saved so much time, as I did not need to bring my laptop to IT solution centers at malls. (Translated from Thai).

Travel content is another genre of social media content that has become popular. Consumers, especially entry-level employees or undergraduate students who have limited income for travel, feel as if they travel with net idols to places they aspire to visit. They learn from net idols how to travel to many different places and live an aspirational lifestyle (Duffy, 2015; Limkangvanmongkol, 2015), which is reiterated by an interviewee in the following:

> Reading travel blogs and watching travel YouTube channels are my favorite. I feel blissful when I watch net idols do local activities and enjoy their sightseeing abroad. I have learned how to adapt to different cultures. (Translated from Thai)

First-time visitors to some countries rely on net idols' videos/posts as information to prepare their own itinerary, as this interviewee mentioned in the following:

บทความนิยม! แก้ปัญหาเครื่องช้าอืดเป็นเต่าใน Win7/8/10 แถมได้ผลชัวร์, แนะนำโปรแกรม Anti-Virus โหลดฟรี

47,203 views · Aug 5, 2018

Figure 11.2 NotebookSPEC's Popular Problem-Solving Clip. Screenshot from NotebookSPEC on YouTube at https://www.youtube.com/watch?v=huwmzk0LaXY on August 5, 2018 (NotebookSPEC, 2018).

> I do not want to miss a thing when I visit Japan. I have searched on many net idols' travel videos, for I could plan my itinerary. I need to know net idols' recommended instagrammable spots. (translated from Thai)

Some consumers rely on not only travel plans by net idols but also content about how to create their look that fits with the temperature of the city they are traveling to and matches with the tourist spots or the ambience of the traveled destinations, as discussed by this interviewee:

> I follow June JellyJune most of the times that I need to travel. She has shared how she has prepared her daily clothes after she finalized her itinerary and plans detailing places she would visit daily during her trip. I want to make sure that my clothes could handle cold temperature, and more importantly, make me look chic and go well with the ambience. (translated from Thai)

#CONTENTCREATORS: INFORMATION SOURCE FOR PURCHASE DECISION PROCESS

Net idols serve as a crucial information source for followers' purchase decision process. Consumers begin the process of information search after they determine they have a need for a product or service. Consistent with other scholars (Hill et al., 2006; Iyengar et al., 2011), consumers make purchase decisions by considering recommendations from others in personal and professional networks (Hinz et al., 2012). Net idols come into play in the process, in particular, for the WOMM recommendation (Limkangvanmongkol, 2018; Limkangvanmongkol & Abidin, 2018). Other empirical evidence also reveals that consumers increasingly rely on advice from others in personal or professional networks when making purchase decisions (Hill et al., 2006; Iyengar et al., 2011). Thai consumers rely on net idols' product or service reviews for informational support, in particular, for products or services that they have never experienced. It is possible that they may be interested in brands recommended by net idols whose posts are considered "useful" in the consumers' minds (see figure 11.3). An interviewee noted the following:

As a foodie person, I shortlist restaurants recommended by Bearhug YouTube Channel and brought the list to pitch with my family members for dining restaurant choices. I find the channel very useful, for it informs me of new restaurants to explore, and teaches me new English vocabularies as it provides both Thai and English subtitles. (Translated from Thai).

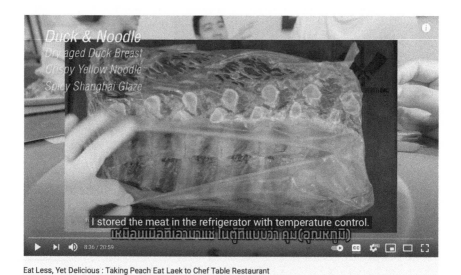

Eat Less, Yet Delicious : Taking Peach Eat Laek to Chef Table Restaurant

1,584,025 views · Dec 7, 2019   👍 34K   👎 614   ↗ SHARE   ≡₊ SAVE   ...

Figure 11.3   Bearhug's Creative Food Showcase. Screenshot from Bearhug on YouTube at https://www.youtube.com/watch?v=_eO2RG_ECWQ&t=516s on December 7, 2019 (Bearhug, 2019).

Followers initially assume that the majority of posts by net idols are sponsored, thus, followers mostly care about "true fact" they gain from useful content. As Solomon et al. (2006) explained, an individual consumer gives a different personal weight to various factors gathered during the information search—product features, price, perceived value, and brand value among others. At best, followers look for honest and deep reviews from net idols who have tried and tested products or services before sharing their experience. Honest and deep reviews create trust, maintain followers' interest in particular net idols' page/channel, and could help followers to evaluate alternative options (Kotler & Amstrong, 2010). In particular, followers want to know not only if the product and service is evaluated as highly recommended or not recommended, but also the rationale why it is evaluated so. As one interviewee put it:

> When I am looking for skincare product reviews, Madam Krian FB page is the first one I choose as I like deep reviews which explain ingredients and cite scientific references. I do not trust before and after photos by net idols who do not provide deep reviews. (Translated from Thai)

The insights from interviews with the two brand representatives who had collaborated with net idols have confirmed net idols' influential power to effectively influence consumers' purchase decisions. In particular, brands no longer expect net idols' WOMM to only raise brand awareness, but they expect an increase in conversion rates and sales as well. The number of followers may not always be important as long as the net idols engage with their followers and ensure high conversion rates and sales for the brand. Managers and communication teams have particular means to prove each net idol's influential power. For example, when brands launch a new collection of lipstick, each color is assigned to a chosen net idol who agrees to create content about that particular lipstick shade on their social media platforms. Beauty assistants help managers to monitor sales of each lipstick color. The higher influential power a net idol has, the more likely their assigned lipstick color will be popular.

#Contentcreators: Entertainers

Thai social media followers usually love entertainment. They find entertainment value to yield a positive influence on their willingness to finish watching an online video or read a post. They are likely to subscribe to or follow channels/pages they find enjoyable and entertaining. To define entertainment value, followers shared different experiences. Initially, followers reported the first impression of net idols' presentability, in terms of appearance, image, and communication skills as an important indicator of entertainment value, as evidenced by this interviewee's following response:

> I need to admit that the attractive appearance of net idols initially draws my attention. However, their effective presentation skills are very important to sustain my attention. From my observations, a friendly but knowledgeable presentation could really capture my attention. (Translated from Thai)

Creativity is also considered a crucial characteristic for net idols to successfully entertain consumers. To illustrate, *creativity* is "the ability to produce work that is both novel (i.e., original, unexpected) and appropriate (i.e., useful, adaptive concerning taste constraints" (Sternberg & Lubart, 1999, p. 3). For Thai followers, the term generally refers to unique and unexpected ideas (see figure 11.4). One interviewee put it the following way:

> Icepadie is very unique. Her social media content portrays colorfulness and fantasy unicorns. Her uniqueness is reflected by her big earrings, colorful eye make-up and outfits. Watching her videos, regardless of content genres, really entertains me (Translated from Thai).

Figure 11.4   Icepadie's Colorful Donut Earrings. Screenshot from icepadie on YouTube at https://www.youtube.com/watch?v=uIwOEUuRi-c on October 5, 2019 (Icepadie, 2019).

In addition to presentability and creativity, a sense of humor is also considered a crucial element for net idols to serve as entertainers. Adding sound and visual effects to the video content help make videos more interesting. For example, one interviewee reported the following:

> I like a transgender YouTuber. She usually adds sound and visual effects to her videos. Though she has very good presentation skills and looks very beautiful and sexy, I feel sleepy or bored when watching a lot of videos in a row. With the sound and visual effects, the videos keep me engaged longer. (Translated from Thai)

Net idols' exposure to trends and current affairs is beneficial. Net idols who create or tie in content of current cultural affairs that have recently garnered massive attention could potentially better capture new followers' attention. Cultural affairs may include gimmicks from Thai soap operas, updates about celebrities, fads, fashion styles, and arts or cultural events.

After the COVID-19 outbreaks, the majority of Thai people were required to self-quarantine and work from home (*Bangkok Post*, 2020). Netflix series (such as *Itaewon Class*, *Crash Landing on You*, and *Money*

#แต่งเป็นยุนเซริ #ของสหายผู้กองรีจองฮยอก #Crashlandingonyou
แต่งเป็น "ยุนเซรี" ของสหายผู้กอง "รีจองฮยอก" จากซีรีส์ดัง "Crash landing on you" | Nisamanee.Nutt

253,169 views · Mar 5, 2020   8K   194   SHARE   SAVE   ...

Figure 11.5 Nisamanee.Nutt's Makeover Clip Inspired by Yoon Se-ri (female protagonist) from the series *Crash Landing on You*. Screenshot from Nisamanee.Nutt on YouTube at https://www.youtube.com/watch?v=uxjjzmIW07E on October 5, 2019 (Nisamanee.Nutt, 2020).

Heist) (Popiko, 2020) have been much talked about on social media, as people watched them during the stay-at-home period. Some net idols make use of such cultural popularity to increase followers' attention to their social media channels. For example, transgender YouTuber Nisamanee.Nutt talked about a popular South Korean series that was released on Netflix, *Crash Landing on You*, especially the lead actor and actress with great admiration (see figure 11.5). An interviewee explained why they followed Nisamanee.Nutt in the following:

> During self-quarantine, I have tried hard to avoid consuming too much news about the COVID-19, and I have randomly found her YouTube channel. As I am very into this series and a huge fan of Captain Ri Jeong-hyeok (male pro-tagonist), I have so much enjoyed Nisamanee.Nutt's makeover YouTube clip to look like Yoon Se-ri (female protagonist) from the beginning to the end. Like other Thai women who are into this series, I wish I could become beautiful Yoon Se-ri. (Translated from Thai).

As entertainers, net idols mainly serve content pertaining to enjoyment and emotional release, as shown by previous literature on social media environment advertising (Edwards et al., 2002; Fischer & Reuber, 2011). Interview results also show that net idols' content of entertainment value helps distract followers during serious situations and allows for imaginative experience as evidenced by the case of Netflix series.

CONCLUSION

This chapter examined online WOMM communication within Thai social media platforms by examining the relationship between net idols, or social media influencers, in the lifestyle sector and their followers. In the digital age, net idols take the opinion-leading role in creating social media content that is co-created and coproduced in their networks. These content creators who have influential power are considered seeds. Marketers select seeds who could potentially communicate about a product to other consumers in a pleasant and presentable way. Our study suggests two characteristics of the co-created and coproduced content within online environments: informative and entertainment. Followers learn and take informative content from net idols into consideration when making purchase decisions. Moreover, consumers need content or elements of content with entertainment value added to the posts or videos. Within the relationships between content creators and their followers, the net idol takes on the role of how-to guru, information source, as well as entertainer. Through these roles, content creators allow for the formation of online communities built on trust, which strengthens relationships with their followers.

REFERENCES

Abidin, C. (2016). Please subscribe!: Influencers, social media, and the commodification of everyday life. https://doi.org/10.26182/5ddc899d698cb

Arksey, H., & Knight, P. T. (1999). *Interviewing for social scientists: An introductory resource with examples.* London, UK: SAGE Publications.

Arndt, J. (1967). Role of product-related conversations in the diffusion of a new product. *Journal of Marketing Research, 4*(3), 291.

Asean Up. (2019). Southeast Asia digital, social and mobile 2019. https://aseanup.com/southeast-asia-digital-social-mobile/

Balter, D. (2005). *Grapevine.* New York, NY: Penguin Group.

Bangkok Post. (2020, March 13). State-run quarantine centres to remain open: govt. https://www.bangkokpost.com/thailand/general/1877564/state-run-quarantine-centres-to-remain-open-govt

Bearhug (2019, December 7). Eat Less, Yet Delicious : Taking Peach Eat Laek to Chef Table Restaurant [Video]. YouTube. https://www.youtube.com/watch?v=_eO2RG_ECWQ&t=516s

Brooks, Jr, R. C. (1957). "Word-of-mouth" advertising in selling new products. *Journal of Marketing, 22*(2), 154–161.

Burt, R. S. (1999). The Social capital of opinion leaders. *The ANNALS of the American Academy of Political and Social Science, 566*(1), 37–54.

Charmaz, K. (2006). *Constructing grounded theory: A practical guide through qualitative research.* Thousand Oaks, CA: Sage Publications.

Chen, Q. (1999). Attitude toward the site. *Journal of Advertising Research, 39*(5), 27–37.

Dehghani, M., Niaki, M. K., Ramezani, I., & Sali, R. (2016). Evaluating the influence of YouTube advertising for attraction of young customers. *Computers in Human Behavior, 59*, 165–172.

Denzin, N. K., & Lincoln, Y. S. (Eds.). (2011). *The sage handbook of qualitative research.* London, UK: SAGE Publications.

Ducoffe, R. H. (1995). How consumers assess the value of advertising. *Journal of Current Issues & Research in Advertising, 17*(1), 1–18.

Duffy, B. (2015). Amateur, autonomous, and collaborative: Myths of aspiring female cultural producers in Web 2.0. *Critical Studies in Media Communication, 32*(1), 48–64.

Edwards, S. M., Li, H., & Lee, J. H. (2002). Forced exposure and psychological reactance: Antecedents and consequences of the perceived intrusiveness of pop-up ads. *Journal of Advertising, 31*(3), 83–95.

Engel, J. F., Kegerreis, R. J., & Blackwell, R. D. (1969). Word-of-mouth communication by the innovator. *Journal of Marketing, 33*(3), 15–19.

Fischer, E., & Reuber, A. R. (2011). Social interaction via new social media:(How) can interactions on Twitter affect effectual thinking and behavior? *Journal of Business Venturing, 26*(1), 1–18.

Glaser, B. (1978). *Theoretical sensitivity: Advances in the methodology of grounded theory.* Mill Valley, CA: Sociology Press.

Group M Thailand. (2019). Thailand digital playbook 2019. https://issuu.com/gr oupmthailand/docs/groupm_thailand_digital_playbook_20

Hennig-Thurau, T., Gwinner, K. P., Walsh, G., & Gremler, D. D. (2004). Electronic word-of-mouth via consumer-opinion platforms: what motivates consumers to articulate themselves on the internet? *Journal of Interactive Marketing, 18*(1), 38–52.

Hill, S., Provost, F., & Volinsky, C. (2006). Network-based marketing: Identifying likely adopters via consumer networks. *Statistical Science, 21*(2), 256–276.

Hinz, O., Skiera, B., Barrot, C., & Becker, J. U. (2011). Seeding strategies for viral marketing: An empirical comparison. *Journal of Marketing, 75*(6), 55–71.

Icepadie (2019, October 5). เปิดกรุตุ้มหู 2019 !!! [Video]. YouTube. https://www.you-tube.com/watch?v=uIwOEUuRi-c

Iyengar, R., Van den Bulte, C., & Valente, T. W. (2011). Opinion leadership and social contagion in new product diffusion. *Marketing Science, 30*(2), 195–212.

Katz, E., & Lazarsfeld, P. F. (1995). Between media and mass/the part played by people/the two-step flow of communication. In O. BoydBarrett & C. Newbold (Eds.), *Approaches to media* (pp. 124–134). London, UK: Arnold.

Kim, Y., Sohn, D., & Choi, S. M. (2011). Cultural difference in motivations for using social network sites: A comparative study of American and Korean college students. *Computers in Human Behavior, 27*(1), 365–372.

Koeck, B., & Marshall, D. (2015). Word of mouth theory revisited: The influence of new actors on seeding campaigns. In K. Diehl & C. Yoon (Eds.), *Advances in Consumer Research Volume 43* (pp. 374–378). Duluth, MN: Association for Consumer Research.

Kotler, P., & Armstrong, G. (2010). *Principles of marketing.* Pearson Education Limited.

Kozinets, R., de Valck, K., Wojnicki, A., & Wilner, S. (2010). Networked narratives: Understanding word-of-mouth marketing in online communities. *Journal of Marketing, 74*(2), 71–89.

Lee, W. N., & Choi, S. M. (2005). The role of horizontal and vertical individualism and collectivism in online consumers' responses toward persuasive communication on the Web. *Journal of Computer-Mediated Communication, 11*(1), 317–336.

Lenhart, A., Fallow, D., & Horrigan, J. B. (2004). Content creation online. https://ww w.pewresearch.org/internet/2004/02/29/content-creation- online-2/

Limkangvanmongkol, V. (2015, October 21–24). Online red carpet: The magic of instaselfie culture in Thailand. Paper presented at Internet Research 16: The 16th Annual Meeting of the Association of Internet Researchers. Phoenix, AZ, USA: AoIR.

Limkangvanmongkol, V. (2018). *When a nobody becomes a somebody: Understanding beauty bloggers in Thailand.* Unpublished doctoral dissertation. University of Illinois at Chicago, Chicago, USA.

Limkangvanmongkol, V., & Abidin, C. (2018). Net idols and beauty bloggers' negotiations of race, commerce, and cultural customs: Emergent microcelebrity genres in Thailand. In C. Abidin & M. L. Brown (Eds.), *Microcelebrity Around the Globe: Approaches to cultures of internet fame* (pp. 95–106). Bingley UK: Emerald Publishing.

Mathew, J. (2008). *Understanding influencer marketing and why it is so effective.* https://www.forbes.com/sites/theyec/2018/07/30/understanding-influencer-mar keting-and-why-it-is-so-effective/

Meyer, Eric T. (2015). The expert and the machine Competition or convergence? *Convergence, 21*(3), 306–313.

McQuarrie, E. F., Miller, J., & Phillips, B. J. (2012). The megaphone effect: Taste and audience in fashion blogging. *Journal of Consumer Research, 40*(1), 136–158.

Mills, J., Bonner, A., & Francis, K. (2006). The development of constructivist grounded theory. *International Journal of Qualitative Methods, 5*(1), 25–35.

Muntinga, D. G., Moorman, M., & Smit, E. G. (2011). Introducing COBRAs: Exploring motivations for brand-related social media use. *International Journal of Advertising, 30*(1), 13–46.

Nisamanee.Nutt (2020, March 5). แต่งเป็น "ยุนเซรี" ของสหายผู้กอง "รีจองฮยอก" จากซีรีส์ดัง "Crash landing on you" [Video]. YouTube. https://www.youtube.com/ watch?v=uxjjzmIW07E

NotebookSPEC. (2018, August 5). บทความนิยม! แก้ปัญหาเครื่องช้าอืดเป็นเต่าใน Win7/8/10 แถมได้ ผลชัวร์, แนะนำโปรแกรม Anti-Virus โหลดฟรี [Video]. YouTube. https://www.youtube.com/ watch?v=huwmzk0LaXY.

Phahulo, S., & Boonnak, P. (2015). Net IDOL. *Thinking, 6*(5), 12. (in Thai).

Popiko. (2020). Top 10 Netflix movies and series for Thai people, updated on Friday 3rd April 2020. https://droidsans.com/top-10-movies-series-netflix-3-fri-april-20 20/ (in Thai).

Putnark, V. (2016). Who are net idol? Why do we react towards their appearance? *The matter.* http://thematter.co/pulse/net-idol-gone-why/11888 (in Thai).

Rettberg, J. W. (2008). *Blogging.* Cambridge, MA: Polity.

Robinson, J. P. (1976). Interpersonal influence in election campaigns: Two-step-flow hypotheses. *Public Opinion Quarterly, 40,* 204–319.

Rogers, E. M. (2010). *Diffusion of innovations.* New York, NY: The Free Press.

Saldana, J. (2009). *The coding manual for qualitative researchers.* Thousand Oaks, CA: SAGE Publications.

Senft, T. M. (2008). *Camgirls: Celebrity & community in the age of social networks.* New York, NY: Peter Lang.

Solomon, M., Bamossy, G., Askegaard, S., & Hogg, M. K. (2010). *Consumer behaviour. A European perspective.* Essex, UK: Pearson Education.

StarNgage. (n.d.). Influencer marketing in Thailand. https://starngage.com/influencer -marketing-thailand/

Sternberg, R. J., & Lubart, T. I. (1999). The concept of creativity: Prospects and paradigms. *Handbook of Creativity, 1,* 3–15.

Turner, G. (2010). *Ordinary people and the media: The demotic turn.* London, UK: SAGE Publications.

Weimann, G. (1982). On the importance of marginality: One more step into the two-step flow of communication. *American Sociological Review, 47*(6), 764.

Zhao, X., & Belk, R. W. (2007). Live from shopping malls: Blogs and Chinese consumer desire. In G. Fitzsimons & V. Morwitz (Eds.), *NA - Advances in Consumer Research Volume 34* (pp. 131–137). Duluth, MN: Association for Consumer Research.

Index

About the Editor and Contributors

ABOUT THE EDITOR

Brandi Watkins, Ph.D. (The University of Alabama), is an associate professor in the School of Communication and Digital Media at Virginia Tech, where she teaches courses in social media and public relations. Her research examines the role of social media in brand communication and as a way to build, enhance, and maintain organization-public relationships. She is the author of the book *Sports Teams, Fans, and Twitter: The Influence of Social Media on Relationships and Branding*. Her work has been published in *Public Relations Review*, *Journal of Brand Management*, and *International Journal of Sport Communication*.

ABOUT THE CONTRIBUTORS

Kelli S. Burns, Ph.D. (The University of Florida), is an associate professor in the Zimmerman School of Advertising and Mass Communications at the University of South Florida, where she teaches public relations and social media courses. Her research interests include social media influencers, social media activism, and the intersection of social media and popular culture. She is the author of two books on the topic of social media: *Social Media: A Reference Handbook* (2017) and *Celeb 2.0: How Social Media Foster Our Fascination with Popular Culture* (2009).

JoAnna Boudreaux is a graduate student in the Department of Communication and Film at the University of Memphis. She also has an M.A. in sociology and a graduate certificate in women and gender studies. Her research focuses on Islam, gendered identity construction among American Muslim youth, and ideologies of womanhood.

Nancy J. Curtin, Ph.D. (Southern Illinois University), is a chair and associate professor in the Department of Communication at Millikin University, where she teaches courses in organizational/business communication, intercultural communication, and gender communication. Her research focuses on topics in organizations and gender.

Karen Freberg, Ph.D. (@kfreberg), is an associate professor in strategic communications at the University of Louisville, where she teaches, researches, and consults in social media strategy, public relations, and crisis communication. Freberg has experience working with brands such as Hootsuite, General Motors, Breeders' Cup, Facebook, and Chipotle. Freberg has written several books including *Social media for strategic communications: Creative strategies and research-based* applications and *Discovering Public Relations*.

Mitchell Friedman, Ed.D., APR, is senior lecturer in the Graduate School of Defense Management at the Naval Postgraduate School. He teaches courses on ethics, leadership, management communication, and organizational behavior. In addition, he serves as Northern California director of the Institute of Advanced Advertising Studies, a program for early-career advertising agency professionals. He also teaches courses on communications campaigns.

Elizabeth B. Jones, Ph.D. (The Ohio State University), is an associate professor and graduate program director in the School of Communication Arts at Asbury University. Her research explores the nexus of communication technology, interpersonal communication, and health communication, often through the lens of lifespan communication. She teaches courses in social media and communication research.

Carolyn Kim, Ph.D., APR, is an associate professor and chair of the Public Relations and Strategic Communication program at Biola University. Her expertise includes public relations pedagogy, digital media, and credibility. Dr. Kim's research has been published in peer-reviewed journals such as *Public Relations Review, Public Relations Journal,* and *The Journal of Public Relations Education.* She has served in a variety of leadership roles in both academic and professional public relations organizations, such as with the Commission for Public Relations Education, the Public Relations Society of America Educators Academy, the Institute for Public Relations Digital Media

Center, and the Executive Board of the Orange County Public Relations Society of America.

Nicole M. Lee, Ph.D. (Texas Tech University), is an assistant professor in the School of Social and Behavioral Sciences at Arizona State University where she teaches courses in strategic communication and science communication. Her research examines the intersection of public relations, science communication, and digital media. She is the author of several articles published in journals such as *Science Communication, Public Relations Review,* and *Journal of Communication Management.*

Corey Jay Liberman, Ph.D. (Rutgers University, 2008), is an associate professor of public relations and strategic communication in the Department of Communication and Media Arts at Marymount Manhattan College. His research spans the interpersonal communication, group communication, and organizational communication worlds, and he is currently interested in studying the social practices of dissent within organizations, specifically the antecedents, processes, and effects associated with effective employee dissent communication, as well as risk and crisis communication. He is currently working on a coauthored book entitled *Risk and Crisis Communication: Communicating in a Disruptive World*, as well as a coedited case study book focusing on mediated communication. He is coauthor of *Organizational Communication: Strategies for Success (2nd Edition)*, editor of *Casing Persuasive Communication*, and co-editor of *Casing Crisis and Risk Communication* and *Casing Communication Theory*: all published by Kendall Hunt.

Vimviriya Limkangvanmongkol, Ph.D., is a full-time instructor in the School of Communication Arts at Bangkok University, in Thailand. She teaches undergraduate and graduate courses related to branding, digital marketing, cross-cultural communication, and media studies to students in Thai and international programs. Her research interest focuses on the commercialization of the Internet, online identity, culture and consumption, media ethics, as well as AI and technology. Particularly, she mainly explores media effects at the intersection of networked technology affordances and appropriation of everyday media use (e.g., Internet celebrities). Her research mostly draws from interdisciplinary areas ranging from new media, technology, gender studies, and marketing. In addition, she is a soft skill trainer certified by the International Soft Skills Standards & Testing and an image consultant certified by the Association of Image Consultant International.

Jenn Burleson Mackay (Ph.D., The University of Alabama, 2008), is an associate professor in the Department of Communication at Virginia Tech. Her research looks at the ethics of journalists and the influence of new technology on journalism. She is coeditor of the journal *Electronic News*. Her work has been published in several journals including *Electronic Journal of Communication, Journal of Mass Media Ethics, Newspaper Research Journal, Journalism and Mass Media Quarterly, Journalism Studies,* and *Journalism Practice.* She has held leadership positions in the Association for Journalism and Mass Communication.

Anne W. Njathi is a second-year Ph.D. student in the Communication, Rhetoric and Digital Media (CRDM) program at North Carolina State University. She currently teaches international and cross-cultural communication in the Department of Communication. As an Associate Chartered Marketer (CIM-UK) with degrees in communications and PR, she has more than nine years of corporate work experience in Africa. Her research interest lies in emerging media technologies and digitally mediated communication such as social media and mobile communication.

Alison N. Novak, Ph.D. (Drexel University), is an assistant professor at Rowan University in Glassboro, NJ. Her research examines digital culture, youth, and digital dialogic communication. She is the author of *Network Neutrality and Digital Dialogic Communication* and *Media, Millennials, and Politics.* Her work was featured on BBC, *Wired Magazine*, and *NBC*.

Sydney O. Scheller is an M.A. student in the digital storytelling program at Asbury University. She originally began investigating megachurch pastors' Twitter communication practices as part of an undergraduate-mentored research experience.

Carrie S. Trimble, Ph.D. (Michigan State University), is an associate professor of marketing in the Tabor School of Business at Millikin University, where she teaches digital media marketing and business writing courses. Her research agenda measures consumer responses to consumer-related marketing and student responses to active learning in travel courses.

Nathan A. Vick is an M.A. student in the digital storytelling program at Asbury University. His research interests involve the expression of theological concepts on social media platforms.

Amanda J. Weed, Ph.D. (Ohio University), is an assistant professor in the School of Communication & Media at Kennesaw State University where she teaches courses in digital/social media and public relations. Weed is an award-winning scholar in the fields of digital technologies and strategic communication pedagogy. Weed's research has been featured in *Telematics and Informatics, Journal of Public Relations Education,* and *Business Case Journal.* She holds Accreditation in Public Relations (APR) from the Public Relations Society of America.

Chelsea Woods, Ph.D. (University of Kentucky), is an assistant professor in the Department of Communication at Virginia Tech where she teaches public relations courses. Her research focuses on crisis communication, anti-corporate activism, and reputation management.

Lightning Source UK Ltd.
Milton Keynes UK
UKHW041530030123
414759UK00015B/310